Messrs. Fores London

Fores's Sporting Notes and Sketches

No. 1 April 1884

Messrs. Fores London

Fores's Sporting Notes and Sketches
No. 1 April 1884

ISBN/EAN: 9783337092436

Printed in Europe, USA, Canada, Australia, Japan

Cover: Foto ©Andreas Hilbeck / pixelio.de

More available books at **www.hansebooks.com**

MESSRS. FORES,

SPORTING AND FINE ART PUBLISHERS,

41 PICCADILLY, LONDON

(Corner of Sackville Street),

Beg leave to announce the following recent Publications :—

THE NIGHT TEAM, by C. Cooper Henderson, forms
Plate 6 of the celebrated Series of Fores's Coaching Recollections, and shows the
night 'Screws' being 'put to,' the duck-toed Coachman looking to the harness,
whilst the Guard affixes the lamps. This is replete with 'character,' and one of
the best of the Series.

Coloured Engraving, 26¼ by 17½ inches, £1 1s.

THE FIRST DAY OF THE SEASON, by Cecil Boult,
Introduces us to a charming young lady on a well-bred chestnut, preceded by
her father on a clipped bay, who is opening a gate into a lane in which are the
Huntsman, Whips, and Hounds.

Coloured, 19½ by 8¼ inches, £2 2s.

THE END OF A LONG RUN, by Basil Nightingale,
Companion to above, presents us with the ultimate of the Noble Sport, 'The
Death of the Fox,' who has just been rescued from the Pack with Brush, Pads,
and Mask intact, the former doubtless intended for the Lady on the well-bred
Chestnut, which forms the centre of the picture. The Huntsman's Bay and
Hounds possess quality and character.

Coloured, 19½ by 8½ inches, £2 2s.

THE HUNTING SEASON IN IRELAND, a pair by
CECIL BOULT. Are humorous atires on the 'boycotting' of hunting ; in one
of the plates a Fox attired as an Irish peasant is defiantly trailing his coat before
a Foxhound dressed as a Huntsman ; in the other we have Mr. Fox, Wife, and
Family, still humorously attired, enjoying a picnic, without fear of interruption
from their old enemies the Hounds.

Coloured, 15¼ by 11 inches, £4 4s. the pair.

SUSPENSE, by Cecil Boult. A model 'Whip,' neat,
muscular, and well dressed, mounted on a good stamp of 'Whip's horse,' at the
corner of a covert where 'Charley' is likely to break. The natural and easy seat
of a perfect horseman is well represented as he turns in his saddle and listens
eagerly to the music of the Hounds in cover. Altogether it is one of the most
sporting bits this artist has produced.

Coloured, 16 by 12 inches, £2 2s.

LONDON: PUBLISHED BY MESSRS. FORES, 41 PICCADILLY, W.
SHIPPERS SUPPLIED UPON LIBERAL TERMS.

2

HIS FIRST AUDIENCE, by A. Harvey Moore. A

Fisher Lad, leaning against the stern of a boat, intently playing on a pipe ; three donkeys standing near appearing absorbed by the musical strains.

Coloured, 14½ by 8½ inches, £2 2s.

FOX HUNTING, by Cecil Boult. A Set of 4 Upright.

1. A FAVOURITE MEET.
2. THROWING THEM IN.
3. IN THE FOREMOST FLIGHT.
4. 'BREAK HIM UP, BEAUTIES!'

Ladies, as well as gentlemen, are here introduced in the varied incidents of the chase. The treatment is sportsmanlike and unconventional, the shape is elegant, and the size convenient for hanging.

Coloured, 21½ by 9 inches, £3 8s. the set of Four.

ON THE ROAD TO GRETNA, by C. Cooper Hender-

SON. Shows that historical vehicle, an old 'Po Chay' and four, going at speed, with a gentleman leaning out of the window offering a purse to the Post Boys—pursuers in the distance. The stamp of Horses and character of Post Boys are admirably given by the above unrivalled painter of Coaching and Road Scenes.

Coloured, 17½ by 11 inches, £2 2s.

FORES'S HUNTING SKETCHES, by Cecil Boult.

PLATE 7.—IN A GOOD PLACE.

A Lady following Hounds out of Cover, with Huntsman in the Distance.

PLATE 8.—A PROMISING YOUNG ONE.

Flying a Brook in first-rate style, ridden and handled by a workman.

PLATE 9.—GOING TO THE MEET.

Two Ladies driving in a well-appointed Pony-trap.

PLATE 10.—HOME AGAIN AFTER A HARD DAY.

A Lady on a 'pumped out' Bay arriving in sight of home.

Coloured, 15 by 10½ inches. 10s. 6d. each.

'LOST AND FOUND,' by Stanley Berkley.

'Weary, and worn, and sad,
By the lamp's cold gleam I stand,
Waiting and watching, sighing and sighing,
For that loved and long-lost hand.'

A large Dog which has been stolen, having broken the rope which held him (a part being still round his neck), regains the door of his old home, and waits eagerly and anxiously on the doorstep in pelting rain for 'that loved and long-lost hand.'

Coloured, 10½ by 8½ inches, £1 5s. Plain, 10s. 6d.

ANGELS EVER BRIGHT AND FAIR, by E. George.

Represents in the Firmament two lovely Female Heads (dark and fair), with flowing gauze drapery : one gazes eagerly and intently upwards, the other 'casts a longing, lingering look' below.

Coloured, 11½ inches circle, £2 2s.

Fores's Highly Coloured Sporting Publications.

FORES'S HUNTING INCIDENTS. After W. H.
Hopkins. Price £6 6s. the set of Four.
1. A View Halloo.   2. A Check.   3. A Holloa Forward.
4. Killed in the Open.

FORES'S SERIES. (A Front and Back View of a
Lady Riding to Hounds.) After C. B. Barber. Price £2 2s. the pair.
1. First at the Fence.   2. Taking the Lead.

FORES'S NATIONAL SPORTS. After J. F. Herring, Sen.
1. The Start for the Derby. Price £3 3s.
2. Steeple-Chase Cracks. Price £3 3s.

FOX-HUNTING.—3. The Meet. 4. The Find. 5. The Run. 6. The Kill.
Price £10 10s. the Four.

RACING.
7. Saddling. 8. A False Start. 9. The Run In. 10. Returning to Weigh.
Price £10 10s. the four, or the Set of Ten Plates, price £26 5s.

FORES'S SERIES of the BRITISH STUD. Portraits
of Celebrated Stallions and Mares whose Performances and Produce are well
known on the Turf. After J. F. Herring, Sen. Price £1 1s. each.
1. Sir Hercules and Beeswing.   4. Camel and Banter.
2. Touchstone and Emma.   5. Muley Moloch and Rebecca.
3. Pantaloon and Languish.   6. Lanercost and Crucifix.
7. Bay Middleton and Barbelle (the Sire and Dam of the Flying Dutchman).

FORES'S STABLE SCENES. After J. F. Herring, Sen.
Price £4 4s. the set of Four.
1. The Mail Change.   2. The Hunting Stud.   3. Thorough-breds.
4. The Team.

FORES'S COACHING RECOLLECTIONS. After C. C.
Henderson. Price £6 6s. the set of Six.
1. Changing Horses.   2. All Right.   3. Pulling Up to Unskid.
4. Waking Up.   5. The Olden Time.   6. The Night Team.

FORES'S COACHINGS. After J. W. Shayer.
The Brighton Coach. Price 21s.
The Brighton Up-and-Down Day Mails passing over Hookwood Common.
Price £1 11s. 6d.

FORES'S SPORTING TRAPS. After C. C. Henderson.
Price 21s. each.   1. Going to the Moors.   2. Going to Cover.

FORES'S HUNTING ACCOMPLISHMENTS, Indis-
pensable with Hounds. After H. Alken, Sen. Six Plates, price £1 5s.
1. Going along a Slapping Pace.
2. Topping a Flight of Rails, and Coming well into the next Field.
3. Swishing a Rasper.   5. Charging an Ox-Fence.
4. In-and-Out Clever.   6. Facing a Brook.

London: Published by Messrs. Fores, 41 Piccadilly, W.
Shippers supplied upon Liberal Terms.

4

FORES'S HUNTING CASUALTIES, that may Occur

WITH HOUNDS. After H. ALKEN, Sen. Six Plates, price £1 5s.

1. A TURN OF SPEED OVER THE FLAT.
2. A STRANGE COUNTRY.
3. DESPATCHED TO HEAD QUARTERS.
4. UP TO SIXTEEN STONE.
5. A RARE SORT FOR THE DOWNS.
6. A MUTUAL DETERMINATION.

FORES'S STEEPLE - CHASE SCENES. After H.

ALKEN, Sen. Six Plates, price £3 3s.

1. THE STARTING FIELD.
2. WATTLE FENCE WITH A DEEP DROP.
3. IN AND OUT OF THE LANE.
4. THE WARREN WALL.
5. THE BROOK.
6. THE RUN IN.

FORES'S HUNTING SKETCHES. (The Right and

WRONG SORT.) Showing a Good and Bad Style of going across Country. After H. ALKEN, Sen. Six Plates, price £3 3s.

1. HEADS UP AND STERNS DOWN.
2. A GOOD HOLD OF HIS HEAD.
3. A CUT AT THE BROOK.
4. CLERICAL AND LAY.
5. A CUSTOMER, AND HOW TO GET RID OF HIM.
6. THE FARMER'S FIELD OF GLORY.

FORES'S SERIES OF THE MOTHERS. After J. F.

HERRING, Sen. Price 7s. 6d. each.

1. HACK MARE AND FOAL.
2. CART MARE AND FOAL.
3. DUCK AND DUCKLINGS.
4. HEN AND CHICKENS.
5. SOW AND PIGS.
6. THOROUGH-BRED MARE AND FOAL.
7. DRAUGHT MARE AND FOAL.
8. COW AND CALF.
9. HUNTING MARE AND FOAL.

FORES'S RACING SCENES. After J. F. Herring, Sen.

Price 21s. each.

1. ASCOT.—The Emperor, Faugh-a-Ballagh, and Alice Hawthorn, Running for the Emperor's Plate, value 500 sovs.
2. YORK.—The Flying Dutchman and Voltigeur Running the Great Match for 1000 sovs. a-side.

FORES'S CELEBRATED WINNERS. After J. F.

HERRING, Sen., and others. Price 21s. each.

1. THE HERO, with John Day, Sen., and Alfred Day.
2. THE FLYING DUTCHMAN, with J. Fobert and C. Marlow.
3. TEDDINGTON, with A. Taylor and Job Marson.
4. BRUNETTE, the celebrated Steeple Chase Mare.

FORES'S COACHING INCIDENTS. After C. C. Hen-

DERSON. Price £4 10s. the set of Six.

1. KNEE DEEP.
2. STUCK FAST.
3. FLOODED.
4. THE ROAD v. THE RAIL.
5. IN TIME FOR THE COACH.
6. LATE FOR THE MAIL.

FORES'S COACHINGS. After J. W. Shayer. Price

21s. each.   UP HILL—Springing 'Em.   DOWN HILL—The Skid.

FORES'S ROAD SCENES. (Going to a Fair.) After

C. C. HENDERSON. Price 15s. each.

1. HUNTERS AND HACKS.   2. CART HORSES.

LEFT AT HOME. After R. B. Davis. Price £1 11s. 6d.

Represents a fine stamp of Hunter, and Hounds of perfect form, excited by the sound of the huntsman's horn.

5

FORES'S
SPORTING NOTES & SKETCHES.

A QUARTERLY MAGAZINE.

No. 1.   APRIL 1884.   PRICE 2s.

CONTENTS.

LONDON :
PUBLISHED BY MESSRS. FORES, 41 PICCADILLY.

SIMPKIN, MARSHALL, & CO.

FORES'S
SPORTING NOTES AND SKETCHES.

THE Proprietor of the above Quarterly Magazine has pleasure in informing lovers of sport that he has made arrangements with well-known authors to supply carefully written and amusing articles connected therewith ; and as full-page Illustrations will be one of its leading features, he has secured the services of eminent sporting artists for this purpose, and will spare no endeavour to make this the highest class Sporting Magazine of the day.

The first number will be published early in April, 1884, and will contain eight full-page tinted Illustrations, and the Articles as enumerated on the other side. The price will be Two Shillings, and may be ordered of any Bookseller, or from the Publishers, Messrs. Fores, 41 Piccadilly, London.

TO ADVERTISERS.

THE Proprietor of the above high-class Magazine begs leave respectfully to direct attention to this valuable medium of advertising every description of property, especially that which is connected with the varied requirements of Sportsmen.

The Publication will be Quarterly, and as one of the leading features will consist of full-page tinted Illustrations, depicting celebrated people, events, sports, &c., the work will be largely one of reference, thereby increasing its importance to advertisers.

FORES'S
SPORTING NOTES AND SKETCHES.

A LONG WAY TO COVERT.

By A. HERON.

SUPPOSE that there is no profession in which, if a man is a sportsman, he can indulge his tastes so fully as in that of a soldier. Quartered here to-day, there to-morrow, with ever a hearty welcome from those living wheresoever it may be his lot to be stationed from time to time, if there *is* sport of any kind to be obtained in the neighbourhood, the 'soldier-officer' is sure to get a chance of indulging in it; at least, so it was when I held Her Majesty's commission in the 1st Hussars. Those were the days when examinations for the Army were within the compass of ordinary capabilities, and but little extra preparation was necessary in the way of cramming to fit a boy coming from any of the public schools to qualify for the test demanded by the Government. In those days even the work we had to perform as officers was light and pleasant, though, to be sure, it *was* an awful bore to have to get up to morning stables in the winter, especially after a 'big night;' but, so long as the necessary work was properly done, leave was nearly always to be had for the asking, and, if one could *possibly* be spared, never refused for sporting purposes.

In those days, if an officer in a cavalry regiment did not care for hunting, he was 'hunted,' and generally found it to his advantage to transfer himself to any regiment which was willing to receive him; for he found the tastes and ideas of his brother-officers quite unsuited to his own, and so, as a rule, *esprit de corps* was further strengthened by *esprit de sport*.

Those were truly halcyon days, and I don't believe that officers were any the worse soldiers, if they were, perhaps, not so talented or so deeply read in 'tactics' and all the etcæteras of learning necessary now-a-days; and it has ever been admitted

that the 'tactics' (if one may so call them) of being able to
keep well with hounds when running a good pace over a big
country necessitates the possession of qualities far more valuable
to an officer than the power of cramming his head with ' conic
sections' and abstruse calculations, which it is necessary for the
unhappy subaltern of to-day to acquire; and the true sportsman
ever makes the best officer.   At all events *we* thought so, and
we honestly believed that we were performing our duty to our
country quite as fully when riding to hounds as when in the
barrack square, even though 'the wish might be father to the
thought.'   Moreover, I am sure our dear old Colonel thought so
too; and there must have been some *very* special reason to
prevent his making one of our party on the coach to covert on a
hunting day.   *Tempora mutantor;* but it is nevertheless pleasant
to recall these memories, and to feel that if 'the dog has had his
day,' he *has* had it, and a very good one too.

The dear old regiment still exists, untouched, thank goodness, as yet, by the hand of the reformer ; and long may it
remain so, true to its motto, '*Conservare.*'   But how many of
those who served in it with me are left in it now ?   But one or
two.   The rest have either gone over to the 'majority' or are
married and ' done for,' myself amongst the latter number.

Once a-year I grow young again, and that is when my wife
and I go to town to stay with my old friend Joe Malton.   Joe
and I, and perhaps one or two of the old lot, get together, and a
real good time we have of it, and sit up to all hours talking
over old days.   Joe and I joined the regiment the same day,
and left it the same day, for he always declared that when *I*
went he should go *too*, and as I was about to get married he
thought he would do the same ; and as my *fiancée* had a very
pretty little sister he, as luck would have it, fell in love with
her, and she, nothing loth, accepted him, and so we had a double
wedding.

Joe never got his troop, but I obtained mine some years
before I retired through the death of my own captain, and
when this event took place Joe at once went to the Colonel and
begged to be posted to my troop as my subaltern ; and the
Colonel, knowing what inseparables we were, at once gave his
consent, and so we always marched together ; and if the annual
move of the regiment took place, as it often did, before the
hunting season was over, we always took our hunting things
with us, and many a day's hunting we managed to steal if the

hounds were out near enough for one or the other of us to get to. If he went, I marched the troop, and if I went he did, and we took it in turns; and so, as our map could show, our experience of different packs was considerable, for we had marked out all the marches we had made, and different meets we had been to, putting special marks against any place from which we had extra good sport. There is one place we distinguished above all others, and the mention of that one particular day was for a long time a sore subject to Joe. I think that, as a rule, persons who are what is commonly called 'quick-tempered,' are also the warmest-hearted, and Joe was no exception. No warmer, more generous heart, ever beat, and he certainly had about the quickest thing in tempers I ever knew : but, notwithstanding, we never but once had a single difference of any kind. I don't know why it was, but he never seemed to mind anything *I* said to him ; but for years after, whenever I alluded to that one particular day, he always winced a good bit. However, he has got hardened to my chaffing him about it now, and so I don't mind repeating the story : besides, I have often told it in his presence, and he now laughs over it as heartily as I do. It is this : After several years of pleasant soldiering in England, it occurred to the authorities to suddenly order the regiment to Scotland. Now neither Joe or I had ever been to Scotland, and our ideas of the country were but limited, and we neither of us had looked upon it in the light of a hunting country, but a sort of mixture of wood, water, and whisky, and covered with perpetual snow all through the winter; and had any one but our old Colonel told us there was decent hunting to be got there, we should hardly have believed it. However, we found by experience he spoke truly respecting Ayrshire, for, as a hunting county, it is nearly perfection, though small in extent, being nearly all grass, and always ' good going.' No matter what the weather is elsewhere, one can nearly always hunt in Ayrshire ; for, from its being near the sea, or some such cause, it is but rarely that frost interferes with the hunting; and, short as is the distance from Glasgow, the latter place may be several inches deep in snow, and yet not a vestige of anything of the sort in Ayrshire, or even a few miles out of Glasgow in that direction, and Joe and I felt our lines had indeed fallen in pleasant places, the only drawback to our hunting being the necessity for always being obliged to train from Glasgow ; and as economy was a consideration

to us in those days, we did not keep our horses at Ayr or
Kilmarnock, as many of the people who hunted from Glasgow did, but had to content ourselves with stabling the few
quads we possessed in barracks, and sending them down by
the early train, on hunting days, to Kilmarnock, whilst we
ourselves followed by the later train which stopped there, and
this gave us plenty of time to have our breakfast comfortably,
and Kilmarnock was a good central point to start from, and
within an easy distance, as a rule, to ride on to covert.

Joe's stable and mine was, as regards servants and requisites,
very much a joint affair, and we had all things in common. His
head man was an odd specimen of the genus 'soldier-servant,'
but my own was the most peculiar one I had ever met. He
had served in the regiment for several years, but a bad fall in
the field had injured his knee, and he had been therefore discharged from the service, with a magnificent pittance wherewith
to support himself and a wife who had as many children as
there are days in the week—there really *were* seven, and we
used to call them 'Monday,' 'Tuesday,' &c. 'Thursday' had
not long arrived when he met with his accident, and when he
was discharged, knowing him to be an honest fellow and a good
groom, I took him into my stable, and eventually made him my
head man : he also acted as my valet and general factotum.
His name was William Buckle—'*Mr.* Buckle,' as the other servants called him, he always insisting on their using the prefix.
He was a good, faithful creature, always cheerful and willing,
honest to a fault, and thought there was no one in the regiment
to compare with me—except himself; and 'our' horses, 'our'
baggage, 'our' everything, was his usual way of describing my
property, and he might have been the very Colonel himself as
regards the overweening confidence he had in his own capabilities. This excess of assurance was the constant cause of
getting him into trouble, and very often me too, for he was for
ever running off to execute an order before he really half understood it, and, putting his own construction upon it, not unfrequently made a mess of it. However, his many good qualities
made up for his few failings, and I might have gone far before I
found a more faithful servant. To *me* he was always truthful,
but to outsiders he used to tell the most Munchausen stories of
the performances of our horses. Joe used to hate him, because
he used to compare the soundness of his purchases unfavourably
with that of my own horses, and would turn round to Joe, after

watching one of his horses, which was always a bad feeder after hunting, refuse his feed, and say, 'Ah! *Our* little brown 'oss he've eat all '*is* corn, and would eat as much again if I give it 'im,' or make some such remark to Joe, which the latter could not stand, for he was always terribly tetchy about his horses; and so, by degrees, he took a rooted dislike to poor Buckle, and never believed he could do anything right.

Well, there is, they say, an exception to every rule, and after we had had a long spell of hunting weather, and some exceptionally good sport, such a swingeing hard frost set in that not even Ayrshire was proof against it, and hunting was stopped. However, after about a week of it the wind suddenly shifted, and as rapid a thaw set in as we could have wished for.

Now the meet was advertised for the next day at a place by the name of Caldwell, a station rather more than midway between Glasgow and Kilmarnock. There were two morning trains which stopped there, but only one (the earlier one) by which we could send our horses; so as Joe's man was ill we decided to send Buckle on with them by that train, and follow on comfortably by the next one: so, sending for him to come to me, I gave him the necessary orders. Joe and I went to dinner that night in high spirits at the prospect of sport on the morrow.

When I was undressing to go to bed that night, Joe came up to my room and said, 'Look here, old fellow! as that beggar Buckle is apt to be a bit of a fool at times, don't you think it would be as well to write out his instructions for him: just to make sure, you know? I always do with my own man, and I find it answers.' So, knowing Buckle's failing, I agreed, and the more readily since he was to take Joe's horse on as well as my own. Accordingly, before going to bed I wrote out, as carefully as possible, the orders for Buckle, and placed the paper by my bedside. Sure enough, in the morning there was Buckle by my bedside, with his usual 'Beg your pardon, sir, Sergeant Reilly said yer wanted me.'

'Yes,' I said, waking up. 'Are the horses all right?'

'Yes, sir.'

'What's the weather like?'

'Thawing and mizzling with rain.'

Why on earth soldier-servants should always describe it as *mizzling* with rain I never yet could understand; but they always do get hold of the most extraordinary words, and Mr. Buckle's vocabulary was quite up to the average.

'Give me that paper off the chair,' I said, 'and bring the candle here. You can read?'

'Yes, sir; I can read all right.'

'Well, anyhow, I will read it over to you.'

And then I read over his orders, as to what hour he was to leave, what train to go by, where to go to, &c., and also to order Joe's trap to be ready for us to go to the station in at a later hour. He seemed quite hurt at my taking all this unwonted trouble, and after folding the paper put it, with a great show of care, into an old pocket-book, which he produced from some inner recess of his coat. Little did I then think how needless all my care would prove. However, he assured me that he quite understood 'heverythink.'

Well, after breakfast, Joe's trap came round; the rain had stopped about an hour before, the air was quite warm, and everything bid fair for a good day's sport. We reached the station, luckily in good time, for generally we only just managed to catch the trains. On our arrival, what was my surprise to see Buckle, whom I believed to have been waiting for us at Caldwell, looking as if he had done something extra smart that morning. On my asking him why he had not gone on with the horses, he said that, as he did not go with them the last time, he concluded I did not mean him to do so. Joe looked black, and muttered something pretty audibly, but as there was no time to waste he ran off to get our tickets, while Buckle took our bags containing our change of clothes, which we always took when 'training,' in case of accidents, out of the dog-cart, running off with them so as to avoid being pitched into, I suppose. Seeing him going off towards the platform from which the trains for Kilmarnock usually started, I called out to him to come back. The only response I got was a frantic gesticulation, accompanied by a shout of, 'This way, sir; the train's a-going.' Seeing a porter, I told him to run and fetch him back, and when he returned I said, 'Where the d—l are you going to?' He replied, 'That's your train, sir,' and I, knowing perfectly well that the train we wanted to go by started from the other side of the station altogether, endeavoured to convince him that it was *not* our train, but he would have it he was right, and was so positive about it, that, seeing Mr. MacWhistler, the station-master, passing by, I asked him if I was not right; and he at once said I was, of course. Buckle looked puzzled, and, putting down the bags in a despairing way, and with an air which implied that, station-master or not, he knew best, said, 'Well, all I know is that the 'orses went away from that 'ere platform this morning!'

Mr. MacW. said, 'Were they *your* horses which went away this morning, sir?'

I replied, 'Yes; I suppose so.'

'Where were they booked to?'

'To Caldwell.'

'To *Caldwell!*' he said. 'Why, your man there, despite all I could say, would have it that they were to go to *Cornwall!!* They have been gone ever so long by the express. We don't, as a rule, send horses by that train, but, knowing you gentlemen, we did it to oblige you; and, what is more, your man was so late with them that the train was late in starting.'

During this we had been walking towards the other platform, and Joe, just then coming up, had overheard the conversation.

Mr. MacWhistler continued: 'The only thing I can do is to telegraph, and try and stop them at Kilmarnock; but I much fear I shall be too late, and if so they will go on to Carlisle. However, you had better go on by this train to Kilmarnock, on the chance of their being there when you arrive.' And off he ran to telegraph.

Never shall I forget the scene which ensued. The story had already reached the train, thanks to the porter, who had overheard and retailed it; and being the first open day after the frost, there were more hunting-men there than usual, who, with their heads out of the windows, were all roaring with laughter at our expense. It was certainly exasperating enough, especially after all my care, and I felt too angry to speak; but Joe, who by this time had taken it all in, could stand it no longer. He cast one despairing look at me, and then seizing the unfortunate Buckle by the scruff of the neck, he shook him like a rat, and fetching him a kick hard enough to kill a horse, sent him flying, bags and all, and was running after him to give him a repetition, and would, I verily believe, have half-killed him had I not implored him to desist. I don't think I ever saw any one in a much worse 'taking on.' However, as we had already delayed the train beyond its proper time, there was nothing left for it but to get in; so, shouting to Buckle to get in anywhere he could, off we started. Bad as it was, it was too amusing, for the bare idea of our horses being sent off from Glasgow to Cornwall for a day's hunting was in itself absurd enough; but the scene between Joe and the wretched Buckle, and the expression of the latter's coun-

tenance, the downfall from his pinnacle of pride—he, *the* Mr.
Buckle, to have made such a fool of himself, and, worse still, to
be kicked and laughed at in front of those before whom he had
swaggered so much and so often, was too much, and he looked
it; while, if ever suppressed hatred was let loose in one kick, it
was in Joe's. I lay back in the carriage—fortunately we were
alone—and *roared* with laughter, and the more I laughed the
more Joe swore. He was always most amusing and original in his
remarks, but I never heard such quaint imprecations before. I
tried to pacify him, and to assure him that it would be all right;
but it was all to no purpose, and it ended in his declaring it
was all my fault : till, last of all, and as even the very worm will
turn, I turned rusty, and we had no end of a row, after which we
both lapsed into sulky silence.

At last, after what seemed to me to be an interminably long
journey, we reached Kilmarnock, and in reply to our questions
were informed, to our relief, that the telegram had been
effectual, and that our horses had been stopped, but only just
in time ; and, sure enough, there they were, being led up and
down by one of the porters. Out of the carriage Joe rushed,
nearly knocking me over; out through the doorway of the
station, seized his horse, tore off the clothing, and jumping
on to her back, without saying a word to me, galloped up
the road at the rate of forty miles an hour, utterly regardless
of where he was going to, and of his mare's legs. I followed
on more steadily, and after a time caught sight of him in the
distance, going off in what I rightly concluded was the wrong
direction; for I had heard that the hounds would most likely
draw towards Kilmarnock, whereas he was going off too much
to the left. However, he never looked back, and it was, of
course, no use to shout to him, so I had to let him go. After
riding on for about an hour I came up with the hounds. Every
one, of course, had heard the story, and I was, as may be
imagined, assailed with no end of chaff about our going to hunt
with old Trelawny from Glasgow, &c. On making inquiries for
Joe, he had not been seen, and, as I supposed, had not found
the hounds. They had had no sport as then, for there was little
scent, strange to say ; but with the day matters improved, and
shortly after my arrival a fox was viewed ' away,' and gave us, if
not, perhaps, *the* run of the season, at all events as good a gallop
as the heart of man could well wish for, and a kill at the end of
it. Just as we got away I saw Joe, who had just returned from

his travels, with the mare all in a muck, and himself too, his hat like a concertina, his coat, which was new, muddy and torn. For a few fields I saw them going like mad a little to the right of me, the mare jumping in a very uneven, slipshod style, and then we came to a fence with a deepish drop into the road beyond it. On landing the mare give a falter and pulled up dead lame, and the last I saw of them was Joe dismounted, standing by her and looking as if he could kill her, and she with her near fore held up in a helpless way. Just then the hounds turned to the left, and, though I felt a bit selfish and guilty, I went on, for the pace was too good to stop.

Later on in the day we found another fox, and had a very nice gallop, but ran to ground ; and I then turned to ride back to the station, where I found Joe, looking the picture of woe. Poor old boy! We both relented towards each other the moment we met. He had had to leave his mare at a farm, too hopelessly lame to be moved, and to drive to the station in the farmer's trap. Bit by bit, on the return journey, he got out of me the details of the day's sport ; but I was most unwilling to say too much about it, or to make it worse for him by letting him know what he had lost. After some time the mare was patched up sound enough to go to auction, and, I grieve to add, only fetched about as many shillings as she had cost pounds. The Vet. said that it must have been disease of some long standing—I think he said 'navicular.' Before this, Joe never would have a Vet's. opinion when buying a horse, but I think he evinced less contempt for professional opinion afterwards, for his succeeding investments in horseflesh proved sounder than his many previous ones had been. An old aunt of his dying soon after, like a good old soul left her town house and well-filled 'stocking' to him, and as *her* investments had been 'sound ones,' he became a comparatively rich man. He and his wife talk of coming to live close to us. I can wish for nothing better than again to have my old friend and brother-in-law near me. Besides, Buckle, who is still with me, requires keeping in order from time to time.

I am glad to say, by the way, that Mrs. Buckle never got beyond 'Saturday.'

'Tuesday,' the eldest boy, is in my stable.

A DAY'S SHOOTING IN THE PYRENEES.

By the Author of 'The Tommiebeg Shootings.'

OMEWARD bound from the East, we found ourselves—Fred Somers and myself—one fine morning
in the first week of October, at Marseilles, and as
neither of us was in any particular hurry to face a
northern climate after twelve months' enjoyment of more genial
temperature—to say nothing of the disinclination we both felt to
relapse into the conventionalities of civilisation after the wild,
free-and-easy life we had been leading—we determined to take
a *short cut* to England *vià* the Pyrenees. The hedge-bound
stubbles and turnip-fields offered no temptation to us after the
wide range, without outsides, we had been shooting over lately on
the shores of the Bosphorus. There must be, we thought, some
sort of sport to be got along the road we traced out on Murray's
map ; at all events we decided on taking our shooting tackle,
which we reinforced by supplies at Marseilles, and having despatched our heavy baggage by the *petite vitesse*—Anglicè, the
goods train—to Paris, we proceeded in light marching order—
that is to say, with a portmanteau a-piece—by railway to Mont-
pellier. Here, at the expense of much palaver and twenty
napoleons, we became proprietors of a dusty, rather shaky-
looking *calèche*, whose principal attraction was the being somewhat better-looking than its fellows, which, like itself, had been
laid up in ordinary for the winter, and were now paraded before
us with much ceremony and more palaver.

Though visibly in a sad state of decrepitude, we thought
there was life in the old thing yet, and trusted to its surviving
yet another month, which we purposed spending on our road to
Pau, where the railway communication recommenced. Travelling post would make us quite independent to go where the
whim took us, to stop *where* we liked, to go *when* we liked.
Behold us, then, fairly *en route*. A day or two's experience of
our vehicle sufficed to set our minds at ease as to its enduring
qualities, and accustomed as we had been for some time to
almost every other description of locomotion—steam, horse,
mule, donkey, camel—there was something luxurious and ex-

hilarating in our novel mode of travel. The merry jingle of the
bells on the horse-collars and harness imposed upon us, by making
us fancy we were going at a rattling pace, and the lively crack
of the postilion's long whip as we entered the towns brought
out all the population to wonder at the apparition of a post-
carriage at a season when the Pyrenees are deserted by ordinary
travellers.

I do not imagine that many travellers have been seduced
into a visit to the Pyrenees for the sake of any attractions they
may offer for sport of any kind. Those that have been so
deluded will not, of a certainty, 'try it on' again; and to those
who may have any idea of making a campaign there with the
double-barrel, we can only say, as *Punch* said to those who are
about to marry, 'Don't!' We say this, however, with a reserva-
tion. If they look for sport—that is, if they measure their
enjoyment by the weight of the bag, and insist on the contents
of that bag being composed of game—legitimate game—we
say, 'Don't!' But if they are 'not proud,' and do not mind
seeing, when the bag is emptied and the results of the day laid
out upon the greensward, a little admixture of the *feræ naturæ*
which their principles and prejudices have taught them to consider *infra dig.*—if they will only substitute the word 'Fun' for
'Sport' (and, after all, old Johnson's first definition of 'Fun' *is*
'Sport'), we bid them follow in our wake, submitting only that
they ought to be well up in French, in order to appreciate fully
the little episodes of adventure and the character of the 'sporting
men' with whom they must necessarily become associated.

Our mode of action was this. On our arrival at any place
whose neighbourhood looked like shooting, our first care was to
take the landlord of our inn or the postmaster into our counsels,
and it is right to say that our inquiries were always met with
the utmost civility, and with the most profuse offers of aid to
further our object. As a rule, we found it as well to take the very
florid accounts we heard of the abundance of hares and partridges
cum grano: it would be safe to divide their sum by a good
round number. But we had become quite used to Eastern
flowers of language, though we hardly expected to find them
flourishing among the Franks.

On arriving at Cauterets on the 3rd of November we had
no little difficulty in getting taken in at an hôtel, for the season
of the *eaux* was long time past. Inns and lodging-houses and
shops were all closed for the winter. The establishment was

partly dismantled, and was left in charge of a jolly-looking old
nondescript, who came out in the several capacities of landlord,
cook, waiter, boots, and chambermaid.

'*Ah, Messieurs!*' said this personage in his character of
landlord, 'it is a *vrai coup de bonheur*'—a regular bit of luck.
'You arrive *au beau moment*'—in the very nick of time! 'Ha!
ha! Messieurs will have a glorious opportunity of distinguishing
themselves. *Ecoutez, Messieurs!*' he went on, in a slow and
measured tone, as if to allow us to dwell upon each syllable of
his communication. 'Listen! To-morrow—to-morrow—one
has organized *une chasse à l'ours—à l'ours!*'—a bear hunt! And
then he scanned our countenances to read thereon the effect of
this thrilling news. Now I had already *assisted* at one or two of
these battues, and having once had a very narrow escape of being
bagged myself instead of Bruin—whom, by the way, I never saw,
and firmly believe to have been a myth—I knew that the field
would be taken by every ragamuffin within a dozen miles of
the place who possessed a gun; not to mention the outsiders,
whose name is generally legion, armed with pikes, and poles, and
pitchforks, or any portable implement of husbandry that might
by ingenuity be converted *à l'improviste* into a weapon offensive
or defensive. So, affecting to be greatly excited by the grandeur
of the enterprise that loomed before us, I nodded my head
mysteriously to mine host, like 'Noodle' in the play, and
made him happy with the words, '*Nous verrons!*' pronounced
oracularly.

'I will tell you what it is, Fred,' I said to my companion as
soon as I had interpreted what had been Greek to him. If you
fancy going out with these fellows, only say the word, and I am
with you; but, *experto crede*, I have no faith in these *chasses*. I
have *been* bear-hunting; and all I know is, that if by chance there
might ever have been a bear within a couple of leagues of us he
always had timely notice given him to quit. You cannot conceive the row—the hallooing, and horn-blowing, and *sacré*-ing,
and *peste*-ing was always something awful; besides the constant
reports of guns going off without meaning it. It stands to
reason no bear would be such an ass as to wait for such fellows.
Now look here! The meet is most probably here in the town;
we will be a-foot in good time, and you shall judge for yourself,
when you see the field, whether it will be worth the risk—of
being shot, I mean. If you don't like the look of it, I will arrange
to have a guide for the mountains; we will take our guns with

Finch Mason

Alphonse Vingt
Ah! c'est magnifique la chasse
à l'anar

See page 13.

us, on the chance, as Mr. Micawber says, 'of something turning up.'

'All right, old fellow! my name's Easy!' replied my companion, good-humouredly. 'But I own,' he continued, 'I should like most uncommonly to have a shot at a bear. I would give a trifle only just to see how he looks in the open.'

'Take my word for it,' was my answer, 'you are just as likely to see a bear on our way to the Pont d'Espagne as you would be if you joined the ruck to-morrow : but, as I said before, if you really wish to go, I am your man.'

The main street of Cauterets presented an animated scene at an early hour on the following morning, when, having despatched our breakfast, we strolled towards the centre, to which every one seemed hurrying. Oh! for the genius of Homer, or the pencil of poor Leech, to reproduce the motley figures, the queer costumes, and the multifarious weapons of the *chasseurs*, as they poured into the little town! Here a fellow, got up regardless of expense, in a tight, close-fitting velveteen coat, long in the skirt, and of infinite pockets, buttoned up to his throat by copper buttons—gems of art in their way, being embossed with sporting devices of rare variety : the nether man encased in yellow gaiters or leggings fastened with straps and buckles ; the whole surmounted by a sort of jockey-cap of black velvet, with wide projecting eave. His rifle or smooth-bore slung across his back by a broad strap, which crossed another broader strap over his breast, belonging to the monstrous *carnassière*, or game-bag, of tawny leather, with an outside of network and a pendant fringe at the bottom. Yet another belt or two, from which were suspended powder-flask and shot-pouch ; and over all a green cord, also across the chest, which ended in two big tassels on either side of a wicker flask, holding about a quart. Here a stout peasant, wearing on his head a red or black *berret*—or bonnet ; his blue blouse, confined at the waist with a red sash or a broad leather-belt—carrying his gun, most likely loaded and capped, pointed at everybody at the same time. But on arriving at the meet in the *Place* our attention was immediately drawn to him who evidently was the leader of the expedition. He was a lively, dapper-looking little fellow, rather fat and very hot, with a round, swarthy face, clean-shaved, with the exception of a very stumpy black moustache, and a round tuft on his chin. On his turnip-shaped head he wore a sort of Vandyke hat, with a rosette at the side, of izard-hair ; and his loose velveteen blouse, with

capacious breast-pockets, belted at the waist, looked comfortable
and workmanlike. He was bustling about and seemed to be
everywhere at once, now giving his orders to a lot of fellows
armed with poles and pikes, whom we took to be beaters ; now
conferring with some of the more extensively got-up sportsmen,
like the one we have described. Seeing him for a moment in
confabulation with our host, we anticipated what presently
happened.

Advancing to us and lifting his hat in the most polite manner,
he began by expressing his sorrow at not having been earlier
informed of the arrival of two Messieurs, who were *amateurs de
la chasse*—that he would otherwise have made it *son devoir* to
have proposed our joining his *partie de chasse.* It was not too
late, he hoped, to insure the pleasure of our company. ' *Ah!*'
he said with great unction, ' *c'est magnifique, la chasse à l'ours !*
C'est moi qui vous le dis'—I give you my word it is all that is
piquant—all that is——' *enfin, c'est superbe !!*'

By this time, however, Fred Somers had been gradually
coming over to my opinion, and having seen the reckless way in
which the guns were universally carried, was quite willing to
agree with me. After a short conference with him, I made a
speech to our inviter, expressive of our gratitude for his polite-
ness, and our profound regrets at being unable to spare a day to
a *chasse* which I doubted not, and heartily wished, would be
crowned with success—that our time was limited—the season far
advanced—that our object was to explore the exquisite beauties
of the glorious mountain country in which it was his happiness
to be domiciled—and so on. Monsieur le Capitaine was *désolé*,
quite. It was *dommage*—it pained him—*mais enfin !*—which
being freely interpreted means, 'Such is life!'

Begging his acceptance of two or three Malta Havannas from
my case, and shaking him by the hand—there ensued a deal
of taking off hats between us and the small circle of *chasseurs*
that had closed round us, and without waiting to see the start
we returned to our hotel, where we found in attendance a cheery-
looking guide, holding by a cord a very untoward-looking, big-
boned, crop-tailed pointer, which he had procured in our behalf
according to my instructions.

This cross-grained brute gave us, during the first part of our
walk, no end of trouble. His national prejudices were evidently
strong, and it was clear he had conceived no great opinion of a
couple of *chasseurs* who had little about them but their guns,

which they carried over the shoulder instead of slung at the back, to qualify them—most likely he missed the big *carnassière*, the tight leggings, and the jaunty, self-satisfied air, to which he had been all his life accustomed. But for the remonstrances of our guide I should soon have started César homeward, in which direction, though held in hand, he persisted for some time in pointing. After a while, however, he became more resigned, and accepted the situation. Fred's knocking over a woodcock, which we flushed unexpectedly on the very edge of the Gave, captivated him at once. He was now on his mettle, and with his assistance we put up two more cocks in a sort of brake of stunted box, one of which we bagged.

Our next achievement was the getting, after much circumventing and stalking, a pair of choughs, of which we came upon a small colony. Their yellow legs and beaks (not red, as in the Cornish bird) distinguished them at once from the vulgar jackdaw. It ought to be known that it was not in mere wantonness we killed them. We had already preserved and sent home the skins of a great variety of birds, and these rare specimens would form a valuable case in the *museum*. We may say, *en passant*, that the only other place in which we found the bird was on the road to the Cirque de Gavarnie ; there, too, we had succeeded in getting a pair, but they were badly shot : those that we now carefully smoothed down and folded in a handkerchief were beautiful specimens, and clean-killed.

We wasted a good deal of time in beating the low brushwood coverts that appeared occasionally on the left of our path, but drawing them blank we pushed on to the Pont d'Espagne at a good pace ; from thence a short but rough walk brought us to the *great* lake of the Pyrenean chain, the Lac de Gaube, which in the Alps would be regarded as a mere pool or tarn. The air was too keen for lounging about, and the dark beetling precipices, which form a sort of wall round the dismal-looking lake, looked too uninviting to induce us to do more than take a hasty survey of this much-vaunted bit of scenery, which may be all very well, and make a very cool and pleasant change, in the height of summer.

On retracing our steps to the picturesque and rather rickety-looking bridge, our guide proposed our crossing it and going a short distance further, to a spot from which he promised us a fine view. There was already, about the level of the bridge, a slight sprinkling of snow, just enough to *tint* the ground, but as we got

higher the white carpet became more and more palpable, till on
arriving at a sort of ridge, from which we looked down into a
valley far beneath us, it might have been perhaps a couple of
inches in depth. Here we were startled at hearing an unearthly
sort of cry, borne to us on the light breeze, and while I was
pondering on its strange effect, the guide suddenly called out:
'Monsieur heard that—did he not? It is the hunters *là bas!*'
—down below us. And, true enough, the puffs of wind brought us
at intervals, with more distinctness, the cries and shouts of men.

'I say, Fred, what did I tell you—eh? Those fellows are
miles from us. Now you don't imagine for a moment that
any sensible animal—and Bruin is by no means a fool. . . . .
Quick! quick! Fred!' I whispered hoarsely to him, for he was
some little way below me. 'Ram a couple of balls over your
loose charge!' And without further ado I proceeded, with a hand
trembling from excitement, to put a ball into each barrel—old
habit had made us always carry a few balls and some patches
in our waistcoat pockets.

'Look here!' I said quietly to the guide, who was seated
upon a stone lighting his pipe, and I pointed at the same time
to a series of big, round footprints in the snow, the surface of
which was brushed by the advance of each foot; 'what do you
call that?' '*Cré mâtin!*' he exclaimed, slipping his pipe hurriedly into his pocket, and looking first at the track, then peering
cautiously round in every direction. '*Pas de doûte! c'est bien
lui! c'est l'ours!*' he said solemnly. And Bruin it most assuredly
was who had left his mark, and who had probably been 'taking
a sight' at the hunt from the very spot on which we were
standing. He had perhaps been disturbed in his chucklings of
delight by the sound of our voices, for there was no doubt in the
world of the recent passage of the animal.

My companion, who knew me pretty well, had acted upon
my suggestion at once, without asking any questions; having
done so, he came up to where the guide and myself were
following the trail. 'What's up?' he asked. 'Only a bear!' I
replied. 'You remember what I told you—here is his line, you
see, pointing this way. It's a burning scent, my boy!'

For about fifteen yards or so he had kept the path, and had
then turned off suddenly to the right, under the lee of a big rock,
and then down a steep incline of some fifty yards in length—so
steep, that we saw it would require some holding on by the
stunted shrubs to follow him. While I was taking a hasty look

at the *country*, in order to take my line, Fred suddenly shouted out, 'By Jove, there he goes!' and bang, bang went his two barrels, giving me time only to see a dark object, rolled up apparently in a ball, disappear suddenly. I should say, if I were very hard-pressed by a very inquisitive and cross cross-examining counsel, just the tick of a clock before Fred pulled the trigger.

The latter was now bolting down an impossible slope, when I rushed forward, at some risk, and gripped him fast by the arm. 'Gently, Fred! gently! Load again!' I said to him.

'But he is down!' he replied, eagerly. 'I saw him topple over.'

'So did I ; nevertheless, load again! If he is dead, he won't run away, you know ; and if he is only scratched—why, then look out for squalls!' I verily believe poor Fred, in his excitement, would have put in the lead first, if I had not suggested that a charge of powder below it would be more to the purpose.

It was no easy matter achieving the descent of the inclined plane ; it looked ugly, too, for we were unable to see what was beyond it. We accomplished it at last by sitting on the ground, and easing ourselves down by holding on to the bushes. It ended by a drop of some eighteen or twenty feet perpendicular fall, at the foot of which was a clear field of *débris* of small stone, partially covered with snow ; but nothing was to be seen of Bruin, and there was not a bush or a twig to hide him. We were at the very spot where we had seen him disappear, and it was easy to see where he had mopped up the snow in his descent, and the still downward-pointing track he had left. I was satisfied that our *Ursa Major* had doubled himself up in a ball, or bundle, *more majorum*, and had dropped himself over the edge.

This, of course, I kept to myself; it would have been an act of wanton barbarity to damp poor Fred's delight at having bowled over a real bear. It was not till he had made two or three rather dangerous casts to find an opening for following Bruin, who, Fred averred, was 'knocked all to pieces,' that the guide and myself became persuaded it would be madness to try further. It was, indeed, an impracticable place ; looking, from where we stood, very like sheer precipice down to the plain.

'Never mind, Fred; it is "hard lines," I admit,' I said to my friend, who was chafing under the disappointment. 'You have seen *how a bear looks in the open*, you know ; and, more than that, have *had a shot* at him, which is about twice as much as you would have done if you had been with those fellows down yonder! It must be confessed Bruin has beat us fairly, but "better luck next time." We are scarcely likely to find any more big game, but we left two or three likely bits of covert lower down the valley, where we may yet pick up a cock or two.'

We were, nevertheless, not destined to have altogether a blank day in the way of *larger game.*

It was with great difficulty I persuaded my companion to leave the scene of his exploit—and the bear, too—behind us; and when, at last, he threw his gun over his shoulder, and turned away from the spot, he left there all his good spirits and light-heartedness. It must be confessed he was very indifferent company now; so much so, that I was fain to join conversation with our guide. He was an intelligent fellow, Pierre Cazus, and he beguiled the way with descriptions of the summer amusements, the excursions and picnics, and the gossip of the season of *les bains.* In the meantime, Fred, whose stock of French was limited, had marched on ahead of us, to indulge, probably, in melancholy brooding over his bad luck.

We had gone on thus for perhaps an hour, when suddenly we heard the report of a gun some little distance before us, and the ringing cry, 'Who-oop!' left not a doubt that Fred had this time really knocked over *something.* Knowing his recklessness and rashness, and having the bear always uppermost in my thoughts, I conjured up at once all sorts of horrible probabilities —the animal wounded, perhaps, and Fred alone! I tore along the rough path, followed closely by Pierre, and we were brought to a sudden halt by a loud shout, apparently issuing from the bed of the torrent below us—another louder hail, and we were plunging down the steep bank, at the bottom of which the Gave was hidden.

'Halloo! Fred!' I sang out, as I caught sight of him up to his waist in the stream, struggling with all his might to reach the other bank, his gun held high above his head.

'All right!' he answered; 'he is on the other side!'

'What is on the other side?' But already Pierre was with him in the river, and before he could answer the pair were landed, not without some difficulty and danger, on the opposite bank.

'What have you done?' I shouted out.

'Oh! never mind, old fellow; you will soon see. I've bagged

him safe enough!' he bawled out, as he scrambled over the rough boulders, making for a large patch of thick, stunted under-wood, some yards above him. This was within easy shot of where I was standing; in fact, I commanded the whole of the slope, so I contented myself with feeling if my charge was tight in each barrel, and waited the issue.

On carefully looking over the ground I espied, among the bushes, a bit of dark colour—*only a bit*, but enough to satisfy me that the object, whatever it might be, was Fred's victim.

'Who-oop!' shouted the latter, as he caught sight of the *object*, and dashed breathless into the low, tangled brake.

'Have a care, Fred! For Heaven's sake have a care, man!' I called out, the bear still before me, and my gun ready to cover the brute if he stirred. But Fred was now standing in pensive contemplation of his quarry, and I was near enough to perceive the shade that came across his face, just now so animated. What could it be?

Pierre had now arrived, and, stooping down, dragged out into the open—what? A bear? No—certainly *not* a bear. By all that is ridiculous! a huge, black, long-haired, long-bearded he-goat, as dead as Julius Cæsar!

It would appear, from Master Fred's account—which, by the way, he was rather chary in giving, for the subject was evidently most distasteful to him—that he had caught sight of a dark animal moving *stealthily* in the bushes. Of course, he thought it was *the* bear—why shouldn't it be? what was more likely? any fellow would have thought so, especially after he had wounded one *badly* so lately—that he had *stalked* to within easy shot of the brute, and only waited till it gave him a chance. Well, at last he saw enough of his broadside to know exactly where his shoulder *ought* to be, and, of course, he was not going to wait till the brute dodged him. How was he to tell, he should like to know, that it was only a beastly goat?

Poor Fred! I believe he would have cheerfully given five hundred francs to have been spared the degradation of paying fifteen for his shot; and five hundred more, at the very least, to bribe me to silence. I have, however, his full permission to tell the story under a pseudonym, and if he ever reads it he will have the consolation of thinking that it may, as I hope it will, afford some entertainment to our readers. They may by the way, be interested in knowing that the bear-hunters had *quite* a blank day.

FULL FORTY YEARS AGO.

By 'ORANGE BLOSSOM.'

NCE upon a time a fond mother was endeavouring to impress upon her little son the excellence of truth, honesty, charity, and other qualities which are more precious than rubies, and very much scarcer. She went on to tell him, as is the wont of good mothers, that in heaven he would meet with the reward of a virtuous life. 'Heaven,' said the child, pondering; 'are there any horses in heaven?' 'No, dear,' was the reply. 'Then,' exclaimed the little fellow, '*I don't want to go there!*' Is it necessary to add that he was a Yorkshire boy? He still lives, and has certainly never faltered in his devotion to the noble animal.

With such enthusiasts vivid recollections remain of days, and men, and horses, during the earliest period of their acquaintance with the Turf. To one, at any rate, as these lines are written, come memories of eager attention in very early life to talk about some famous racehorses of that time. The most prominent of them were Beeswing, Lanercost, and Charles XII.; but another celebrity was Mr. St. Paul's Calypso, who 'split' Beeswing and Lanercost in a splendid race for the Newcastle Cup, the 'old mare,' as she was fondly called, being victorious, whilst the redoubtable Lanercost finished last. A great treat, and vast incentive to make nearer acquaintance with the beautiful creatures about which, as it then seemed, all men spoke so often and so admiringly, was the occasional stolen examination of a portfolio full of prints, some plain, some coloured by hand. Various sporting subjects were represented, but the bias of the owner's taste was shown by racehorses largely predominating. When the vigilance of parents and custodians had been eluded—the precious portfolio propped against the back of a sofa, and the door shut—what delightful half-hours were spent in examining the sheaf of portraits! Those of horses cantering and galloping were the favourites, especially if their riders wore showy jackets. The period must have been shortly after that in which Lanercost and Beeswing fought their great battles, and set all the north country in a flame. The newest portrait was that of Blue Bonnet,

and so fascinating was the tartan and yellow-sleeved jacket which
adorned the body of Tommy Lye, that many were the attempts
made to reproduce its glories by the aid of a shilling paint-box,
after a rude pencil imitation had been produced of the galloping
filly and her queer, old-fashioned pilot. No colours were, for a
time, more popular in the north of England than those of Blue
Bonnet's owner. When a second and third St. Leger fell to his
lot, a demand had arisen for silk handkerchiefs having in the
centre a representation of the Derby winner, or the hero of
Doncaster, printed in colours. In one of the little north-country
towns in the Middleham neighbourhood a great sale was expected
for these exceedingly flash articles. When they arrived, it was
discovered that, although the yellow sleeves and cap of the rider
were correct enough, the tartan was not the exact one so familiar
to followers of Van Tromp and The Flying Dutchman. So,
instead of purchasing, the expected customers turned up the
nose of disdain ; the handkerchiefs had to be returned, and
others procured more satisfactory to the eyes of such exacting
critics.

But to go back to the portfolio. To the child poring over
the prints they appeared marvels of art. Now-a-days, perhaps,
they would not pass muster so readily, but assuredly many
of them were full of spirit, and often the likeness of the jockey,
as well of the horse, was good—a point in which many more
recent portraits fail dismally. One specially admired was that
of the 1820 St. Leger winner, St. Patrick. Perhaps this was
owing to a family story as to the origin of the horse's name.
Local associations made Reveller, Antonio, and Jack Spigot
favourites, although there was a coarseness about the second of
these that ever caused some of his more elegant companions in
the portfolio to be preferred. At Jerry a long pause was always
made. The colours were striking, and there was vigour and
character about both horse, jockey, and the whole of the little
group in the foreground ; whilst in the rear, glancing anxiously
at Mr. Gascoigne's black, Tom Shepherd was stripping off his
overcoat, allowing a glimpse to be caught of the white-and-
crimson sleeves that were presently to appear above Canteen's
back. Shepherd was an inhabitant of the town where the owner
of the portfolio resided, and many years after the date mentioned
still lived there, ready to tell stories of races which his knowledge of pace had enabled him to win on horses of which
Revolution, I think, was one. Occasionally he acted as starter

at the local races; but, eventually, his sufferings from gout, or
rheumatism, compelled him to cease visits to the breezy moor.
Tarrare, looking rather weak-backed as he cantered in the
St. Leger preliminary, under the light blue and white stripes
of Lord Scarborough, was always attractive, and so was the
varmint-looking Matilda, special interest attaching to Mr. Petre's
filly because an eye-witness of her famous Doncaster race had
told, in the child's presence, how the false starts caused Mameluke to turn so restive, that the application of a cart-whip was
inefficacious to make him start. With what awe was the story
heard as to how he was left far behind when the race did commence, and how he gradually drew on Matilda as told in the
most spirited verses ever written by a lover of the racehorse.
Margrave was another of the coarse class, but with an honest
look about his big head that caused him to be regarded with
friendly attention ; and a suspicion has always lingered that the
colourer had not been very true to the real thing when endeavouring to represent the Mostyn banner as carried by Queen
of Trumps. But the portfolio was a source of great delight, an
extra relish being imparted by knowledge that inspection of it
was a forbidden enjoyment. For the parents of that precocious
Yorkshire boy had a wholesome dread of the Turf and its temp-
tations, and sought, by all reasonable means, to discourage the
passionate fondness for everything pertaining to the sport that
he soon exhibited. But their well-meant efforts availed nothing;
and those were happy hours indeed when again and again he
turned over the beloved prints of St. Leger winners, hastily
laying aside the portfolio at the sound of approaching footsteps,
or listening anxiously for the voice of the old clock on the stairs
to tell how much longer he might draw delight from the glorious
thoroughbreds.

Then came the time when real live racehorses were seen for
the first time. It was rather a disappointing experience, as,
walking in their clothes, and ridden by stable-lads in homely
garb enough, they contrasted unfavourably with the bright-
coated, brilliant, galloping creatures like Tarrare and Blue
Bonnet in the pictures, and the gay jackets of the jockeys
were altogether wanting. Still, it was a memorable and deeply
interesting sight. From the place and time at which they presented themselves, it is exceedingly likely that they were a lot of
platers. But what wotted the excited looker-on of that ? Of
their names nothing was known to the young woman in attend-

ance on the child. How the incidents of that sunny morning come back! The girl spoke of those delightful animals vaguely, and not without awe, as 'the racehorses,' and, as experience has taught, only affected to take umbrage at some complimentary remark addressed to her by the lad or man in charge of the string. From the sweet, soft breeze—the time was between eleven and twelve in the forenoon—the month must have been May or early June. May in those days was often that May of the poets that, in these unsentimental times, has been succeeded by one of quite another sort. All was very still. Down below, in the sloping pasture where the ladies' smocks grew, the cows were cropping. Beyond, the narrow, rapid river wound and gleamed in the sunshine. Farther away still woods hung thick and long on the precipitous side of a valley, with great patches of grey rocks standing out sturdily here and there. Presently, made drowsy by excursions after buttercups and daisies, and by the warmth of the sun, the boy lay down and dozed, with the nurse-wench looking after his safety. There was nothing to threaten it, probably, except the field mice, and the bonny martins that built their nests in the sand-quarry close by. Then a distant bell proclaimed, not unmelodiously, to some mill hands that noon was come; and the dozer, rousing and blinking in the sun dazzle, was aware of trampling hoofs, and had sight, for the first time, of the creatures that were greatly to influence his life.

In that district it was almost impossible for any one with a natural liking for racehorses to escape from their influence; the talk, the sights, the sounds of each succeeding day, lead the mind so much in that direction. Old men there were to relate legends drawn from the two famous moors hard by, and from half-a-dozen racecourses within tolerably easy distance. Young men, fresh from stirring scenes on one or other of those courses, fired the imagination with descriptions of famous horses and riders from the south they had just seen, and told of the stout struggles in which they had beaten our northern champions, or set a York, Doncaster, or Newcastle crowd roaring with delight when the crack from Newmarket or Hampshire succumbed. Many of the ancient dames of the little town—they live to vast ages in the air of those wild hills and fir-clad valleys— could tell stories of old racehorses and of their roystering, debauched owners, that to some youthful ears were more delightful than any tale of fairy or magician.

Is the legend still remembered there of one of the Huttons

of Marske and the Cup race won by Silvio? By-the-by, was
it Silvio or Navigator? Silvio, I think. It has been related
before, but incompletely. Well, for four successive years Silvio
had started for the Gold Cup, then but just established, and a prize
most coveted by men who ran horses at what was then nearly
the most important meeting in the North. Each time he had
been beaten by Dainty Davie, once perhaps by mischance, owing
to coming into collision with a horseman, as not unfrequently
occurred in those days of ill-kept courses. Still later in life
he was thrown out of the same race by running against a post,
so his owner's experience of the great Gold-Cup contest was
very disagreeable. Now, in 1763, Dainty Davie ran his last
race; so, with this terrible opponent out of the way, Silvio's
chance for the Cup of the following season was, no doubt,
thought a great one. At that time betting between horses was
often very heavy. In whatever way Silvio's owner had wagered,
it is certain (so the old story said) that he had far more money
on the Cup than he cared to lose, and, when the hour for its
decision arrived, left the moor and walked away in the direction
of his own residence, unable to bear the sight of his pet's defeat,
if beaten he was to be. Silvio was not favourite, starting at
three to one, whilst odds were betted on Mr. Fenwick's Shuttle.
According to the legend, Mr. Hutton lingered by the roadside in
great anxiety, until a man came, lurching but merry, along the
path from the racecourse, raising his voice now and again in a
half-tipsy shout for 'Bonny Hutton!' That uneasy gentleman
recognised in the noisy wayfarer one of his tenants, occupant of
a small farm.

'Which horse has won the Cup?' he inquired, anxiously.

'Why,' said the man, staring stupidly, 'you've won—Silvio
won, sir.'

'Then,' exclaimed the relieved Mr. Hutton, 'you shall have
your farm rent-free for life!'

In this handsome reward for information there is something
rather characteristic of the manners of men in the district at
that period. Some of them are known to have been very free-
handed and generous. At the same time the truth of this
portion of the story has always seemed to me rather doubtful.
The facts might still be ascertained. But now about Silvio.
Mr. Hutton's horse was apparently the first on record to bear
the name. What was its origin? The question was discussed
not very long ago, without a satisfactory conclusion being

reached, when Lord Falmouth won the Derby with *his* Silvio.
I forget whether any allusion was made to the occurrence of the
name in Andrew Marvell's *Nymph Complaining for the Death of
her Fawn*. This always appeared to me a probable source
from which Mr. Hutton obtained the name. Most people will
remember the opening lines,—

> ' *The wanton troopers, riding by,*
> *Have shot my fawn, and it will die.*'

But some of them may have forgotten that she goes on to
tell of

> ' *Inconstant Silvio, when yet*
> *I had not found him counterfeit,*
> *One morning (I remember well),*
> *Tied in this silver chain and bell,*
> *Gave it to me.*'

Andrew Marvell was Member for Hull, and native of that
town. He died in 1678. Silvio was foaled in 1754, when
Marvell's memory would be green enough in Yorkshire.

Let a man be enthusiastic as he may about horse-racing, no
such pleasure awaits him after becoming an active participator
in the sport as he enjoyed at the first half-dozen meetings visited
in early life. With what rapture used the early arrivals of
sporting men, of list sellers, of dingy, mysterious people of no
certain occupation, of travelling shows, and of organ-grinders
to be watched on the eve of the little country two-days' meeting!
Many of the horses engaged used to walk over from their
training quarters, and there was keen relish in encountering
these strangers, and offering conjectures as to their worth or
name. What agonies of mind were suffered lest rain should
cause the ruling domestic powers to refuse at the last moment
the promised visit to the course! One companion of those
youthful holidays has since confided to me that he was in the
habit at such times of offering up private prayers for fine
weather. Broken rest and loss of appetite betokened the fever
of the mind. But then the delight when the afternoon proved
fine, perhaps after one or two forenoon showers had plunged
the young expectants into despair. And, oh, that first glimpse
of the course, with its familiar aspect completely changed by
ropes and rails, and a crowd blackening the turf generally so
beautifully green! The flapping of banners, the long row of
booths, the blare of music, the songs of itinerant minstrels, the
sight of jockeys' shoulders and caps above the heads of the mob

—it was almost too enchanting for endurance. How vividly
are retained the incidents of some petty race run on one of those
charming afternoons! Not all the after-experience of eventful
turf occurrences has wiped out the recollection of seeing a filly
belonging to the late Lord Zetland, called Diavolina, slip up at a
turn forty-two years ago, or of the dimmed jacket of the little
boy who rode her. Galaor won the race, and his owner, Mr.
Vansittart, must have loved the romance of Amadis de Gaul,
even if his admiration was somewhat weaker than that of the
crazy Don. For his Darioletta was dam of Galaor, and of
Perion besides, the second horse in the famous Derby won by
St. Giles.

Lists sold much better than did cards in those days, and
nasty, flimsy, ill-printed things they often were, rendered useless
at once if rain fell. 'Return Lists,' too, must have gone off
pretty well in the evening, as they supplied the place of the
results now published by the special editions. To people accustomed to the rich stakes of the present time, it must
appear that their fathers were content to run horses for absurdly
small sums, especially as regards added money. In the year
when Charles XII. won the Goodwood Cup for the first time—
and to win a Goodwood Cup was a great feat—he commenced
the season by running for a stake worth but 50*l.* at Catterick
Bridge—a subscription of 10*l.* each with no added money.
Beeswing was more than once started for a race even less in
value than that just mentioned as won by Charles XII. At
such paltry stakes owners would now-a-days turn up their
noses. Added money, when any was given, frequently did
not exceed 20*l.* Sometimes it was no more than 15*l.*, and this
trifle occasionally attracted horses better than those that win
monster races of the present time, with their 500*l.* or 1000*l.*
added money. One barbarism that flourished 'full forty years
ago' has, it is pleasant to think, quite disappeared. That was
racing in heats. The country-folks liked them, because a meagre
card was sometimes spun out by their aid. Now and then they
did so with a vengeance, sport being protracted until darkness
came down, and it was no longer possible to race with safety.
These heat-races were occasionally most severely contested.
Men who have much acquaintance with Yorkshire turf history
must have read of the famous 100*l.* plate run over a two-mile
course at Doncaster in 1797. Warter, a three-year-old by
King Fergus, had to cover no fewer than twelve miles before

he won, and in the second and fifth bouts he and Pepperpot
ran a dead heat. Stamford, who had finished second for the
St. Leger and won the Gold Cup earlier in the meeting, was
amongst the half-dozen defeated by Warter. It is worthy of
mention that in 1798 Stamford again won the Doncaster Cup,
after a dead heat with Timothy. Warter was third, and a couple
of days later carried off a 50*l.* plate in two three-mile heats. So
the exertion of the terrible six heats in one afternoon of the previous summer had not greatly affected him. At about that date
the northern turf knew horses that were paragons of stoutness.
In after years a great heat-race for producing close struggles
was the Queen's Plate at Carlisle. That queer little man,
Tommy Lye, figured to advantage in its annals, and had the
mount on the strapping Sampson, who won for the Duke of
Cleveland, after a dead heat with a horse belonging to Mr.
Ramsay. Brandyface and Sylvan had each won a heat before
Quadruped settled their pretensions for the Queen's Plate in
1848; and in 1850 Jenny Lind carried off the first heat by a
short head. Then Flash, with Tommy Lye up, beat her for the
second by a head, and, according to the return, gained the final
one by 'half a head.'

Whether it is for good or evil that prophets should have
increased so marvellously since one's youthful racing days cannot here be discussed. Many readers of these lines will remember a time when the brotherhood was a very small one.
Mr. Ives, Mr. F. Clarke, and Mr. Harrison, were amongst the
early ones to achieve distinction, and the sporting magazines
had writers who ventured on prediction with more or less
success. Who, by-the-by, was 'Uncle Toby,' of the *New
Sporting Magazine?* Some rather clever prophecies in verse
appeared in *Bell's Life* from the pen of 'Agrippa,' who died
about 1844. He was, I believe, a Southampton gentleman
named Hunter.

A successful prophecy, even if delivered by word of mouth
only, is a source of great gratification to a youngster. When
grey-headed grandpapas, and fathers whose complete knowledge
of everything no man can doubt and still live, have pronounced
strongly in favour of a particular horse, whilst the tall cousin,
who in so many ways renders himself an object of hate, has
declared for another, what a proud triumph to choose one that
beats them both and wins! Perhaps the 'pick' of the fledgling
is pooh-poohed. He is scornfully told that it was beaten off at

Liverpool, or must be held quite safe on the York form ; and the tall cousin, with a snort of contempt, avers that the owner but now told him that the horse has no chance. How delightful when, in the face of such adverse criticism, the chosen one leads almost from start to finish, and wins cleverly ! Be sure that the old grandpapa is delighted, and applauds the youthful predictor as ' the best judge of us all.' The father's gratification is modified by the reflection that his reputation for infallibility has somewhat suffered. As for the tall cousin, he turns yellow, and either walks away in a fume, or, if more practised in giving annoyance, pretends to have forgotten the successful ' tip ' altogether. Under such circumstances, either Cranebrook or Lightning once, in the long ago, made me supremely happy.

Whilst on the subject of prophecies, there can be no harm in telling the true story of a baulked one, although the disaster occurred considerably less than ' forty years ago.' The date was September of 1861. Prior to the Derby or St. Leger, it was my wont in those days, and for a long time afterwards, to contribute to *Bell's Life* what was courteously called a ' poetical ' prophecy. It was nothing but a rude jingle—but that is now of no moment. Well, the week before the St. Leger arrived, and, from some process of reasoning now forgotten, or out of sheer impudence, or inspired by a dream, or possessed by a devil, I had determined to ' go ' in my rhymes for Caller Ou. The ' prophecy ' was written, and I proposed sending it to the old office in the Strand on the Wednesday evening of the week before Doncaster races. On the afternoon of that day I was in the City, and some evil influence suggested to me to call at ' Joe's ' in Finch Lane. That once famous eating-house has disappeared, but for a great number of years it was a favourite resort, not only of City folks, but of people who came from other parts of the town to try the capital soles, steaks, and chops that were cooked in the dark dining-room, before the eyes of intending feeders. Occasionally a party of officers from the Tower would appear there at luncheon-time, and wash down with port the relays of smoking rumpsteaks. How tastes change! Who now-a-days thinks of such a combination as beefsteaks and old crusted ? This very port wine of ' Joe's ' was it that spoilt my St. Leger prediction ! When about to quit the room a friend entered, and begged me to share with him a bottle ; I complied, and the delay was fatal. On leaving Finch Lane I ran against a man whose opinion on horse-racing was then of great value. Naturally the conversation

fell on the St. Leger, and in reply to a question as to which
horse 'Orange Blossom' would select, I replied 'Caller Ou.'
Such a storm of ridicule did the statement evoke, that my
intention of voting for her was reluctantly abandoned. Had I
adhered to it, the famous 'Vates' prediction of Phosphorus
for the '37 Derby would have been rivalled. True that the
success would only have been a day's talk amongst racing men.
But it is something to be famous even for a day.

THAMES TROUT-FISHING.

By J. P. WHEELDON.

TO kill a Thames trout of any considerable size is to
render one's name now-a-days—so far, at least, as the
opinion of all angling society goes—for ever famous.
There are men whom I know personally, and who
have been trying hard all their lifetime to effect this greatly-to-
be-envied feat, and have never yet succeeded ; nor are they, in
my opinion, ever likely to do so. The reason for this is, that
they trust a little too much to haphazard practice, and far
too infrequently to the more certain results of a deliberately
prepared plan of attack to be presently directed against an
exceedingly wary and cautious foe. It is the fashion, and
particularly amongst folks who don't know, to assert that the
art and accomplishment of killing a salmon is the very highest
niche of skill attainable by practitioners in the silent craft.
On the contrary, nothing is more erroneous ; and, to my mind,
there is no branch of the sport of angling which has had so
much 'high falutin' nonsense talked and written about it as
that of salmon-fishing. The simple truth is, that any one who
can throw a long cast with a trout-fly, cannily and clean, and
just such a fly as is necessary, say, to effect a kill, upon the
Wandle or the Old Barge Water at Winchester, in the height of
the season, and when the trout there located know a hare's ear
from a humblebee—why, that man can also throw a salmon-fly
with a double-handed rod. This reasoning being accepted, it is
simply necessary that such an expert should have the opportunity
given him of casting over a pool full of lively, fresh-run fish,
eager to get higher up still, or upon 'catches,' where fish are in
the habit of lying and 'taking,' for his success to be assured. He

will naturally, if his angling capacity be worth a dump, have made himself acquainted with the best and most killing flies in vogue upon the particular river he may have at his service, and he will equally naturally, by virtue of his trouting education, pick a fly suitable to the conditions of the atmosphere and the size of the water. That being so, I think it is quite likely that the novice would stand a fairly equal chance with a far more experienced rod. I am perfectly well aware that there is very much to be done afterwards, even supposing one gets him 'on,' in the matter of playing and killing a large and powerful fish; but even then, I think the man who has once circumvented one of those cunning old Hampshire veterans would be likely enough to play the very dickens with any ordinary salmon, eventually creeling him under fairly short notice. Such, at least, has been my experience with such fish as have come within my own ken. I have killed a few in my time, and found little difficulty about it either. It is true, I have never had the good fortune to get fast in one of those monstrous beasts that take five and six hours to settle handsomely. I devoutly wish I had, and I might then, perhaps, be able to estimate, at a better and more brilliant figure, the general surroundings of the sport of salmon-angling. Lest, however, it should be thought that I am underrating the characteristics of a branch of the art which should be upon its own merits—apart from the beautiful and romantic accessories which it is nearly certain to possess, in the shape of surrounding scenery—at the very top of the tree, I will give one or two reasons for saying that there is, and always has been, a lot of 'high falutin' nonsense talked about it, and which practical experience has entirely failed to support. I have fished one or two notable rivers in past days, and have seen so-called salmon-fishers—men who could talk glibly, as so many highly educated parrots, about toppings and wings, hackle, tippet, tag, and all the rest of it; and those very men were in the habit of lugging great salmon out, just as boys would serve eels in a mill-pond, by the aid of a stout line, a stouter hook, and a great bunch of worms attached thereto. Probably, at the end of a non-taking day, when every other honest and hard-working flyman had come home 'clean,' these identical fish had all been killed, 'dear boy, with a fly I tied myself, something like a Silver Doctor, you know, but with an Indian yellow hackle at the shoulder, gallina over, and a bit of kingfisher and chatterer feathers at the cheek.' Why, certainly.

Then, I once saw a noted salmon-fisherman, owner of a high-sounding name, too, who was spinning in a pool literally swarming with up-running fish, and the little bait he was using, if it so pleases you, was a ten-inch phantom, with large dependent triangles thereto. Every ten minutes he hooked a fish foul, and oftener than not broke away with the slight hold obtained. Not a few, however, he landed, and I dare say he and other excellent practitioners of the same kidney called all that kind of thing salmon-fishing, but I didn't.

To return to our trout. There are spinners and spinners, comprising nearly every grade and variety in that branch of human craft under the sun. There is your pike-spinner, who is perfectly happy and content in the possession of fifty yards of line, a swivelled trace, and for bait a villainously ugly American spoon. There is another of the same variety, who simply substitutes a natural roach or dace for the spoon, and by virtue of the substitution thinks himself an exceedingly finished artist. Then there is the really good pike-spinner, who fishes with a neat gut trace, and puts his bait on nicely into the bargain, together with men who fish up stream and down, with eel's tail, parr's tail, fresh and salted minnows, others preserved in spirits, and either used upon modern drop-tackle or, perhaps, in a few cases, upon Hawker's clumsy old principle; and all these are spinners—after a fashion. But, I say, and very seriously too, put any one of them upon an open Thames reach, or at the head of a weir where there is a big trout feeding, and that man would inevitably be lost. For this reason: there is no fish that swims which requires at once such careful and scientific fishing to effect his capture as your Thames trout, while there is none so easily alarmed and made shy. The tackle used must be of the neatest and most delicate quality, while the bait selected must not only be the best and cleanest, but 'put up' in the most thoroughly workmanlike manner. A great authority, and none less than Mr. Francis Francis himself, once asserted, 'the great art and mystery of Thames trout-fishing is unwearied perseverance.' Perfectly true: but he then goes on to say, 'If the angler can make up his mind, when he has "spotted" a fish to sit and spin over him for hours, and keep up his expectation of a run for every minute in the twenty-four, perhaps for a week or more, he may, if he has luck, get a fish in the course of a week or two; but even then it is no certainty.' That may be the experience which Mr. Francis has obtained, but I am bound to

say it is not mine. If I had 'spotted' a trout, and a big one
to boot, and took my punt down with the fixed intention of
spinning over him for hours, I should, to my fancy, be laying
myself open to a grave suspicion of lunacy. The best chance
would be with the first half-dozen throws, and even then always
supposing that the punt had been dropped down without
the slightest noise or disturbance. If he did not come then,
I should rest him for an hour, and, not seeing him feed, try
perhaps half-a-dozen more. Still no results. Well then, upon
mature reflection, I think I should go home. I venture to think
that a man, casting for hours over a large, and, necessarily, very
wary trout, would effectually 'put him down' for good, just in
the same way as a man continually throwing over a salmon that
has once 'offered,' but thought better of it, is simply destroying
all the chances he might originally have possessed.

It may perhaps be worth while, as the gloriously uncertain
sport of Thames trouting has just opened, to give a few hints,
not necessarily addressed for the benefit of novices and aspirants,
but as a kind of general reminder, with regard to the style and
quality of the tackle that should be selected. That having been
ventilated, I propose to offer certain suggestions as to the
localities where trout are usually found, and the ways and means
best adapted for getting on the side of their better confidences.
First, then, as to the rod. To have a complete outfit I would
choose two, one for weir-spinning and one for casting from a
punt. In the confined and narrow limits of a punt, a 12 or
13 foot rod is quite sufficient for comfort and nice power of
direction, but in the case of spinning a weir this length is nothing
like enough for effective work, and also in successfully getting
the bait into queer and artful corners; and it is just in such places
that the best fish of all lie. The rod should be made of the best
West India mottled cane, as free as possible from knots and
burrs. It should be light and limber in the hand, with a fairly
good amount of spring and play from top to butt—not stiff in any
event, and yet have such a power of resistance as would be effectual
in bringing a powerful fish to the top should he be intent upon
making desperately for an undeniably ugly place. It may be remembered that it is for just such places as I have last mentioned
that old and cunning veterans invariably do make. *En passant,*
the very biggest trout I ever hooked in my life—a fish, I think,
of fully 16 lbs. weight, if he was an ounce—beat me in this way.
Just below where he fed there was a lot of old stumps and

He had broken me!

boughs of trees jutting out into deep and heavy water. At the very last blink of daylight, just at that mystic hour when the thrushes' song grows fainter in the far-off copse, and the first bars of a low, beautiful night melody, as full of pathos and feeling as any of Mendelssohn's songs without words, floats out from the exquisitely attuned throttle of the shy bird of eve, this big fellow splashed up with a sounding roll, plunged through the swift waters, and I was fast ! Every drop of blood in my body ceased running, and I felt as though my veins were filled with congealed oil. Hurrah ! Fast in ' the ' big one of all at last, after days and days spent patiently within ken of his lair. My puntman was quick as lightning, and knew what to do without any telling. In an instant he had cast the punt adrift, and was pushing her hard across for the opposite side of the river, and so out of the stream. My lethargy had lasted just so long as the startled fish had been seen plunging about on the top. The very instant that he turned downwards, with a last flourish of his grand broad tail aloft, I was fully awake to the exigencies of the situation. I had him tight in a second, and the very moment he felt the restraint upon his head away he went, leaping, plunging, and tearing through the water like a mad thing. Talk about your salmon ! the best and gamest salmon that I ever saw hooked and killed in my life never went with half the strength and velocity with which that trout sped down stream. It was something wonderfully and marvellously beautiful to see that gloriously shaped fish, a blaze of pellucid silver, with a tinge of crimson here and there flecked on his broad deep side, out of the water time after time, falling with a sounding plash, and beating up fretting waves and huge rippling eddies, while, alas and alack-a-day ! I had only a thread to hold him with ! I verily believe, in his indignation and mighty rage, he had forgotten all about that hideous arrangement of stumps and stakes; but, all in an instant, ah me ! memory seemed to prick him more keenly even than my little triangle hook did, and, turning, he flew up stream for their shelter. With a lot of loose line between the trout and the winch, it was impossible to get it up quick enough, fast as the handles of the Nottingham went round. When I did get it taut, it was only to find that my splendid prey had made good his rush for shelter, *and had broken me !* That lesson will last me for a lifetime. The reason why I lost him was that, through using running tackle totally inadequate to his great strength and resolution, I was obliged to let him have his head too freely in

the first dash away. This, of course, is necessary in nearly all
cases; but there may be too much of a good thing, and here there
was unquestionably, for I could not get the line back upon the
winch-barrel half as fast as he came through the water, whereas,
if I had had him more under control and less line out, the issue
might have been different.

A shocking digression; but somehow, when chatting upon
fishing, one naturally drops into anecdote just as easily as Silas
Wegg occasionally dropped into poetry. To go back again,
therefore, to trouting rods, they should, as a matter of course,
always have standing or upright rings, while the best winch that
can possibly be used is the double-actioned Nottingham. By
double-actioned, I mean that which is so arranged that by the act
of pressing a little spring down on the reverse side to the handles,
the user gets a check movement instantaneously, while, by revers-
ing it, the smooth, fast, Nottingham action, is obtained at once.
If an angler be proficient in the use of the Nottingham winch,
and fully confident of his ability to control its velocity by the
pressure of his finger on the outer rim, I would always advise him
to play a fish by this means, and no other; but if he be not perfectly *au fait*, then by all means use the check, care only being
exercised in seeing that the tension is not too heavy or resistant.

In the matter of traces for spinning purposes, I would advise
an aspirant for trouting honours never to use shop-tied and
bound goods upon any consideration whatever. I know of no
such prolific source of aggravating smashes, even under the very
best management, as shop-bound traces. In buying them, simply
insist that every link between the swivels, and every joint between
the separate lengths of gut, be knotted neatly, and the binding
left out altogether. The latter frequently serves to cover bad
and imperfect knotting, while without it even a tyro can see
whether the knots are tied properly, or the reverse. Trouting
flights are tied now-a-days upon both gimp and gut. There is
only one reason why I incline to the former in the smallest
degree; which is, that by virtue of the hooks being mounted
upon fine gimp, one stands less chance of the flight being
rugged and torn by the teeth of the swarms of big and little
pike, which would invariably seem to delight in spoiling a bait
meant for their betters. At other times, of course, and when their
visitations might be tolerated, and even approved of, they keep
discreetly and judiciously at a distance. As a rule I hate and
abominate gimp. There is at once nothing so difficult to get

good, and nothing which is equally difficult to prevent going
wrong during service. At the present time, however, the better-
class tackle-makers keep a supply of especially fine white
gimp ; and this is generally good in quality. Hooks tied upon
short lengths of this 'stand up' exceedingly well, while its
colour assimilates also with the lustrous silvery hue of the little
natural bait used. For a few times, if I could see in the outset
that it was very closely wrapped with wire, and yet felt supple
and flexible in the fingers, I might feel fairly safe ; but after
that I am afraid I should get more fidgety every day, owing to
the quickness with which I have found very good gimp, in
appearance, getting rotten and useless after very little service.
Generally, therefore, I cling to gut ; and if it does get bitten
through now and again by pike, why even that is better than
losing an undeniably big trout through the gimp giving at the
very moment when the exhibition of its quality of excellence
was most to be desired.

In choosing hooks for spinning flights, never be led into
buying such as only look small, neat, and pretty. Bear in mind
the fact, that it is hoped at least, that one's tackle will be called
upon to antagonise a fish every bit as powerful as a salmon,
and in water quite as heavy as salmon are usually found in.
Hooks, therefore, should be fairly large—small pike triangles, in
fact, or about as large as those used for chubbing with cheese.
The wire should be stout, and the barbs large and well defined.
The flight pattern I use, and practice has proved to my own
satisfaction, at least, that it is the best form I can get, consists of
four simple triangles and a lip-hook. This lip-hook is best used
loose and hanging from an eye tied at the top of the shank. The
'bite' is then obtained by wrapping a bit of the wet gut carefully
round the shank of the hook, after the distance between the
nose of the bait used, and the bend of the hook itself, has been
determined upon. Many dodges have been adopted for getting
a good and lasting bite, because upon this, and the fact that it
keeps the bait straight, the accuracy of the spinning movement
very greatly depends. At one trouting station—say Great
Marlow, for instance—one finds a man using a lip-hook, with
an eye at top and bottom of the hook shank, while the gut
has been put through with a half-hitch round the shank itself.
At another, and Maidenhead to wit, the next angler one meets
is using a hook slipping up and down upon a tiny length of
quill cut from a starling's wing, and so on ; while probably each

experimenter swears by his own pattern. Very good ; let them
do so, say I. Mine is an old form I am willing to admit, but
sometimes experience proves that it is difficult to improve upon
old things. Old port, old friendships, old cigars, old easy-chairs,
old coats, old homes, and goodness knows what else besides,
are all barely capable of improvement, so why not old patterns ?
It may be that the remark applies to both cabinet ministers
and trouting flights alike.

The trace should have five or six small neat swivels set
below the lead, and all of these should be kept carefully cleaned
and oiled. There is no necessity to have any swivels above the
lead, because this is intended to hang stationary, and merely·
act as ' a steadier ' upon the flight, trace, and bait. There is no
better form of lead than 'the Field,' while the trace itself should
be, so far as length goes, a yard and a quarter full. I need hardly
suggest that the best and roundest gut procurable should be used,
and that it should be perfectly free from stains and blotches.

In baiting the flight, care should be used in picking a bait
which from its own dimensions fits naturally upon the length
of gut or gimp upon which the hooks are tied ; that is, that the
bottom triangle being fixed at the root of the tail, the top should
be found just level with the shoulder. The best of all trout-
spinning baits are bleak, and next to them a small dace. Now
and then, in a very bright and low water, a gudgeon is effective,
and always, at least, spins well. So also a big, plump, green-
bellied minnow. Before handling the bait at all, and as it lies
kicking about in the dip-net, first wet your fingers thoroughly.
This does away in a great measure with the likelihood of rubbing
away half the scale and bloom of the little bait, which after all
forms its most attractive qualities. The bleak having been
killed by a smart flip on the back of the head, administered by
the forefinger, take him up ' tenderly, fashioned with care,' and
holding him equally gently, put one of the hook points of the
bottom triangle right through the rays of the tail in the exact
centre of the fork, and bring it through the fleshy root just clear
of the back-bone. See that the hooks lie regularly, and, taking
the lateral line as your guide, push the second triangle well
home along the line and level with the setting of the ventral
fin. The third should nick in midway between that and the
line of the pectoral fin, and the fourth close up to the gill-plate
into the thick of the shoulder. One glance will give the length
of the gut necessary to take up for binding round the shank of

the lip-hook; and this being done, the point of that hook should be pushed through the centre of both lips and brought clean through, so that the bait hangs exactly in the middle of the bend. The bait should also hang perfectly straight and true, with a nicely defined, gentle curve at the tail. That having been obtained it ought to spin like a top. If it wobbles it is useless. A pike may, and will if he has a chance, snap at it where a trout won't. It ought to come through the water with the regularity of a screw-propeller, and look like a little streak of bright light. It now and again happens that a bait put on very truly won't spin at first, try it as one will. Why I know not. If such a thing happens, and the operator is satisfied that it hangs straight and true, it might be useful to give it a sharp pull or two through the water and against the stream before entirely condemning it. This treatment, which apparently settles all things into their proper places, is frequently productive of a splendid spin.

In casting from a punt the better plan, supposing there is no heavy, gusty wind blowing, is to have the line coiled neatly on the till: that is, always supposing that the operator is unable to work the line from a coil in the palm of his left hand; or, better still, throw from the winch. A high wind is at all times a terrible nuisance, and if such prevails one's only chance would be to drop the line neatly upon the bottom boards, care being exercised that neither the legs of a Windsor chair, nor the lace-hooks on one's boots, form component parts of the coils. The great difficulty about throwing from the winch with the ordinary trouting lead arises from the fact that it is almost always too light to give sufficient impetus to the cast. This may be obviated in some waters by using a much heavier lead; but even then, unless the rod be in a master's hand, the little delicate bait gets torn and warped, and hence speedily useless. The better plan, therefore, would seem to be to cast from the hand-coil; a process which may be learnt very easily, and improved upon every day. In throwing from a coil, a fine eight-plait silk line, well and evenly dressed, supple and smooth to the touch, is as good as can be adopted; while in throwing from a winch, always the safer process, if a little more troublesome, an undressed silk line of similar pattern is as good as one can use.

To attempt thus early in the season the task of pointing out where it is certain that an angler may meet with the best Thames trouting would be to attempt a very difficult task. Difficult, because the everlasting traffic on the river, a disturbance

everlastingly increasing, causes the best fish to take up now and
again with very queer quarters. One ought to find them upon
sharp scours and at the tails of swift, impetuous eddies : one
finds them instead frequently located in dull, motionless, pike-
like holes. That is, because their sensitive shy natures cannot
make a stand amongst the uproar consequent upon the plash
and noise incident to cockney oarsmen, or the tumultuous
churning, shrieking, and groaning of a whole fleet of steam-
launches. Generally, however, trout lie, in the earlier portions
of the year, upon shallow lengths and the tail of gravelly scours,
shifting up to the weirs as the nights get hotter and the water,
perhaps, drops a little. This reasoning hardly applies, of course,
to such places as Maidenhead and Marlow, where, year after
year, the enterprising supporters of the local preservation
societies put in numbers of good fish. There they are found
in all parts of the stream, and it becomes difficult to say where
trout are not. Still, however well they may do, and however
handsome they may grow, these Wick fish are not Thames
trout, and therefore enter not into the calculations made in this
paper. Last season heavy trout were to be found all over the
river, and, unless I am very greatly deceived, they will be heard
of somewhere near their old locations, and perhaps in far larger
proportions, this year. Kingston, Hampton, Sunbury, Chertsey,
Staines, Windsor, and Datchet, all had their big fish to boast of,
and there probably they will be found again. If I might be permitted to 'spot' the two stations where I think the largest
number of heavy trout are likely to be found, I should infallibly
put my finger upon Kingston and Windsor.

Big trout, singularly enough, always have their fixed homes,
in which they take up their residence year after year. If a good
fish be killed during the season from some particular hole, the
next there will assuredly be another, which has taken the place
of his relative gone before. Up at the weirs it is just the same.
There are always one or two particular 'runs' where, year after
year, good fish take their stations. In spinning a weir there is
one good, general rule, which it might be well to always remember : 'Keep out of sight.' First spin all the white water close up
to the fall over the camp sheathing or cill, and next all those
beautiful little back-eddies which come surging up between the
two foam-capped runs ; because that is where big trout lie. And,
whatever else you do, my advice is—fish them carefully, perse-
veringly, and 'keep out of sight.'

A FAMOUS MATCH.

By ALFRED E. T. WATSON.

STRICTLY speaking it was not a match, but a cup race, for which there might have been a large field; nevertheless the struggle I am writing about was reduced to a match, for the presence of two champions made opposition from manifestly inferior animals hopeless. It is to the last meeting between those doughty rivals, Bend Or and Robert the Devil, at Epsom, on the day when the victory of Thebais in the Oaks was overshadowed by the interest attaching to the race for the Gold Cup, that I refer; and as, so far as I know, the real facts connected with this famous match have never been fully published, it may be well to glance at the career of these two grand horses, and relate the circumstances of their final appearance side by side.

Which was the better of the pair? The generally accepted opinion is, that over the Derby course the handsome chestnut son of Doncaster and of—shall we say?—Rouge Rose was superior, while over the Cesarewitch course the plainer but sturdy and approved good son of Bertram and Cast Off could always have held his own. This may be right, but for reasons that will appear in the course of this sketch I do not think it is by any means certain.

As a two-year-old Robert the Devil was out twice, and won both his engagements. Bend Or was out five times, and won all his races. The preponderance of success was with the chestnut, but the bay had done all that was asked of him, and could do no more; so that when they met for the Derby of 1880 the partizans of both were comfortably confident of success. The one thing against the chance of the Bertram colt was that Cannon, who would otherwise have ridden him, had been claimed to ride a brute called Mariner (a 50 to 1 chance), and Rossiter, a clever lad in the saddle, when anything short of a supreme effort of judgment and skill was required of him, rode Mr. Brewer's animal; Archer being on the Duke of Westminster's representative. Both were in the pink of condition—to use a not very easily explicable phrase—and in the face of the freely expressed hope of victory of the Robert party, it was no doubt the fact of Archer being on Bend Or that reduced the odds against him to

2 to 1, while 7 to 1 was offered and freely taken about the other, who, with 4 lbs. the worst of the weights, had been beaten a head by Apollo at the Newmarket Craven. What justification backers had for their confidence was shown in the result. The flag fell and the field started for the memorable Derby. From long before the distance it was seen that there were only two in the race, and it was almost equally evident that the better of the two was Robert the Devil. They came on, locked together, but always with an advantage for the bay, who shot out a dozen lengths from home and seemed to have the race at his mercy. His backers had already opened their mouths to shout in honour of his victory, when, guided by his evil genius, Rossiter turned his head and looked round to see what Archer and Bend Or were doing. His curiosity was fatal. Archer saw his rival's indecision, gathered his horse together for one final and desperate dash, and just got home by the shortest of short heads. Archer had beaten Rossiter; that was all that could be said. Whether he would, under similar circumstances, have beaten so cool, wary, and experienced a horseman as Cannon is another affair; nevertheless in the first duel between them the triumph was with the chestnut.

Sensational events followed. It was rumoured that Bend Or was not Bend Or at all, but a colt called Tadcaster, by Doncaster —Clemence, and an objection was lodged. It need hardly be said that no one for a single moment suspected any of the Duke of Westminster's agents, infinitely less his Grace himself, of intentional deception. What was suspected was that, by an accident of a groom, confusion had arisen between the sons of Clemence and of Rouge Rose, Doncaster being the sire of both; that they had been incorrectly entered in the Duke's stud-book, and that it was the son of Clemence that had won the Derby. Investigation, followed by a confirmation of the judge's verdict, was the consequence, and Bend Or was finally recorded as the winner of the Derby.

Bend Or followed up his success by winning the St. James's Palace Stakes at Ascot, but only by a head from Fernandez, an own brother to Isonomy. Robert went to Paris and distinguished himself (Rossiter riding) by securing the Grand Prix, worth over 6000*l.* It was not till the St. Leger that the pair met again. On a dreadfully wet day both went to the post for the first Northern race, Cannon this time being on Robert, Archer resuming his guidance of Bend Or. The Derby winner was a hot favourite, odds of 6 to 4 were laid on him, 4 to 1 being readily obtainable about Robert; but the calculations of the 'talent' were completely upset. Robert the Devil avenged his Epsom defeat by winning with the utmost ease by three lengths; Bend Or finished just in front of the pulling-up division, and the question of superiority was once more in abeyance. Could it have been the extra distance that told against Bend Or? Would he have won over a somewhat shorter course, where speed as against endurance would tell? This was the question discussed till the pair met once more in the Great Foal Stakes at Newmarket. When it came to the point, however, the ring disdained the idea of Bend Or's all-superior speed. Odds of 7 to 4 were laid on Robert, and 9 to 4 was forthcoming against Bend Or. Cannon was on the former, Archer on the latter; but though the event proved backers to be right, their excessive confidence was felt to be misplaced. Robert won, but only by the shortest of heads, and so very narrow a result left the question again in doubt.

Robert's next achievement, however, was a grand one. As the winner of the St. Leger he had to carry 8 st. 6 lbs. in the Cesarewitch, a most severe weight for a three-year-old, especially seeing that so good a horse as Petronel met him in the race with only 7 st. 5 lbs. Cannon rode again. No such weight had ever been successfully borne by a horse of any age, yet this three-year-old not only won over the severe two miles and a quarter of the Cesarewitch, but won with the utmost ease. Robert's star was in the ascendant; nevertheless, when in the Houghton Meeting the two rivals met, there was only the very faintest shade of odds between their favouritism—11 to 10 against Robert the Devil, 5 to 4 against Bend Or; but here the former won by a dozen lengths. Such a win may mean anything; that is to say, it may show that, ridden out, the second was hopelessly inferior; or it may show that an experienced jockey, believing that his chance was hopeless, had ceased to persevere and distress a valuable horse. Neither side, therefore, accepted the verdict as final. To have beaten Robert in the Derby was a great achievement for Bend Or; to have won the Cesarewitch under an unprecedented weight was a notable performance for Robert the Devil. Bend Or had only got home at Ascot a head in front of Apollo, but then, at a difference of 4 lbs. in favour of Apollo, that colt, a son of Kingcraft and Silverhair, had actually beaten Robert. Thus collateral running showed here that the two great

rivals were as equal as they well could be. Excuses were made
for Bend Or's defeats in the Leger and subsequently at Newmarket
in the Champion Stakes, on the ground that he was 'off' on
both occasions, and in the Great Foal Stakes there was only a
head separation. No wonder, then, that both sides argued for
their champion. The thing was to see what would happen next,
for their three-year-old careers had settled nothing decisively,
though it had suggested on the whole that the Bertram colt was
better than the Doncaster.

Next year Robert was out first. He ran in a Newmarket
Biennial, but nothing was proved by the race, for he had only a
couple of very bad animals to beat. Long odds were laid on
him, and he was never extended, winning with superlative ease.
The contest was, in fact, a mere exercise gallop, except that
probably in his gallops he usually went faster at home. Far
different was the reappearance of Bend Or. In the City and
Suburban he was burdened with 9 st. That grand horse Peter
(Hermit—Lady Masham) was a year older, and had 2 lbs. more
to carry ; Petronel had 21 lbs. less ; Foxhall, then a three-year-
old, had 6 st. 8 lbs. only, which was making the great American
colt to be a very liberal 21 lbs. worse than Bend Or at weight for
age ; and the world knows what marvels Foxhall performed when
William Day had charge of him in the autumn of this year. In
spite of the *prestige* accruing to Bend Or for the reason that
Archer rode, some half-dozen horses were more fancied in the
market. A victory under such a weight was, in fact, regarded
as in the highest degree improbable ; but in a field of just two
dozen competitors, Bend Or won from the mighty Foxhall by
nearly two lengths. Here was ' cakes and ale ' for the friends of
the chestnut ! 'Would Robert the Devil have won with nine
stone on his back ?' was asked ; and notwithstanding that there
was nothing whatever to guide the inquirers to a reply, the answer
' No !' was fearlessly given. Robert walked over for 50*l*. at the
Newmarket Second Spring, a performance which merely showed
that he was presentable, and neither was out again till what
I have called the ' Famous Match.'

Five horses were coloured on the card for the race for the
Epsom Gold Cup. Three of the five, however, declined the contest, and the two 'cracks' were left to fight out again over the
same course the duel which they had fought in the Derby just a
year before. They were saddled in good time, paraded, and cantered gently to the starting-post, where a long delay occurred.

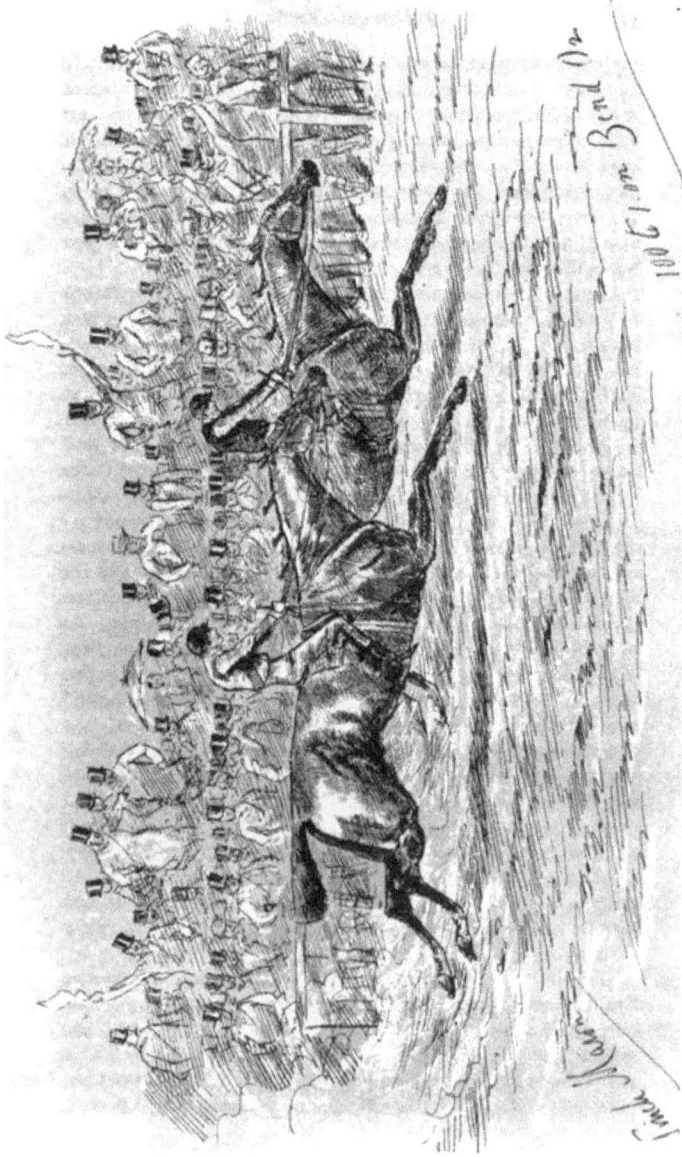

1001 Glen Bend Or

The race which was to have come between the Oaks and the Cup—a Juvenile Selling Stakes—was declared void. Not knowing this, the starter and his assistant had gone up to the five furlong starting-post, beyond Tattenham Corner, so that till they arrived and the time fixed for the race had come there was leisure to inspect the champions. The Cesarewitch winner was a warm favourite. Odds of 6 to 4 and 7 to 4 were cheerfully laid on the bay, though the chestnut was by no means without friends. Cannon in the white and blue belt, Archer in the yellow and black cap, showed that everything jockeyship could do for either would be done. But of the horses themselves, as in the midst of an admiring crowd they stood still or walked to and fro about the Derby and the Cup starting-post? There was plenty of time to take careful stock of them, and the opinion of experts was that, well in themselves as both appeared, neither was thoroughly wound up. Cannon's cheery face told nothing of what might be passing in his mind ; possibly it was a shade less cheery than usual, but anxiety might perhaps have explained this, and Archer's more saturnine expression was equally inscrutable. From the ring came shouts which seemed ever to increase. For both there was so much to be said that both sides grew more sanguine as the time approached. Robert's victories in Cesarewitch and Leger, and his two defeats of Bend Or, encouraged his supporters. On the other hand, over this very course Bend Or had beaten Robert; there had only been a short head between them on another occasion ; and then, over a mile and a quarter of this course, there was the brilliant success of Bend Or in the City and Suburban to be taken into account. So apparently even a fight had rarely awaited the signal for a beginning, and presently the starter reached the spot. The time had come. A swish of the red flag, the lowering of the white, sent them on their journey. The famous match had begun.

Robert, who had been a bit fretful before starting, and would have been more so but for Cannon's gently restraining hand, dashed off with the lead ; Bend Or, who had comported himself in the most placid manner possible since he emerged from the paddock, following contentedly in the rear; and so they mounted the hill on the far side of the course. The pace was fairly good. Robert, always some two lengths in front, had no difficulty in retaining his position ; Bend Or, however, making no attempt to wrest it from him. So they approached and rounded Tattenham Corner, fairly entered the straight for home ; and then it was

first suspected that the favourite was not having it all his own
way. The yellow jacket gradually crept up ; the wearer of the
white and blue belt seemed uneasy on his horse. At the distance
they were head and head, and Tom Cannon, whose patience and
judgment are always to be trusted, took up his whip—a fatal
sign, for he never draws it till need has arisen either to hit or to
threaten his horse. To him in the saddle, as to experienced
watchers on the stands and carriages between which the pair of
rivals sped, the result speedily became obvious. Bend Or was
going strongest and best. Cannon rode his horse hard with the
reins, but did not hit or spur him. Archer had only to sit still,
and, thus sitting, he passed the post—winner by a neck. Cannon
had been forced to make play it will have been seen, and the
famous jockey always calculates that, with any but a very free-
going animal, this necessity is equivalent to 7 lbs. the worst of
the weights.

And now, which was the better horse ?

Unfortunately the race really did nothing to show. The
truth is that Robert the Devil was not nearly fit to run. A leg
had given his trainer great anxiety, and it had been found quite
impossible to prepare him for the Epsom Meeting. Robert was
sent to Epsom, partly because it was thought that his arrival
would scare Bend Or from the field, and partly because one of
Robert's owners had complicated matters by promising some
friends who had backed the horse to run him for the Cup if it
could be done with any degree of safety, without the imminent
risk of breaking him down. On the other hand, when the
Bend Or contingent discovered that Robert was not fit, in consequence of his leg having shown symptoms of giving way, the
Derby winner was allowed to take it easy in the matter of his
winding-up gallops, it being imagined that the appearance of
the chestnut would inevitably be the signal for the striking out
of the bay.

A very anxious little group assembled in Robert's box at
York House, Durdans, the night before the match, and the manner
in which the horse flinched as Cannon felt his leg made the
anxiety, if it were a question of winning a great race, exceedingly reasonable. It was the public that jumped at conclusions,
knowing nothing of facts, and backed Robert till he became a
warm favourite. It can hardly be that his immediate connexions
backed him.

Thus, then, once more the question of supremacy was left

A former trainer Bend Or.

A distinguished amateur

Hooray! Bend Or's won

Lookers on at the famous Match.

What does the Mate think about it?

See page 44.

unsettled; and the pair never met again. Bend Or came out refreshed and well some five months later, and won the Champion Stakes from Scobell and Iroquois—the latter the Derby winner of the year. He was backed warmly by Lord Alington, and started first favourite at 9 to 2 in a field of 32 for Foxhall's Cambridgeshire; he showed prominently at the Red Post, but died away to nothing just as Archer was beginning to look about him and see what he had to beat. So he finally disappeared from the race-course. Robert's leg stood moderately well, and he was prepared for Ascot, where, though he went very short, he won the Gold Cup from Petronel, Exeter, Zealot, and Foxhall, the last-named, however, upset by his journey back from Paris, where he had won the Grand Prix at the beginning of the week. The Alexandra Plate from a couple of opponents also fell to him next day, and his last race was run.

Tom Cannon, who knew Robert well, is of opinion that for a mile Bend Or was the better; over that distance he believes that Robert could always have beaten the Duke of Westminster's colt.

After all, was the winner of the Derby in 1880, and of the Gold Cup next year, the veritable Bend Or, the son of Doncaster and Rouge Rose? What evidence was adduced to prove this when the investigation was made I have no idea, and therefore I feel special delicacy in speaking on the subject, the more so as the Duke of Westminster was doubtless himself convinced; for had he not been he would have eagerly accepted the verdict of disqualification in order that justice might be done.

At Stockbridge races, however, last year, Garb Or, a son of Doncaster and Rouge Rose, an own brother to Bend Or, was being led about in the paddock. The familiar question : 'What's that?' was constantly being put by men who joined the group that surrounded the horse.

' Brother to Bend Or, is he?' a well-known trainer and shrewd judge of horses exclaimed, looking him over carefully. 'Well, he's wonderfully like one that I had in my stable—the worst I ever did have, I think—Tadcaster.'

' Why, that was the one the objection was raised about ! The objectors said that Tadcaster was the son of Doncaster and Rouge Rose, and Bend Or the son of Doncaster and Clemence,' I replied.

' How's that one, Garb Or, bred, do they say?' my friend asked.

' By Doncaster—Rouge Rose,' I answered.

'Well, then, I should say Tadcaster was bred the same way,' was the response.

'Then the beast you had in your stall, and could not do anything with, was, you think, Bend Or, and Tadcaster won the Derby?' I continued.

'That's what it seems to me if looks go for anything,' he said.

Beyond all doubt, in disposition as well as in looks, Tadcaster and Garb Or closely resemble each other.

YOUNG NIMROD AT ETON.

By FINCH MASON.

> 'Twelve years ago I made a mock
> Of filthy trades and traffics ;
> I wondered what they meant by stock ;
> I wrote delightful Sapphics ;
> I knew the streets of Rome and Troy,
> I supped with fates and furies ;
> Twelve years ago I was a boy,
> A happy boy at Drury's.'　　PRAED.

WHEN old Mr. Nimrod sent the younger ditto to Eton, he had considerable doubts in his own mind as to what sort of a boy that youth would turn out eventually ; in fact, the old gentleman was very uneasy indeed on that score.

During the three years Master Nimrod had been at a private school there had never been so much as a single complaint made against him, of any sort or description ; on the contrary, at the end of every term, not only had he invariably brought home with him prizes for scholarship in its different branches, but a special prize for 'good conduct' as well ('I should like to have seen *myself* getting a prize for good conduct,' would remark Nimrod senior on these occasions) ; and once he outdid all previous performances, by bringing home a prize for *gardening* (his father had an attack of gout on the spot). Finally, when he took leave of Doctor Dulcimer's establishment, if that worthy gentleman was to be believed, 'Never, no, *never!* amongst the large number of pupils he had turned out, had he had under his charge a boy who had done his school one half so much credit as Master George Nimrod.'

Now, needless to say, nine parents out of ten would have been in the seventh heaven of delight at the bare idea of being the possessor of such a paragon of perfection as the Doctor made young Squire George appear to be ; but the worthy old gentleman, his father, was cast in a different mould to most parents, and he failed to see the virtues in his son that Doctor Dulcimer appraised so highly. In fact, he was one of the old school, who loved what he called a 'varmint' from the bottom of his heart. He himself, if he was to be believed, was, when *he* was at Eton, as promising a vessel of wrath as was ever flogged of a frosty morning by the celebrated Keate. He it was who held the paint-pot whilst his friend, the Honourable Brownlow Brontie, attired in a three-cornered cocked hat and gown, exactly similar to those worn by the terrible Doctor himself, went round at midnight and decorated half the doors of the College with green paint, under the very eyes of the college servants, who really thought it was the great man himself indulging in a little piece of eccentricity, and could, in consequence, scarcely believe their eyes. He also prided himself on being one of the rebels who were ordered suddenly out of bed on the night of the Doctor's celebrated *coup d'état*, when he flogged several divisions one after another, innocent and guilty alike ;—thereby establishing himself on the throne firmer than ever.

As the Squire then sat in his dining-room over his wine, the night he returned from Eton, where he had left his son, he pondered deeply within himself.

'You see, my dear,' he said to Mrs. Nimrod, 'I want to stick him in the cavalry or send him to Christchurch before he settles down here as M. F. H. and all the rest of it ; and they don't want young gentlemen there who go in for good-conduct prizes and gardening, and such-like. It's not, you know, my love, as if I wanted him to go into the Church.'

'Ah, poor lamb !' sighed Mrs. Nimrod, a subdued-looking lady, with drab-coloured hair and blue eyes, who would have liked nothing better than to have watched her son qualifying for a bishopric.

'Poor *lamb*, indeed !' growled the Squire, with a snort of disgust. 'Poor devil, *I* should say. However, we'll hope for the best, my dear,' added he, consolingly. 'I tipped young Charlie Rattlepate handsomely before I left this morning; and told him to show George all that was to be seen, and let me know how

he got on. So here's both their healths, and "*Floreat Etona!*"'
And the worthy old gentleman tossed off a bumper of claret
with infinite gusto to the time-honoured toast, second only in the
Squire's eyes to that of 'Foxhunting.'

A week afterwards arrived, to Mr. Nimrod's great joy, the
following delectable epistle from his young friend and relation,
Master Charles Rattlepate :—

Eton College, Bucks,
Feb. 18, ——.

My dear Uncle,—

Immediately after pupil-room, on the morning you left Eton,
I proceeded in search of George, and, as luck would have it, ran him to
ground, as *you* would say ['Funny rascal!' chuckled the Squire], just at
the corner of Weston's Yard, looking disconsolately after your fly,
which was just disappearing over Barn's Pool Bridge. As I came up
he was being asked his name for the first time by a little knot of boys.
'What's your name, you fellow?' demanded Tottleby minor. 'Nimrod,'
says George, meekly. 'Nimrod!' exclaimed Tottleby, to the great mirth of
the others, bonneting him on the spot; 'why, blowed if that ain't the
name of our cook at home!' ['Ha! ha! ha!' roared the Squire; 'what an
impudent young blackguard!'] George looked *nasty*, Sir, I can tell you;
and the clenching of his fist and the angry light in his eye showed me
that for two two's, as the saying is, he would have gone for Tottleby there
and then. And perhaps it was lucky I came up when I did; indeed, I
thought it advisable, in order to soothe his ruffled feelings, to take George
to see Spankie, who was sitting at his usual place at the wall. He was
down on me, of course, directly, in his usual style—*you* know, uncle.
'Touching that little account, Sir—thirteen and seven, Sir—shall I write to
your father, Sir? or shall I speak to your tooter, Sir?' said he, in his
unctuous voice. 'Neither, Spankie,' quoth I; for, thanks to you, Sir, I
have, I am happy to say, been enabled to pay off all my debts from last half.
'Nimrod, Sir?' continued Spankie. 'did you say was your friend's name,
Sir?' 'I knew your father, Sir,' said he, turning to George, who was quite
delighted, 'and I trust the good gentleman is well, Sir.' ['I'll send
Spankie some game, hanged if I don't!' said the Squire. 'Remind me,
my dear, will you?'] 'I've got tarts, cakes, and buns, Sir; a bun and
greengage jam, Mr. Nimrod, Sir, you'll find very pleasant, Sir.' And so,
uncle, George proceeded to eat for the first time one of Spankie's celebrated buns and jam. Having taken leave of Spankie, we wandered
further along the wall, where we encountered Joby. (I forget whether
Joby was going or not in your time, uncle; if he wasn't, I may as well
tell you that he sells buns and jam like Spankie, at the wall: besides
which, he stands umpire at cricket-matches and football.) 'Seen the
hounds go by, Joby?' I inquired. 'No, I ain't,' says Joby; 'but they
won't be long fust, I know, for there goes Charlie Wise.' And, sure
enough, the Wise man and young Charlie emerged from their yard just
as he spoke, old Charlie in his green coat with the brass buttons, the

On the Eton Playing Fields

How's that Toby.
H'out!

See page 98

white cords and the butcher boots, looking as spruce as a game-cock as
he replies to the chaff of the boys standing by. A couple of minutes
after the Royal hounds made their appearance. You should have seen
George's eye light up, uncle, when he saw Charles Davis for the first time
on his snaffle-bridled chestnut. ['I'm glad of it! heartily glad of it!'
remarked the Squire. 'His eye lit up, did it!—good.'] George said he
never saw such boots and breeches, or such a seat on horseback, before
in his life; and being a son of a Master of hounds, of course he ought to
know. But I remember I've heard you say, uncle, that you never saw a
more graceful horseman in your life than Charles Davis. We'll shirk
eleven o'clock school and cut over to Salt Hill and see the meet before
the end of the half; see if we don't, Sir. ['Ha, ha! that's the way to
make a man of him, Charlie, my boy!' chuckled the Squire.] The
hounds having disappeared, we wended our way to George's dame's,
in Weston's Yard, to inspect his room, which I notice you have
taken good care to stock well with sporting prints. I have recommended, in addition to those he already has, Will Long on Bertha
and Charles Davis on Traverser, and George and I are going to
buy 'em at Runacles's in the course of the day. ['Fine boy,
Charlie!' remarked the Squire: 'just like me in all his tastes!']
Talking of Charles Davis being a swell, as we walked across Weston's
Yard we came across another swell, though in another line of
country; to wit, Dr. Hawtree, the venerable Provost. George was im-
mensely struck with his frill and his general get-up, and said he should
like to get his recipe for boot varnish as a present for you. ['Devilish
thoughtful of the boy, upon my word!' said the Squire.] The Doctor is,
indeed, a smart old gentleman, and well deserves the title once bestowed
upon him of 'Nitidissimus Hawtree.'* It being a half-holiday, the
first thing I did after chapel was to escort George to Webber's. He
admired Miss Polly very much, he told me, and no doubt he'll be a
great patron of the establishment before long. We then looked in
at Williams's, as he wanted some school books. 'Who's your tutor?'
asked Giles. 'Mr. Old,' replied George. 'Don't call him "Mister,"
you fool!' interrupted a boy standing by; 'we don't "Mister" 'em here.
Say Johnny Old; that's about the ticket: ain't it, Giles?' George blushed.
He is rapidly falling into our ways, Sir; you see—he'll soon be one of us.
['I devoutly hope so!' said the Squire.] After that, I got old Culliford
to let us up into the Swishing-room, where George was much struck with
the architectural beauties of the block. He'll be more struck when he's
been held down once or twice: won't he, Sir? ['Ha, ha, ha!' roared the
Squire.] We went from there to the upper school, to have a look at the

* The facetious William Bolland one day came down to Eton with
'I Zingari,' to play the boys. In the course of the afternoon he presented Dr.
Hawtree, on behalf of the club, with the freedom of I Zingari, in a deal
box, winding up a neat speech with the following appropriate toast: '*Floreat
Etona!* et vivat *Nitidissimus* Hawtree!'

names cut there. We found your name, and a lot more of your family, much to George's delight. I must tell you that he made rather an unlucky remark before we left. Turning round to a boy named Mopson, commonly called 'Mops,' who was with us, he asked him if *his* ancestors were at Eton. Mops replied, he did not know; but the fact is, it is pretty well known here that Mops senior in early life pursued the calling of a navvy. It is also, I am afraid, a fact, that when Mops *père* comes down to Eton, which he does about once a half, in a dirty shirt and diamond studs, Mops *fils*, if he knows he's coming, gets out of his way if he possibly can. You see, Sir, Mops always has such a lot of money, that his parental governor's visit does not do him any good, and as his appearance is against him he would just as soon have his room as his company. Well, uncle, I think I have now shown George nearly everything. We are to meet at Brown's to-morrow morning, after seven o'clock school, for a hot buttered bun and coffee. Mr. Brown, I must tell you, in case you don't remember him, is a great admirer of our hereditary legislators, for whenever he enters from the back of the little shop, with a relay of hot buns, he cries out, 'Now, then! *Lords* first!'

I will now conclude, and with love to my Aunt,

Believe me,

Your affectionate Nephew,

CHARLES RATTLEPATE.

To George Nimrod, Esq. M.F.H.

On repairing to Harkaway Hall one fine day, to pay my old friend Mr. Nimrod a visit, I found him, though suffering severely from gout, in an unwonted state of cheerfulness.

'And how is George getting on at Eton?' I inquired. (It was his third half there.)

'How's he getting on, Sir?' said the Squire. 'Why, I'm thankful to say I have every reason to be proud of him, Sir. Damme, Sir, he's a credit to the Nimrod family in every way. Here's a delightful letter I've just got from him, and another from his tutor. Read 'em, Sir! read 'em!' said the worthy old gentleman.

The contents of Master George's letter were as follows:—

WASN'T it hard lines? I got swished and turned down this morning for being at Windsor Steeplechases. Poppleton minor and me had just tipped one of those chaps who sell sham sovereigns for a shilling off his stool, upsetting all his money, and were bolting from him, he after us, when we ran clean into Stiggins's arms. We should have been on Poppleton's brother's drag in another minute. Wasn't it a sell? I *think* we're going there to-morrow again. Will you please send me a ferret or two, if Tom can spare them? One of mine died the other day, and the other got hung up in a hole at Ditton last Saturday, and we

The War Man & starting from Sack Hill

Finch Mason.

had to leave him. ['Why, he'll be another Poacher "Phinn,"* the dog!' chuckled the Squire, as I came to the above paragraph.] I shall also be glad of some more tin soon, as I am rather short.

Best love to my Mother,

Your affectionate Son,

GEORGE NIMROD.

The other epistle from the young gentleman's tutor was simply to the effect that young Squire George was utterly callous to any punishment, and begging Mr. Nimrod senior to remonstrate with him seriously.

'Charming letters, aren't they?' said the Squire, as I returned them to him, putting them fondly into his shooting-jacket pocket, with delight written on every feature of his face.

Charming, indeed, thought I, as I wended my way homewards across the park; and, at the same time, I could not help thinking how very appropriate the reply was of the old Eton dame, who was asked by a fond mother, bringing her son there for the first time, as to the state of the boys' morals. 'Morals, ma'am!' said the old lady, holding up her hands in astonishment. 'Morals, ma'am! *Why, they haven't got a moral among 'em!*'

---

* The late Mr. Phinn, Q.C., whose old Eton nickname of 'Poacher' stuck to him through life.

Fores's Highly-Coloured Sporting Publications.

FORES'S CONTRASTS.

Illustrative of the Road, the Rail, &c. After H. ALKEN. Price 10s. each.

1. THE DRIVER (Coachman) of 1832—THE DRIVER (Engineer) of 1852.
2. THE GUARD (Coach) of 1832—THE GUARD (Locomotive) of 1852.
3. THE DRIVER OF THE MAIL of 1832—THE DRIVER OF THE MAIL of 1852.
4. ST. GEORGE'S (our Jeames)—ST. GILES'S (our Jim).

A STEEPLE CHASE IN THE OLDEN TIME.

After H. ALKEN, Sen. Six Plates, price £3 3s.

EXPLOITS OF DICK KNIGHT OF THE PYTCHLEY HUNT.

After C. LORAINE SMITH, Esq. Eight Plates Coloured, price £ . Very Scarce.

FOX HOUNDS.

After T. WOODWARD and W. BARRAUD. Price £1 10s. the Pair.

1. COMPANIONS IN THE CHASE.   2. GONE TO EARTH.

AN EXTRAORDINARY STEEPLE CHASE

FOR 1000 SOVEREIGNS,

Between Mr. Geo. Osbaldeston on his 'Clasher,' and Dick Christian on Capt. Ross' 'Clinker.' From Great Dalby Windmill to within a mile of Tilton-on-the-Hill. The five miles were done in 16 minutes.
After E. GILL. Price £2 2s.

RETURNING FROM ASCOT RACES.

(A SCENE ON THE ROAD.)
After C. C. HENDERSON. Price £2 2s.

EPSOM.

After J. POLLARD. Six Plates, price £3 3s.

1. SADDLING IN THE WARREN.   4. THE GRAND STAND.
2. THE BETTING POST.   5. THE RACE OVER.
3. PREPARING TO START.   6. SETTLING DAY AT TATTERSALL'S (OLD YARD).

FORES'S SPORTING SCRAPS.

After H. ALKEN, Sen.   Price 10s. per Sheet of four.

1. STEEPLE CHASING.   2. HUNTING.   3. HUNTING.   4. HUNTING.
5. RACING.   6. COURSING.   7. BOATING.

Sheets 2, 3, 4, form a consecutive series of twelve Hunting Incidents.

FORES'S HUNTING SCENES.

After H. ALKEN. Price 12s. each.

PLATE 1.—THE FIRST INTRODUCTION TO HOUNDS.
PLATE 2.—RENEWAL OF ACQUAINTANCE WITH HOUNDS.

FORES'S ANATOMICAL PLATES of the HORSE.

THE AGE EXHIBITED BY THE SHAPE OF THE TEETH.   Price 6s.
THE AGE EXHIBITED BY THE TABLES OF THE TEETH.
THE STRUCTURE OF THE FOOT CLEARLY DEFINED.   } Price 5s. each.
THE MUSCLES AND TENDONS ACCURATELY DELINEATED.

LONDON: PUBLISHED BY MESSRS. FORES, 41 PICCADILLY, W.
SHIPPERS SUPPLIED UPON LIBERAL TERMS.

2

THE BILLESDON COPLOW RUN.
After R. FRANKLAND.   Six Plates.   Price £2 2s.   Scarce.

THE SMOKING HUNT AT BRAUNSTONE.
After C. LORAINE SMITH, Esq. Six Plates. Price £4 4s. Scarce.

IN LUCK AND OUT OF LUCK.
After T. EARL and W. BROMLEY.   Price 15s. the Pair.

1. IN LUCK.—A Bull Terrier with Pipe and Grog.
2. OUT OF LUCK.—A Scotch Terrier with Empty Platter, &c.

ROUGH AND READY.
A Scotch Terrier's Head looking through a broken Hoarding. After G. STEVENS.
Price 5s.

WIDE AWAKE.
A Rough Terrier's Head Watching. After J. S. NEWTON. Price 5s.

MISCHIEVOUS MODELS.
A Puppy and Kitten in an Artist's Studio. After R. PHYSICK. Price 7s. 6d.

FORES'S ILLUSTRATED SPORTING WORKS.

THE SPORTING SCRAP-BOOK.
Forty Plates Coloured, price £4 4s.
HUNTING, RACING, STEEPLE CHASING, COURSING, SHOOTING, YACHTING,
BOATING, COACHING.

SCENES ON THE ROAD.
By C. B. NEWHOUSE. Eighteen Plates Coloured, price £3 3s.
A Pictorial Gallery of Coaching Incidents, spiritedly pourtrayed.

THE HORSE'S MOUTH
(SHEWING THE AGE BY THE TEETH).
By EDWARD MAYHEW, M.R.C.V.S. Demy 8vo. Price 10s. 6d., with Coloured
Illustrations and Woodcuts. 4th Edition.

ROAD SCRAPINGS.
By C. C. HENDERSON. Twelve Plates Coloured, price £2 2s.
Travelling Scenes in England, France, Spain, Flanders, Italy, and Switzerland.
Each Sketch carries a History of the Road with it, truthfully
and artistically detailed.

THE COMBINATION HUNTING AND CARD RACK.
Designed to hang or stand.
A receptacle for the Meets of Three Packs of Hounds; also Documents, &c. Price 15s.

LONDON: PUBLISHED BY MESSRS. FORES, 41 PICCADILLY, W.
SHIPPERS SUPPLIED UPON LIBERAL TERMS.

3

FORES'S STEEL-PLATE ENGRAVINGS.

THE FAREWELL CARESS.
Painted by C. Burton Barber.   Engraved by F. Stacpoole.
Artist's Proofs, £8 8s.   Prints, £2 2s.

NO FEAR OF THE HOUNDS.
Painted by C. Burton Barber.   Engraved by W. H. Simmons.
Artist's Proofs, £8 8s.   Prints, £2 2s.

A PROMISING LITTER.
Painted by C. Burton Barber.   Engraved by W. T. Davey.
Artist's Proofs, £8 8s.   Prints, £2 2s.

CHRISTIAN GRACES—FAITH, HOPE, CHARITY.
Painted by G. E. Hicks.   Engraved by F. Holl.
Artist's Proofs, £6 6s.   Prints, £2 2s.

IL PENSEROSO.
Painted by G. E. Hicks.   Engraved by F. Holl.   Artist's Proofs, £3 3s.   Prints, £1 1s.

L'ALLEGRO.
Painted by G. E. Hicks.   Engraved by F. Holl.
Artist's Proofs, £3 3s.   Prints, £1 1s.

LINKS OF LOVE.
Painted by G. E. Hicks.   Engraved by F. Holl.   Artist's Proofs, £3 3s.   Prints, £1 1s.

THE PAST AND THE FUTURE.
From the Original by Miss Gillies.   Engraved by F. Holl.
Artist's Proofs, £3 3s.   Prints, £1 1s.

SISTER ARTS.
Painted by W. J. Grant.   Engraved by F. Holl.
Artist's Proofs, £3 3s.   Prints, £1 1s.

THE HUNTSMAN AND HOUNDS.
Drawn by Sir Edwin Landseer, R.A.   Engraved by H. T. Ryall.
Artist's Proofs, £2 2s.   Proofs, Tinted, £1 1s.   Prints, 10s. 6d.

MIRANDA AND DOROTHEA.
Painted by John Faed, R.S.A.   Engraved by W. Holl.
Artist's Proofs, £3 3s.   India Proofs, £2 2s.   Prints, £1 1s.

London: Published by MESSRS. FORES, 41 Piccadilly, W.
SHIPPERS SUPPLIED UPON LIBERAL TERMS.

4

MESSRS. FORES,

SPORTING AND FINE ART PUBLISHERS,

41, PICCADILLY, LONDON,

CORNER OF SACKVILLE STREET,

BEG LEAVE TO ANNOUNCE THE FOLLOWING RECENT PUBLICATIONS:

THE SPORTSMAN'S DREAM,

BY R. M. ALEXANDER,

Representing a tired and sleeping sportsman reclining in his easy chair before a comfortable fire dreaming of the following Sports, which are cleverly depicted in the wreaths arising from his half-smoked pipe, viz. :—Hunting, Yachting, Coaching, Pigeon Shooting, Billiards, Golf, Deer Stalking, Grouse Shooting, Steeple Chasing, Salmon Fishing, Boxing, Racing, Polo and Cards.

Coloured, 14 × 11 inches, £1 1s.

SALMON FISHING,

BY W. BRACKETT,

In four subjects, entitled "The Rise," "The Leap," "The Struggle," "Landed," are clearly the work of a Salmon Fisher, and being replete with artistic finish, will surely commend themselves to lovers of the sport.

Coloured, 11 × 8 inches each, £3 13s. 6d. the Set of Four.

FOX'S HEADS

(A PAIR),

BY C. BURTON BARBER.

HARD PRESSED!

An old "Dog," supposed to be on the point of being "run into," with glaring eyes and open jaws, evidently determined to "die game."

ESCAPED!

Is a panting "vixen," who has doubled upon her pursuers, and by her expression shows the hounds are "at fault."

Coloured, 15 × 12 inches, £2 2s. the pair.

TWO SHILLINGS

FORES's
SPORTING NOTES
&
Sketches.

Nº 2 July ·1884·

Contents:

EIGHT TINTED FULL PAGE ILLUSTRATIONS,
By FINCH MASON
& R·M·ALEXANDER·

PUBLISHED QUARTERLY BY
MESSRS FORES' 41 PICCADILLY, LONDON.
SIMPKIN MARSHALL & Cº

ROWLANDS' ODONTO

is the best tooth powder whitens the teeth and prevents decay; contains no acid or gritty substances. Avoid worthless imitations, and buy only Rowlands' Odonto.

Sold everywhere.

IMPROVED BREECHLOADERS.
LARGEST STOCK IN LONDON.

Latest Improvements. Hammerless, or with Hammers below line of sight, Compressed Steel Barrels, Choke Bore, &c.
Superior Guns, in Pairs and Sets of Three, fitted in same case, ready finished as in Stock, or made to order.

SPECIAL PIGEON GUNS,

Of great power, Hurlingham weight, Whitworth steel tubes, marvellous pattern.
Trial at our private shooting grounds.

HAMMERLESS GUNS.

Further Improvements. TOP LEVER, SIDE LOCKS, SAFETY SCEARS, WITH BLOCK INTERPOSING, DISLODGED BY THE TRIGGERS IN FIRING.

Second-Hand Central Fires in Good Condition.

EXPRESS DOUBLE RIFLES. ROOK AND RABBIT RIFLES.
IMPROVED RIFLING. REDUCED BORE. ACCURATE SIGHTING.

E. M. REILLY & Co.,

277, OXFORD STREET, W. 16, NEW OXFORD STREET. RUE SCRIBE, PARIS.

OLDRIDGE'S

SIXTY YEARS' SUCCESS.—The best and only certain remedy ever discovered for preserving, strengthening, beautifying or restoring the Hair, Whiskers, or Moustaches, and preventing them turning gray. Sold in bottles, 3s. 6d., 6s., and 11s. by all chemists & perfumers, & at 22, Wellington Street, Strand, London, W.C. For Children's and Ladies' Hair it is most efficacious and unrivalled.

BALM OF COLUMBIA

1

FORES'S
SPORTING NOTES & SKETCHES.
A QUARTERLY MAGAZINE.

No. 2.   JULY 1884.   PRICE 2*s*

CONTENTS.

LONDON:
PUBLISHED BY MESSRS. FORES, 41 PICCADILLY.

SIMPKIN, MARSHALL, & CO.

Fores's Sporting Notes and Sketches.

THE Proprietor of the above Quarterly Magazine has pleasure in informing lovers of sport he has made arrangements with well-known authors to supply carefully-written and amusing articles connected therewith ; and as full-page Illustrations will be one of its leading features, he has secured the services of eminent sporting artists for this purpose, and will spare no endeavour to make this the highest class Sporting Magazine of the day.

The first Number was published last April, and met with unqualified success. The favour with which it was received may be estimated by the opinions of the Press, which are reproduced on the opposite page. The Illustrations included characteristic Portrait Sketches of Sir Robert Peel, Bart. ; Earl of Hardwicke; Mr. Peck; A. Coventry, Esq.; Earl of Rosebery; Sir J. Astley, Bart.; Lord Falmouth ; Mr. Matt. Dawson ; Fred. Archer on 'Bend Or,' led by Mr. Porter ; T. Cannon ; Mr. Wise; and Old ' Joby ' of Eton, and proved quite as attractive a feature as was anticipated, and will doubtless induce a continued demand for the part, a few copies of which are still on sale, price Two Shillings, and may be ordered of any Bookseller, or from the Publishers, Messrs. FORES, 41 Piccadilly, London, W.

TO ADVERTISERS.

THE Proprietor of the above high-class Magazine begs leave respectfully to direct attention to this valuable medium of advertising every description of property, especially that which is connected with the varied requirements of Sportsmen.

The publication will be Quarterly, and as one of the leading features will consist of full-page tinted Illustrations, depicting celebrated people, events, sports, &c., the work will be largely one of reference, thereby increasing its importance to advertisers.

SCALE OF PRICES.

Full Page ... ... £5 | Half Page £3
Quarter Page £2

As the number of advertisements will be limited, intending advertisers are advised to secure space without delay.

FORES'S SPORTING NOTES AND SKETCHES.

Opinions of the Press.

'FORES'S SPORTING NOTES AND SKETCHES, a new quarterly magazine, published by Messrs. Fores of Piccadilly, is brightly written by experts in the several divisions of outdoor sport—hunting, shooting, fishing, and cricket; but the charm of the first number is in the spirited, life-like pencillings by that chief of graphic sportsmen, Finch Mason. Seven characteristic designs from his hand, as sure of catching a likeness as his namesake Finch of wicket-keeping fame was of catching a ball that came in his way, illustrate four of the half-dozen literary contributions, one of which, the last, is the artist's own. His cross-country sketches go without saying. The two which embellish Mr. Heron's paper, "A Long Way to Covert," are as good as anything that John Leech ever turned out. The caricature—for such it is, though within the limits of becoming mirth—which represents Monsieur Alphonse equipped for a bear-hunt in the Pyrenees, is irresistible. In "A Famous Match" the likenesses "all over" of Archer and Cannon, with various thumb-nail portraits thrown in, are superlatively true to form, feature, and expression. But finest of all is the character sketch of old Joby, dealer in buns and jam, and umpire at cricket. "Young Nimrod at Eton," written and illustrated by the same hand, is a fresh and lively contribution, full of animal spirits and shrewd reminiscences. Mr. R. M. Alexander, in his illustration to the article on "Thames Trout-Fishing," shows himself well up in his theme. Altogether, the magazine starts with a fair breeze on the sea of public favour.'—DAILY TELEGRAPH.

'MESSRS. FORES, of Piccadilly, have just issued a new quarterly sporting magazine, which they have designated *Sporting Notes and Sketches*, and the opening number fully bears out their title. Hunting, fishing, shooting, racing, are all treated in what may be called a bright, taking way, and, in addition, each article is illustrated by some really clever and characteristic full-page sketches, which are for the most part spirited and realistic. No less than seven of the sketches are from the hand of Mr. Finch Mason, who also supplies a very amusing story of, shall we say, pre-university life, called "Young Nimrod at Eton." The sketch of the college umpire given with this story is really excellent, and decidedly one of the best in the magazine. Mr. Mason has given us "Joby," as he is called, to the life. To our mind the really best sketch in this number is the single one supplied by Mr. R. M. Alexander to "Thames Trout-Fishing," written by that well-known fisherman, Mr. J. P. Wheeldon, a supplier of piscatorial literature to many papers and magazines of the present day. Mr. Watson tells the story of the meeting of those two equine wonders, Bend Or and Robert the Devil, in what he may certainly call their "Famous Match." "Orange Blossom," the celebrated poetic tipster of *Bell's Life*, contributes some racing lore, which he terms "Full Forty Years Ago." A humorous account of "A Day's Shooting in the Pyrenees," by a couple of *voyageurs* on their way back from the East, is not at all dull reading; and the hunting article is from the pen of Mr. A. Heron, and is entitled "A Long Way to Covert"—capital reading for a railway journey.'—THE FIELD.

'SPORTING NOTES AND SKETCHES, published quarterly, by Messrs. Fores of 41 Piccadilly, is to hand. This well-designed and got-up little book, and the eight illustrations by Finch Mason and R. M. Alexander, are most admirable, and remind us forcibly that Leech and Doyle. Finch Mason's horses in particular are horses, and one seems to know instinctively how they are going to "negotiate" their next fence. We can only say that in the story, "A Day's Shooting in the Pyrenees," we have had an almost similar experience ourselves; and the figure in the foreground is an old acquaintance of ours, and by no means overdrawn. We heartily commend the book.'—UNITED SERVICE GAZETTE.

'FORES'S SPORTING NOTES AND SKETCHES.—This is a new venture, which seems likely to be a successful one, an illustrated sporting magazine to be published quarterly by Messrs. Fores, 41 Piccadilly. The contents of No. 1 include a hunting sketch by Mr. A. Heron, called "A Long Way to Covert," with two pictures tinted, full pages, by Mr. Finch Mason, who, indeed, has done all the illustrations one fishing picture by Mr. R. M. Alexander. "A Day's Shooting in the Pyrenees" forms an excuse for the introduction of the conventional French "sportsman." "Orange Blossom" gossips very pleasantly of the Turf "Full Forty Years Ago." Mr. Wheeldon contributes a fishing paper, and Mr. Alfred E. T. Watson, in an article called "A Famous Match," compares the careers of Bend Or and Robert the Devil, including a description of their race for the Epsom Gold Cup. Mr. Watson does not seem to be quite satisfied yet that Bend Or is Bend Or. In hitting off the likenesses of well-known racing men Mr. Finch Mason has been singularly successful, in spite of the smallness of his sketches. A very cheery sketch, "Young Nimrod at Eton," by Mr. Finch Mason, concludes an excellent number.'—ILLUSTRATED SPORTING AND DRAMATIC NEWS.

'FORES'S SPORTING NOTES AND SKETCHES.—Seldom has a candidate for public favour made such a good first appearance as this new quarterly magazine, published by Messrs. Fores, the well-known sporting printsellers of 41 Piccadilly. There is not a dull line between the two covers, and the illustrations by Mr. Finch Mason are quite beyond the sporting pictures which are usually to be found in pages meant for sportsmen. Indeed we may say that few artists in black and white can compete with Mr. Mason in the delineation of the horse, and the spirit with which he contrives to invest his animals while in movement reminds us of the drawings of John Leech, whose humour he also seems to have caught. The literary merits of the magazine are of a high order, as may be guessed from a mere reference to the title-page, for we have contributions from Mr. Alfred E. T. Watson, Mr. J. P. Wheeldon, Mr. A. Heron, the author of "The Tommiebeg Shootings," Mr. Finch Mason, and "Orange Blossom," who gives us one of those pleasantly written chatty articles on sporting lore that almost compel one to become *laudator temporis acti*. The merits of the new magazine are undoubted, and if Messrs. Fores will but keep to the standard shown in the first number, *Sporting Notes and Sketches* should be a great and permanent success.'—BELL'S LIFE.

'JUST on going to press we received an advance copy of the first number of *Fores's Sporting Notes and Sketches*. Of the sporting tales and essays by Messrs. A. E. T. Watson, Heron, Finch Mason, "Orange Blossom," and others, we will not say anything till next week; but we will remark that the

7

illustrations, of which there are eight, all by Mr. Finch Mason, are amongst the best pictures from the field that have been issued for many a long day. These drawings, which abound in portraits of well-known sporting men, are quite stirring. They are reproduced in black and white by a most effective method, and for the sake of these pictorial sketches alone the number is worth more than the florin asked for it.'—COUNTY GENTLEMAN.

'FORES'S SPORTING NOTES AND SKETCHES.—We have received the first number of Messrs. Fores's, the well-known sporting-print publishers of Piccadilly, new quarterly magazine, which contains some spirited articles, the first of which is "A Long Way to Covert," by A. Heron, which is certainly amusing. "A Day's Shooting in the Pyrenees," by the author of "The Tommiebeg Shootings," is in the style which may be expected. "Thames Trout-Fishing," by J. P. Wheeldon, beautifully illustrated by R. M. Alexander, is a very good article. "A Famous Match," by Alfred E. T. Watson, on which subject the author is quite at home, is cleverly written, and so is the last article, "Young Nimrod at Eton," by Finch Mason, who is as good with his pen as he is with his pencil. This number contains several full-page sketches by him in his well-known and characteristic style. The present number is certainly what the proprietors claim for it, the first instalment of a high-class magazine.'—LAND AND WATER.

'FORES'S SPORTING NOTES AND SKETCHES.—Messrs. Fores, of 41 Piccadilly, have issued the first number of their new quarterly magazine. It is excellently printed and illustrated by several charming sketches by Finch Mason, which are alone worth the value of the number. The contributors include Messrs A. Heron, J. P. Wheeldon, A. E. T. Watson, Finch Mason, and the author of "The Tommiebeg Shootings." The articles are all well written, and there is not a dull page in the magazine.'—THE SPORTSMAN.

'A VERY high-class magazine, called *Fores's Sporting Notes and Sketches*, is being published quarterly by Messrs. Fores, of Piccadilly. The illustrations by Finch Mason are on a scale not often attempted in this class of work, whilst the names of "Orange Blossom," J. P. Wheeldon, and Alfred Watson, signed to articles in the first number, which is now before us, speak for the literary merit of the publication.'—SPORTING TIMES.

'FORES'S SPORTING NOTES AND SKETCHES.—This new magazine, to be published quarterly, has made its first appearance, and bids fair to form a valuable and welcome addition to high-class sporting literature. Finch Mason has so ably proved himself a master of the sketching art, that his name needs only to be mentioned in proof of the excellence and originality of the illustrations. Hunting, racing, fishing, shooting, and cricket, have capitally written stories devoted to them, and A. Heron, Alfred E. T. Watson, J. P. Wheeldon, and "Orange Blossom," are names which will guarantee the respective subjects being done justice to. We heartily wish *Fores's Sporting Notes and Sketches* the success to which it is entitled.'—SPORTING LIFE.

'FORES'S SPORTING NOTES AND SKETCHES is the title of a new quarterly magazine, published by Messrs. Fores, the well-known sporting printsellers of 41 Piccadilly, London. The calibre of the contributions to this new candidate for popular favour may be easily inferred from the names of the contributors. A. Heron furnishes an excellent paper, entitled "A Long Way to Covert;" the author of "The Tommiebeg Shootings" supplies "A Day's Shooting in the Pyrenees," and the accomplished "Orange Blossom" discourses on things that happened "Full Forty Years Ago," telling us in that pure English prose for which he is as famous as for the gracefulness of his verse, how he just missed 'tipping' "Caller Ou in *Bell's Life* for the St. Leger she won, and thereby rendering himself famous—at least for a day. J. P. Wheeldon is always at home in describing feats of piscatorial skill, and the votaries of the rod and reel will find him at his best here, discoursing of "Thames Trout-Fishing." "A Famous Match," by E. T. Watson, is a graphic description of the grand race between Bend Or and Robert the Devil for the Epsom Cup of 1881, introduced by an allusion to the great race the two horses made for the Derby of the previous year, and the sensational objection to the winner which followed. It is astonishing how many people still believe that Bend Or was the son of Clemence, and not of Rouge Rose at all; and their argument certainly derives some force from the fact that Tiarb Or, who ought to be own brother to Bend Or, is not the least like him, but is the model of Tadcaster, who was credited to Clemence, but was said to be the real son of Rouge Rose. Nobody supposes for a moment that the Duke of Westminster's servants, much less the Duke himself, wilfully lent themselves to a fraud that could not benefit them in the slightest degree; nevertheless, there is a strong suspicion abroad that there may be some truth in the statements of the discharged groom, and that the colts may have got "mixed up" somehow either in the stable or the paddock. "Young Nimrod at Eton" is a very amusing paper by Finch Mason, whose facile pencil also furnishes the eight full-page illustrations with which the number is embellished. These are all spiritedly drawn in the style which "Phiz" made familiar to the last generation of sportsmen in his *Racing and Chasing*, and the tone of the paper on which they are printed—a yellowish sage-green—gives them a very attractive appearance. Judging by this initial number, we can honestly say that the new sporting quarterly is full of promise, and we heartily wish it every success.'—SPORTING CHRONICLE, MANCHESTER.

'FORES'S ILLUSTRATED SPORTING MAGAZINE is a new candidate for public favour, and we venture to predict that it will be extremely popular. R. M. Alexander, the name of one of the artists, is new to us, but a man who can draw so well, and whose touch is so delicate, and yet so full of vigour, is sure to make his mark. The American magazines are so far ahead of us in the matter of illustrations that we gladly welcome a sketch as spirited and as graceful as that of Mr. Alexander.'—SOCIETY.

'FORES'S SPORTING NOTES. (Messrs. Fores, 41 Piccadilly.)—This interesting magazine is to hand, and we have nothing but the very highest praise to award to it. The letterpress is very good throughout, and the eight tinted full-page illustrations by Finch Mason are, of course, admirable. There ought to be a very brilliant future for this new magazine.'—SHOOTING TIMES.

8

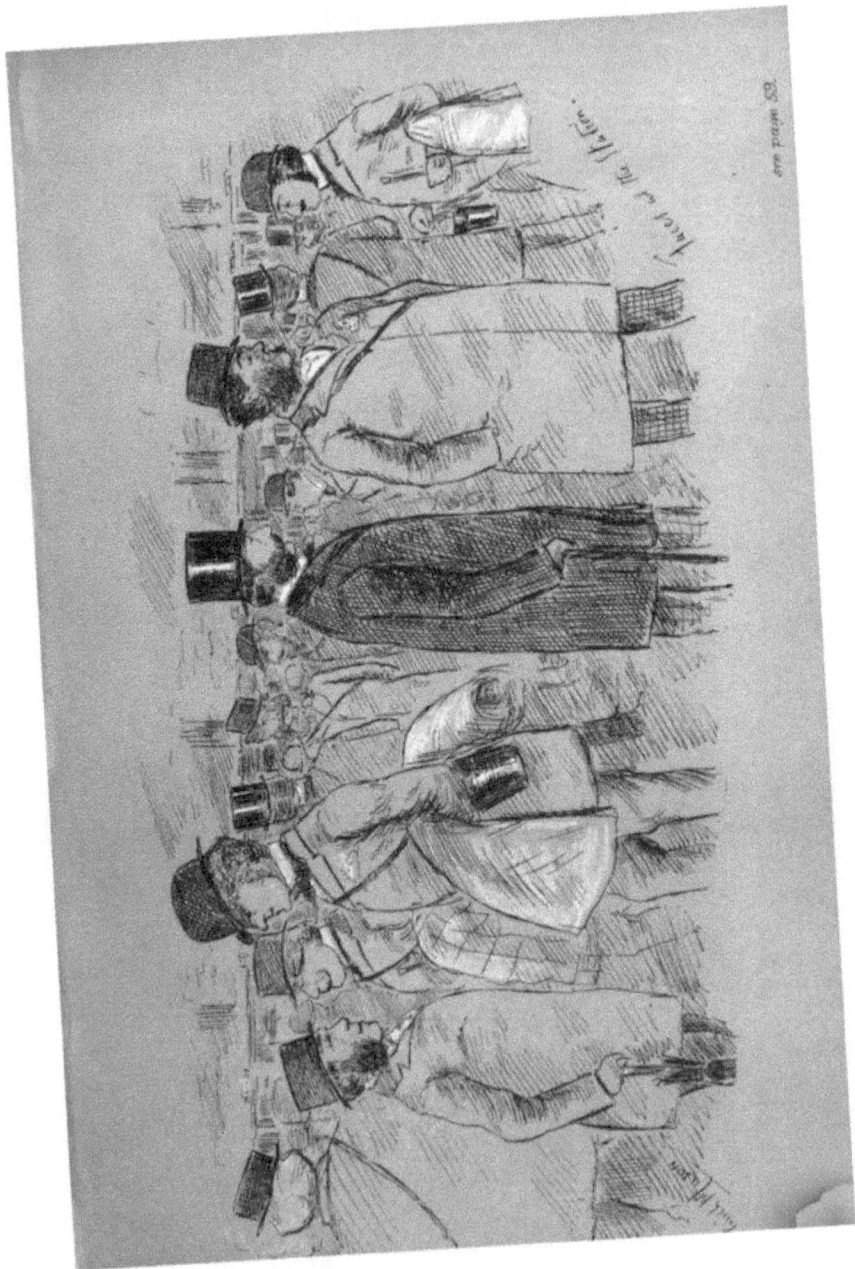

FORES'S
SPORTING NOTES AND SKETCHES.

THE OLD RACE AND THE NEW.

By 'ORANGE BLOSSOM.'

HEN our grandfathers were very young, a day's racing was enjoyed, maybe, but seldom, save by people resident at Newmarket, or those who made the Turf their business. Travelling was slow and expensive; the number of race-meetings small as compared with the vast crop that sprung up of late years; at many 'places of sport' funds were not easily procured, even for the one annual meeting. 'Gate-money' was a term as yet unknown.

In some parts, where training-stables happened to be numerous, races were held at the central town of the district, and at other places not very far from it. In such cases, certain of the inhabitants of the chief town—the lawyer, the doctor, a few of the plodding tradesfolk, who rarely permitted themselves a little relaxation—made holiday perhaps twice or thrice in the season. If a dozen miles or so had to be traversed before the course was reached from their starting-point, they jogged thither on horseback, or drove to it in high-wheeled gigs. Were such vehicles unprocurable, a homelier conveyance was borrowed or hired for the day, and a little party droned along the rough roads in a roomy cart. But the favourite plan was to make the journey on foot, starting with plenty of time in hand, so as to reach by noon the house of some friendly farmer or miller, who, in accordance with long custom, on that day hospitably entertained his gossips or customers from the market-town. The descendants of these honest folks would elevate the nose of contempt were they invited to join in the stroll through fields and lanes, or to partake of the substantial fare on which the companions subsequently regaled. I am old enough to have heard the walk and banquet described by men who had taken part in both.

The little company, four or five in number, marched on soberly and silently enough until the town was left behind, and then, avoiding the high road, made for their destination through woodland paths, by short cuts across fields, along the banks of the rapid river, that in those days so teemed with trout. Plenty sail there still ; but in the time of our grandfathers one noted angler, a pedagogue in the small town, would, after dismissing his pupils at noon, seek the stream, fly-rod in hand, and by the time his early dinner-hour sounded would be home again with a pannier half filled with the spotted beauties. The talk of the wayfarers may hardly have been very refined, and turned not, I expect, much on politics, or even on war, although those were stirring times for Englishmen, when the few newspapers that reached such country places might bring tidings of a victory won by our armies in Spain. Neither, probably, was the afternoon's sport made subject of long discussion. Our holiday-makers did not lack love of the racehorse, but for betting they cared little. Indeed, in their simple world, he who was known habitually to risk money in such a way stood not well with his sober-going townsmen, who delighted to make money truly, but only after the fashion that had been handed down to them by their industrious and thrifty ancestors. Cosily and easily the walkers progressed towards their destination, caring little for the lovely scenery that familiarity had caused to lose its charm ; if, indeed, in their prosaic eyes it ever had charm at all. Anon the discourse was seasoned by some fat jest, provoking a burst of rather boisterous laughter from listeners for whom broad humour alone had a relish : and at last, when these good folks were waxing hungry (they knew little of deep nightly potations and breakfasts contrived for jaded appetites), the house of their jolly host was reached. Year after year they sat down to a dinner varying not the least from its predecessor at race-time, twelve months before. There was a large roast loin of veal, and a Yorkshire ham, and quantities of vegetables from the prolific garden beside the mill-stream. The sharp-set company cut and came again. Then appeared a huge plum-pudding ; and these good things were washed down by home-brewed ale, strong, and rather sharp. The miller's cellar boasted neither port, nor sherry, nor madeira, and he had never even tasted champagne—an unknown drink, moreover—(how things

have changed!—to every one of his guests. When the cloth
was removed the company enjoyed themselves with rum-and-
water and long pipes, until it was time to traverse the mile and
a quarter that still separated them from the course.

The entertainment there provided for them would now-a-days
be considered very tame. A few shows were to be seen, and a
sprinkling of drinking-booths. The company, on the whole,
was of much better class than most race-meetings now attract.
A duke or two had been driven to the course in great state
and splendour, and there were lords and baronets in plenty,
and great numbers of the county gentlefolk, with a noble show
of carriages. But the racing was not abundant. Handicaps
there were none, and all the stakes had but small value. Our
little party from the market-town would first stare at two
or three starters for a produce sweepstakes, run on a two-miles
course. The conditions, which they probably did not read, were
that the stake was for two-year-olds; colts 8 st. 3 lb., and fillies
8 st. Then, and for long after, horses took their age from May-
day; and this little country meeting was held early in April.
Next would come a five-guinea sweepstakes for hunters not
thoroughbred, ridden by gentlemen, a race in two-mile heats.
Last on the programme was probably a 50*l.* Maiden Plate, also
run in heats. If it was the Gold Cup day sport was sometimes
a little better. The spectators would see Sir William Gerard's
pink-and-white striped jacket, perhaps carried by Young Chariot;
they would see Lord Strathmore's black banner; and Mr. Pierse's
straw-and-white quartered. There, too, would be the white-and-
crimson sleeves of Mr. Mellish. But, whilst Streatlam Lass
bore his colours on the oval northern course, her owner was far
away on the great south-country heath, watching his Stavely
trying in vain to give Meteora 5 lbs. across the Flat; whilst
Lucks-all, by Stamford, presently turned the tables on Lord
Grosvenor when he raced with Iris over the Abingdon Mile.
Very scanty accommodation was provided our little party of
tradespeople for seeing the racing, and the more daring spirits
would convert a low tree into a natural grand stand. I remember one of these worthies relating how, in the descent
from this point of vantage, serious mishap occurred to a pair
of nether garments, donned for the first time that day, and
regarded with complacency by reason of their cut, and fit, and
fashion. In those primitive times men were not ashamed of
their occupation, and ready to drop amusement for business at

brief notice. So, whilst the owner of the rent garment lamented, a townsman, who pursued the useful calling of tailor, drew a 'housewife' from his pocket, and mended the tear there and then, in the face of the noble array of dukes and grandees. When the day's racing was at an end our little band of holiday-makers would return on foot to the town, calling once more on the miller for a parting glass of rum-and-water, and lingering in the spring evening by the dam, where grayling rose now and then, and some big chub lurked. Ere finally seeking their homes another halt would be made at the dingy town tavern, where their cosy club was held. Over tobacco and one taste more of the right Jamaica would the cronies conclude the holiday, reaching their respective domiciles not, perhaps, entirely undeserving of reproach from their spouses, but poorer by a crown at most in the way of bets lost, and prepared to turn to work with a will on the following morning.

How differently do men take their pleasure in this good year of 1884! Say I have occasion to wait for some twenty minutes at the Slowington Station, the London terminus of the famous Snoozely line. A great race-meeting is in progress, and people bound thither crowd for places in the trains. I buy a card from a large sheaf that lies on the newspaper counter, and retiring to a quiet corner away from the crush straight fall a musing on the changes in the ways of horse-racing, and in the men who affect the sport, since the days when our grandfathers were young. Why, here is one stake on the card worth more money than all those contested in half-a-dozen years at the meeting to which our holiday-makers walked early in the century! In what shoals the people come streaming past my retired nook! Many of them bright, smart, and trim, like the British gentlemen they are; some the sort of folks you would rather not meet on a dark night in an out-of-the-way London street, or in a lonely country lane at any hour. A little earlier in the day villainous faces would have been still more plentiful. The personage with whose buffalo-hide sack St. Medard interfered to such an unjustifiable extent by the lone Red Sea, could supply his larder thoroughly from the cheap trains on a great race-day. Probably he only bides his time.

What would the revellers, who feasted so contentedly on a plain joint and beer nearly eighty years ago, have thought, could they see the elaborate luncheon-hampers that are borne past to the train! And how those honest burghers would have been amazed could they, innocent of before-noon drinking, notice how many of the young fellows enter the refreshment-bars. I do not say the liquors sold are deleterious. Years ago a luckless scribe was mulcted in heavy damages, if I remember rightly, for impugning the quality of the soup or the tea supplied at a certain establishment for the vending of such light stimulants. So I shall guard against all risk of legal threats by the assertion that the whole of the refreshments sold everywhere are pure, wholesome, and conducive to health. This being the case, the young gentlemen who are preparing to take train for the races must be exonerated from rashness, though thus early they have drunk eagerly from the brandy and soda, or the whiskey and potass goblet. Our grandfathers, in their ignorance, would have hinted that any youth imbibing spirituous liquors immediately after breakfast was on one of the shortest roads to the churchyard.

Still the cabs come rattling up to the station. Catch the exquisites, who descend with such an air of what may be styled wooden dignity, walking when a Hansom is within call! Many of these beardless dandies are of a type familiar to the observant man who goes a racing. They do not know Tristan from a yearling, or Corrie Roy from Voluptuary. Their income is but small; they will not or cannot work; but they want money, and at a race-meeting there is the chance of getting some without much trouble. So they read all the 'tips' on the day's races, and consult such friends as are supposed to be well informed about the sport. If they follow a successful adviser, they assert that the money won was solely gained through their own judgment; if they depend on an unlucky one, he is stigmatised as an ignoramus. Those smooth-faced, straight-haired lads just passing, belong to another stamp. For betting they do not care much; but how terrible is their talk about horses and jockeys! Such noodles, not always harmless, it is who babble nonsense about the filly being stopped in the Two Thousand, and the old mare not trying in last year's Cesarewitch. They have no belief in man's honesty apparently, but are firm in the faith that Archer can win on any horse, and that Captain Machell has forgotten more about racing than is known to all the remainder of the turf world. Somewhat akin to them are the fable narrators, also of comparatively tender years, who raise their voices to tell a companion in a railway carriage that they backed every winner in two days at Newmarket last week. Although sufficiently ad-

vanced in wickedness to fib so dreadfully, they are still ' green '
enough to believe that the other occupants of the compartment
credit their statement.

Now come a batch of men who, unlike the pretenders preceding them, are great judges of horse-racing. That shrunken,
gray-haired veteran, carrying the thin ash stick, was a shining
light amongst steeplechase riders when the sport was almost in
its infancy. Few are sounder critics of condition, or offer a
more valuable opinion when the weights for a great handicap
are published, than the next passer-by, owner of a horse that not
long ago carried off the race that wins men fortunes more frequently than any other. There, grave and stepping out briskly,
is the favourite of fortune, whose white-and-red banner now
carries all before it. More cabs, more luncheon-hampers! Why,
the platform is almost impassable! and the confusion would be
dreadful did not the policemen understand their business so well.
What a departure for a day's racing, as compared with that of
the north-country cronies whose walk was recorded above!
The next two trains will convey almost as many people as
stood on the little Yorkshire racecourse to see Young Chariot
win.

The stock of race-cards at the counter is dwindling rapidly.
Nearly every man who passes buys one, and many are provided
besides with a ' *Ruff*,' with little books containing the returns of
the season's running almost up to the day, with another 'Guide to
Form,' made delightfully easy for reference. For amongst the many
thousands that take train to-day, those who have no expectation
of getting, at any rate, the ' ex's ' by a bet or two, are but few.
Here, however, comes one who, whether winner or loser, will
have a pleasant time in the paddock amongst the horses he loves
so well. A capital man across country, as those know who hunt
with Sir Nathaniel de Rothschild. May the fates be propitious
to the blue-and-white stripes on Doncaster town moor! There
goes a duke, to get a place in the train if he can ; pushing his
way through the crowd and unnoticed by the many. What a
contrast to the pomp and pageantry when the retinue-accom-
panied noblemen set out for the country course in 1806! Much
more like an ideal duke is the charming writer, pleasant alike
whether he gossips of racehorses or rehearsals, who now passes
my nook. Glad to see him about again. Now a lucky backer
approaches. That neat-looking man with the iron-gray hair has
for a time seemed to win at will. May it last! A constant loser

follows. The burly, discontented-looking individual behind him, has, according to his own showing, found but one balance on the right side since Lincoln. Yonder, with his clerk beside him, steps on quickly Mr. Help, most solid bookmaker, most shrewd observer of men. Ready of repartee, too, as a burst of laughter proclaims often enough at one of the 'Gaiety' tables when the evening is old. 'You laid me under the price that horse!' once said to him querulously at Newmarket a gentleman not supposed to be in the habit of booking less than the proper odds. 'Kindly repeat that, Major, aloud, before my comrades here,' was Mr. Help's reply, as he glanced along the rails, 'and I'm certain they'll present me with a medal!'

A mixed group hurries by. The first of them knows why Daniel O'Rourke was driven to 100 to 1 just before the Derby of 1852. Phantom, a stable-companion, that accompanied Mr. Bowes's colt to Epsom, was injured in his box just after leaving Malton, and an incorrect 'office' that the accident had befallen Daniel caused some London speculators to operate, so away went the little Irish Birdcatcher horse to apparently 'hopeless' odds. Trying to squeeze their way to the ticket-box in front of the not-to-be-thwarted gentleman in black who saw Matilda beat Mameluke, and has attended every St. Leger since, come the hotel-keeper, the tailor, the hatter, and the saddler, who, unlike the Yorkshire friends, contrive not only to attend to their business and make money, but to visit all the race-meetings about London, and many held much further afield—all posted in the business done at the morning resorts, where horses may be backed, all eager to discover if any one else knows a 'good thing,' yet preserving discreet silence respecting money-bringing information that has reached themselves. In the arrivals on the platform there is no diminution, and noon is so near that I must no longer delay securing a seat in the special. There is nothing attractive in the prospect: the 'gassing' youngsters, the fib-tellers, the rogues with the shifty eyes and fingers itching to filch something, the ceaseless talk of 'good goods' and 'wrong 'uns,' are hard to endure. I should have preferred the four miles' walk with the uncultivated but honest-minded folks who strolled to the little Yorkshire meeting in 1806.

ABOUT A TUNE ON AN OLD FIDDLE.

By FREDERICK GALE.

OME two or three-and-twenty years ago Frederick Lillywhite, son of the old veteran bowler, solicited my aid in preparing some legal documents connected with an advance of a large sum of money by the late Mr. F. P. Miller for the purpose of publishing the *Scores and Biographies.* 'I did the deed,' and preferred accepting a copy of the four volumes as my *honorarium* instead of filthy lucre, the subject-matter being Cricket, and the client a professional. Mr. Miller, as I expected, and as I warned him, never saw his money back, for the undertaking was hopeless as a commercial speculation, and the cost of warehousing the enormous bulk of unbound copies being very heavy, and a threat having been made by Lillywhite's creditors to seize it as 'assets,' to which they had no earthly right without paying Mr. Miller 2000*l.* and interest. With the remark, 'I'm not going to law, and if the public won't buy the book I will have a flare-up for my money,' Mr. Miller hired a furnace, burnt the stock, leaving the ashes for any claimant, and so my four volumes now are almost priceless, because the book is not procurable, and the four volumes are ' the old Fiddle' which form an accompaniment to my tune, and to which I invite Wykehamists, Etonians, and Harrovians (naming you in seniority of foundation) to dance. You must not be offended if I speak of you as 'boys;' I can't call you 'youths,' 'lads,' 'chappies,' or 'gents:' I only want to distinguish you when *in statu pupillari* from cricketers who have entered life.

From 1805 till 1824 inclusive Eton and Harrow met at different times at Lord's: from 1825 till 1854 inclusive Winchester appeared, at intervals, until 1834, and from that date, for twenty consecutive years (excepting 1837), all these schools met and played two matches each. As a rule, most of the eleven of Gentlemen who appeared against the Players were educated at one of these schools.

Please, you of modern days, bear in mind that cricket came to you cut and dried, and that your fathers or grandfathers had to carry out the sport under great difficulties and no little danger

when they had to meet terrific fast-bowling without pads and
gloves, and bowling which had as much break, spin, and pace, as
any of to-day. Don't you make any mistake about it.

Those whose auburn locks have, through the influence of
time, turned, as mine have done, into an iron-gray clothes-brush,
must remember how, in the old days of Greenwich Fair, the offer
of a glass of rum each to a knot of Greenwich Pensioners would
at once unearth *the* very man who 'caught Nelson in these
blessed arms, Sir,' *the* British Tar who ran up the Admiral's
celebrated last signal; and the inquirer was always fortunate
enough to find that all the members of *the* very group present
heard the dying sailor say, ' Kiss me, 'Ardy.'

There was a *great* deal of miscellaneous information to be
picked up at Greenwich Fair, and knowledge of the world and
of the art of self-defence were useful, when, as it sometimes
happened, the mazy dance was stopped for a gentleman to fight
his *vis-à-vis*. On the same principle, I have no doubt, if an old
nonagenarian could be found at Harrow who had been prompted
a little in advance, and knew that a gentleman wanted information about Lord Byron, who played in the first Harrow match,
he would 'call to mind how he had seen his Lordship hitting the
*H*eton bowling all over the field : had watched him many a time
walking with a beautiful lady—the Bride of Abydos they had
used to call 'er ;' had dandled Childe Harold, ' a lovely boy, Sir,
on his knee ;' and it seemed to him only yesterday when they
put his Lordship's bust (which I believe still wants a home) in
Westminster Abbey ! ' The *h*old 'Arrer gentlemen as was there
all shook 'ands with him and said. "Orner, here's a pot, or a
suvverain," as the case might be.'

I always reject all senile testimony unless it bears strict cross-
examination ; and I will at once give you my authorities for
what I am going to write :—(1.) The late Mr. William Ward,
one of the fathers of cricket whom I knew well, and my friend
the Rev. James Pycroft. (2.) The present Bishop of St. Andrews,
Dr. Charles Wordsworth, who came to Winchester as Second
Master in 1835 (when I was there as a boy), ten years after the
first Winchester and Harrow match, which he inaugurated in
1825, when a Harrow boy ; his brother Christopher, now Bishop
of Lincoln, captaining Winchester, and Cardinal Manning playing for Harrow. (3.) Mr. George Richmond, R.A., whom I have
known for the third of a century, the oldest *habitué* at Lord's
with a thorough knowledge of the game. (4.) Frederick Lilly-

white's *Scores and Biographies*. (5.) My own eyes, ears, memory, after nearly half-a-century in the cricket-field. And so let us first agree that, according to printed records, Eton and Harrow only met in 1805, 1818, 1822, up to 1824 inclusive : and let us also agree that I do not pledge myself to give you a perfect list of past heroes or to make this an entire calendar of school cricket from 1805 to 1854. I am going to talk to myself out loud about good men and true, and if you don't like my chattering go and listen to some M.P. on the stump, who will tell you that England was never so happy and prosperous as now, and that our hearts ought to be as light as our half-sovereigns.

SOUND THE GONG AND RAISE THE CURTAIN.

1822, enter Herbert Jenner (E.), king of wicket-keepers. 1825, first appearance of Charles Wordsworth (H.), Christopher Wordsworth (W.), and Cardinal Manning (H.), and also of Meyrick, Wright, Price, and Knatchbull (all W.), declared by W. Ward and old Caldecourt, the veteran umpire at Lords, to have been the finest quartette of fielders ever seen ; Meyrick (W.), mighty hitter, his last scores being, in his second year, 50 and 38 (not out) *v.* H., and 4 and 146 (not out) *v.* E. 1826, E. H. Pickering (E.), afterwards E. Master ; C. J. Harenc (H.), bowler, very good. 1825-7, Lord Grimston and Hon. E. Grimston, brothers (H.). 1829, G. B. Townsend (E.). 1832, Hon. F. B. Ponsonby (now Earl of Bessborough), the 'Fred Ponsonby,' the twin-pillar of Harrow cricket, 'Bob Grimston,' the late Hon. R. Grimston, being the other. 1833, Ryle, now Bishop of Liverpool (E.); Walmisley, really good wicket-keeper ; Wilde, now Lord Penzance ; G. B. Lee, now Warden of Winchester (all W.), bowlers. 1834, C. G. Taylor (E.), the Gilbert Grace of the game ; Alfred J. Lowth (W.), left-handed, best gentleman bowler in England. 1835, T. A. Anson (E.), gigantic and fearless wicket-keeper. 1836, C. G. Bondier (E.), founder of Eton 'Sixpenny,' and Pakenham, now Lord Longford (W.), tremendous hitter. 1838, Emilius Bayley (E.), admirable cricketer, scored 152 *v.* H. in 1841. 1839, Villiers Chernocke Smith (W.), 'Podder,' terrible at the Winchester 'Barter hit ;' smashed old Lillywhite's bowling in Oxford *v.* M.'C. C. so utterly to pieces that he threw the ball down and said, ' 'Tain't cricket ;' scored 91 *v.* Eton in 1843. 1841, W. Nicholson (H.), wicket-keeper for England ; George Yonge and Harvey Fellows (E.), unsurpassed for years as bowlers. 1842, C. H. Ridding (W.), longstop to England Eleven ; A. Haygarth (H.), 'stone wall' batsman, and compiler, *ex amore*, of Lillywhite's *Scores* ; Hon. C. B. Lyon, now Lord Strathmore (W.). 1843, H. Gathorne

(H.), very good left-hand bowler. 1844, Chitty (E.). Lord
Justice, matchless for brains, muscle, and pluck, ashore or
afloat. Coleridges (2), Patteson, afterwards Colonial Bishop
(all E.). 1845, Vernon (H.), Dewar (W.), left-handed bowler,
founder of cricket at Scutari and in Crimea ; lost seven officers
out of his eleven in storming of Redan. 1846, Aitkens (2),
Deacon, and Whymper (all E.). 1847, W. Ridding (W.),
wicket-keeper for All England ; Reginald Hankey, splendid bat,
and Hon. E. Chandos Leigh (H.) ; Trevilian (W.), his last score
68 and 48 *v.* H., and 126 and 2 *v.* E. 1850, A. H. Walker (H.),
the first of *the* famous family ; T. O. Reay (E.), a very fine all-
round man. 1851, G. B. Crawley (H.), R. A. Fitzgerald, Secretary to M. C. C. (H.), Hon. Wingfield Fiennes (W.), bowler.
1852, Austen Leigh (H.), H. H. Gillett (W.), and little Bramly
(W.), taken in as substitute *v.* Eton, about 5 foot nothing—a
midget ; afterwards fine bowler in 1853-4 ; killed, when little
more than a boy, in leading forlorn hope in Indian Mutiny.
1853, Lord Garlies (H.) and V. E. Walker (H.), unquestionably
the best all-round man on a side ever seen in any age (barring
Gilbert Grace), and wholly unsurpassed as Captain. 1854,
G. L. Hodgkinson (H.), fine bat ; F. H. Norman, very fine
bat (E.).

I saw all the above cricketers who played, and all the
matches, from 1841 to 1854 inclusive, and very many of those
of earlier dates, who played for the Universities, or their counties,
or the M. C. C. ; and some few of the names I have recorded
are from my own knowledge, and their praises are unsung in
Lillywhite's book.

Now, for what it is worth, here is the humble opinion of one
who has seen men and cities, the old style and the new ; and
having analysed the performances of those who before and up to
the discontinuance of the matches between the three schools at
Lord's, I have come to the end of my tether, *quâ* those most of
whose performance I saw at Lords as boys. You will meet on
any cricket-ground those who can take up the tale after 1854
till now ; and a splendid tale of grand cricketers it is. I have
been once or twice, for a short time only, at Lord's during the
last thirty years, at Eton and Harrow match, and I saw Winchester play at Eton once in 1855, and *never* afterwards ; for,
though old Eton fellows were very kind, and asked me to
lunch with the Eleven, and tried to make me at home there,
I pined for the old 'Cockpit' at Lord's, the neutral ground
where the schools met and played two matches each in the
holidays, and not as now, *coram magistro*, and played them

out, and when often each won and lost a match. Those were
the days when there was no boundary, barring the Pavilion,
and fellows got run out by long throwing, caught out long outside the present ring sometimes; and it was 'boys'' cricket,
without artificial excitement beyond the friendly chaff of their
partisans, and there was room to move about, and to see one's
friends of either school. And so, with a hearty groan for the
folly of those who believed only their own story, and who shut
their ears to the entreaties of men of the past, and ignored the
pietas and *prisca fides* of troops of those who in Church and
State, as senators, judges, and in all the professions, had made
their own way, and destroyed a happy annual gathering, I
address now a much larger audience, composed of all the great
schools in England. Honestly it is now a case of *Tros Tyriusve*
as regards amateur cricket, and both Universities' and the
Gentlemen of England's Eleven are open to the schools of the
whole world; and, speaking below my breath almost, I believe
that an eleven from the Universities against All England would
be a better test as to who the eleven very best men in England
are than Gentlemen and Players. It is absurd to ignore the
fact that careful training has not brought boys' cricket to greater
excellence as regards a whole eleven than it was under the
régime, when only two or three bright stars shone occasionally;
but I should like to see in every boys' eleven, as we used to
have, one, or even two, very fine fields, who are desperate
'hitters,' who could be sent in when the bowling was a little
loose. C. J. Thornton, of course, was one in a thousand; for
he not only had the tremendous hitting power against any
bowling, but he could shut off the steam in a moment, and stop
a ball dead. I have all my life seen numberless young fellows
from the different schools, and played against them and with
them in elevens, and most certainly they can stand against and
play good professional bowling better than their fathers, who
had never been coached, probably could; but on the score of
safety they do what their fathers would *not* have done, when
they let a slow long hop off the wicket-pass, making up their
minds that it is a dangerous head-ball, and ought *not* to be
hit. I think their fathers, with youth and strength at their
backs, would have disturbed the glass and china in the booth.
A little more 'devil' sometimes would improve boys' play, just
as a little lemon and cayenne make mock-turtle almost equal to
real. When Peate—a most admirable bowler—first appeared

against Surrey, a kind of preliminary funk set in about the mode of playing him, and Mr. Roller, then quite a young gentleman, with admirable eye and power, solved the difficulty by hitting him three times into the Pavilion. Just as Ullyett puts the bowler out of his pain, if he is doubtful about the infallibility of his style, by lifting him over the boundary.

When the world was younger, in the pre-railway days, the only boy 'cricket world' was at Lord's during the three matches; for the M. C. C. was almost the only world-known Club. Cornwall and Inverness were further practically from London than India is to-day. University Elevens now are cosmopolitan, and composed of all schools; and I will, please, extend my audience to all schools everywhere.

In saying a few farewell words, I don't care a straw what all the rest of the world, ancient and modern (whose cricket has got mixed up with squabbling and dissent), say. I hold with Lord Bessborough's and poor Mr. Grimston's opinion that, barring Dr. Gilbert Grace, Fuller Pilch had the finest defence ever seen, and he learnt it without pads or gloves against 'demon bowling,' and taught the whole world who saw him; and when I was a very young man he tried to teach me, and I have tried to teach his principles to hundreds of youngsters on a village green, many of whom have made a good name in counties.

By-the-by, here is an old cricket 'Church Hymn,' possibly sung formerly before Sunday afternoon cricket practice (*vide* Miss Mitford's *Tales of Our Village*). It is clearly a veritable Sternhold and Hopkins' old-version tune. In my brother's parish in Wiltshire there is a sheet-iron bass viol, made by the village blacksmith eighty years ago, and used by him in the church choir. There it is at Milton Lillbourne; I have seen it; and I should not be surprised if this hymn has been sung to that old viol :—

HYMN APPROPRIATE TO A CRICKET MATCH.

LET those who want to plaie the game
  To Fuller Pilch attende,
What he tolde me I'll tell the same
  To all who ears will lende.

Five yards behinde ye stumps first stande,
  And let ye umpire bee
Where he doth judge ye bowler's hande
  Will let the balle go free.

And let ye middle stump be seen
  In line 'twixt him and you,
And in that very line I weene
  Will be your block so true.

Behinde ye crease your right foot place,
  All of the wicket cleare,
Your left leg forward throwe, and face
  Ye bowler without feare.

If your left shouldere you can see,
  And ye bowler's hande alsoe,
With a straight bat you'll surely bee
  All ready for the foe.

Keep that left shouldere up and wait,
  Watch where the ball doth bounde,
And on her put your bat full straight,
  And drive her on ye grounde.

Beware of balls that never rise,
  To play low doe not fail,
For shooters sinners doe surprise,
  They're like ye serpent's traile.

And if you thrive before you die,
  Till a hundred years be past,
They'll say he 'scored a centurie,
  And his bails are off at last.'   Amen.

I have trained, as I have said, many a youngster (and there
is no difference in teaching cricket to the village baker's or
carpenter's son, or a duke's), with the aid of a good professional
who can bowl well, ' on the lines' that Fuller Pilch taught, and
Felix, whom I knew well, wrote. And what a trainer should
try to do is to teach a boy to *hit* loose balls as well as defence,
but not by blind swiping; and if he has got into a good free
defence he ought not to be checked if he sees a ball a little
overpitched, and steps in and hits her right away. Who is to
say that there are not moments in a boy's life when quickness
of hand and eye, backed by courage and a broad pair of
shoulders, do not authorise a little risk?

If he *will* ' board the vessel,' let him remember Felix's advice:
' If you do go in, go *far* enough. You may be just as well four
feet as four inches off your ground, if you *are* stumped.'

Remember, I was brought up in a school which looked kindly

on a straight ' Barter ' * sometimes. It *was very* risky ; but, oh, *so* sweet when it *did* come off ! and the ball sailed steadily away ' over the garden wall,' to the dismay of the bowler.

Fielding can only be kept up by incessant hard practice.

I am as big a boy at heart as any of you, and I beg, in saying farewell, to include in my audience all the great schools in England. You have a noble mission before you—that is, the promotion of pure, honest cricket ; and, though now at school, the time will slip by so quickly that before you know it you will be in the stream of life, with two paths open before you, in one of which you will find only real sportsmen, whose aim is the promotion of good sport, and fellowship, and honest enjoyment for all ; , the other is only frequented by flash, vulgar, selfish fellows, who think to attain position by sport, and whose hearts are not in the game, and whose chief pleasure is in the applause of the pothouse and the ring. You will find that the latter have a mighty desire to get their sport for nothing, and never give a shilling out of their own pocket for the sport of others if they can help it, and that the professionals who touch their caps to them despise them in their hearts.

Just as I lay down my pen, in comes a sketch of a man on horseback, with a mild request from Mr. Fores that I will write something about it. Well, it reminds me of the parson who received a request from a brother-parson to preach for him, and said, ' Please pitch into the baker, who won't pay his tithes.' The only man who *could* rouse the audience was the man who had been *bilked* of tithes. However, I looked at the man on the horse, and said to myself, ' Oh, no ; this has been done to death by numberless writers, and hunting is all over.' On second thoughts, that horseman comes in handy, like the ram caught in

---

* The late Warden Barter, a giant in stature, was a brilliant scholar and athlete, and a tremendous hitter, and a ' half volley ' was called a ' Barter,' after him. At Winchester Hospital there ' came to hand ' one day a poor fellow dying of consumption. He was the celebrated American giant, a *soi-disant* prize-fighter, 6 feet 10½ inches in height. His rough life had left his religious ideas somewhat hazy, according to the Chaplain's gauge, and directly he saw the grand old Warden—a daily visitor almost at the hospital—he ' threw up the sponge ' for his own ideas, and put himself into the hands of the Warden, who tended him like a child till he died, and then buried him. It was a very remarkable funeral, as the dead man was 6 feet 10½ inches. Ben Caunt, chief mourner and ex-champion, was 6 feet 2½ inches, and the Warden was *bigger* than Caunt.

the thicket ; as a child I pitied that ram, and wished that in the story he had *not* been killed. So people must read the last paragraph of this article, and when read must look at the bold horseman, and put two and two together, and when found make a note of it.

Follow the noble example of the late President of the M. C. C., who spent a lifetime amongst the boys of his old school at Harrow, and who turned out some of the best and truest cricketers in the world, and whose feelings were outraged by the very semblance of foul play—a man who, whether in the cricket-ground or the hunting-field in his favourite 'Vale,' though sometimes to outward appearances displaying a some-what hasty temper on the spur of the moment, at heart had an innate respect for all who promoted honest sport for sport's sake, and stood up for fair play. We can say of him, as the immortal Harrovian, Lord Byron, sang of Sheridan,—

> 'Grieving that Nature formed but one such man,
> And broke the die in moulding Sheridan.'

TROUT AND SALMON FISHING.

By 'ROCKWOOD.'

N the Scripture angling is always taken in the best sense, and that though hunting may be sometimes so taken, yet it is but seldom to be so understood. And let me add this more : he that views the ancient Ecclesiastical Canons shall find hunting to be forbidden to Churchmen, as being a turbulent, toilsome, perplexing recreation, and shall find angling allowed to clergymen as being a harmless recreation—a recreation that invites them to contemplation and quietness.' Such is the remark of ' Piscator' in Walton's *Angler* when discoursing on his favourite subject ; and in it there is no doubt a great amount of truth, though the modern parson of the type of the late Rev. ' Jack' Russell would be inclined to dispute the assertion that hunting is a ' turbulent, toilsome, perplexing recreation.' It is satisfactory to find that angling from the earliest has been recognised as an orthodox sport in these days, when so much sickly sentiment is floating about, and a sportsman of any class is looked upon as an unhealthy specimen of humanity—a kind of kestrel hawk,

that hovers over the hen's brood of the 'unco guid.' It will be
a long time, however, before angling as a pastime will be condemned as cruel, for even when man to man the whole world
o'er 'shall brothers be,' the brotherhood will likely keep the
friendship closely cemented by occasional days with the rod by
the river-side. So let the shallow-headed sons of sentimental
mothers turn æsthetic and talk of the poor, wriggling worm, or
the hook and the gasping fish, till their heart's content ; honest,
strong - minded men will stand by their favourite pastimes,
knowing well that the love of field-sports has been implanted
in the bosom of man with reason ; and he that has no game, no
exercise, no recreation, no safety-valve, is nursing physically a
fever for himself, and morally a bilious and corrupt spirit,
dangerous not only to his neighbours, but to all mankind. So
who *will* that *may* sit by the fireside and squirm at sportsmen of
all classes, I will to the river, with my memory full of

> 'The jealous trout that low did lie,
> And rose at a well-dissembled fly.'

There are few northern anglers who have been anglers from
their boyhood that fail to recollect their first trout. As a rule,
when a lad knocks over his first grouse, his first partridge, or his
first pheasant, he is pretty well into his teens, for unless he has
had a gun specially made for him he will find the distance
between the heel-plate of the stock and the trigger a little too
long for him. That was our experience ; and long did we yearn
for that extra growth of arm which would allow us to get the
first finger-joint round the magic spring with ease, and without
that throwing back of the head, which so much interfered with
the taking of our aim, for we were not so ambitious as to try
and get on to the wing all at once. With one's first trout it is
very different, for that is generally captured ere his pop-gun
days are well over. We were, to use a horsey expression,
'rising nine' when we first resolved to make war against the
finny inhabitants of a mountain-stream, in which we had harm-
lessly 'paidled ;' for, owing to the depth in places and the sizes
of the stones under which the trout lay, we found we were not
equal to 'guddling,' the nice back - tickling work which the
stream-poacher so much delights in. So we hunted the smaller
eels, and watched their eccentric manœuvres, after we had tied
knots on their tails, or tried to spear a regular big one, an
inch thick and about nine inches long—need we say ineffectu-

ally?—with our brand-new, two-bladed pocket-knife. But our first trout . . . ah! well, we have caught many trouts, but never such a trout as that. It was in the spring-time, or rather early summer; the buds were on the trees, the bluebells and the primroses were decking the banks, the birds were singing sweetly, when, having become the happy possessor of some hooks 'buskit' with horsehair, and a piece of 'drow,' that we sallied out in search of a fishing-rod. We were indeed earnest, and heeded not the young rabbit, which at other times would have called for a hunt; and we scarce gave a thought to the cushat, as she sat on her broad twig nest on the larch, rocking to and fro, with her burnished bosom scarce covering the pale white eggs which would have rolled over if not held firmly down. Carefully the hazels were scanned, but in vain, and it was not till we came across a rowan growing from the root of a precipice that we found the rod with which we were destined to catch our first trout, and acquire our first fame as a fisher. Notching right round at the root, a twist broke it off, and then it was carefully pruned to the top. Perhaps some of the town-reared anglers will laugh at such a fishing-rod when they think of their own, with the brass mountings, patent splices, and gaudy reel, whose birring sound is a soul-stirring tune to all writers of fishing-songs. Still, it was a first-class rod; such, too, as were used by the old school of village anglers—the Weaver Will and Tinker Toms of Conquetdale and Nithsdale side—and who were better or keener fishers? That night of the cutting of my new rod saw the descent of the rains which the farmers had been wearying for after the long drying east winds, which had allowed them to prepare the ground and get the seed in. Down it came in straight lines of big drops, slanted at times to a mild south-west wind, which was carrying away up the hillsides the reeking hot mist which bespoke the sun-heat, and the strong growth in all vegetation. It was a West of Scotland burn, and wimpled through many a wooded and pastoral glen to the Firth of Clyde, away o'er which, when the rains took off at early morning, we could see the burns foaming down the sides of the Arran hills to the sea. Better view than that was our own burn, which was, to use a Scotticism, 'down;' that is, its waters had risen, and were rising steadily.

As we worked on our worm, dug from the rich, moist, earthy bottom which marked where had stood till the thrasher required an oat stack, we could see the water 'lapping' on the stones

which we knew marked the favourite crouching-places of trout,
and which, no doubt, with a rising stream, were on the feed.
We were old enough then to know that a burn should be fished
up with the worm, and so commenced by dropping our bait just
forward of the stones, so that when our line became perpendicular
our bait would roll down naturally. Slowly our line worked
down with the current, then stopped. There was a slight vibra-
tion in the line, with an electric feeling in our rod hand, a rush
and a pull, and then, with the boy's notion of worm-fishing
firmly believed in, we tossed it high overhead, and had the satisfaction of seeing the liveliest and bonniest three-quarter of a pound
trout—so at the time we thought—that was ever seen wriggling
amongst the wet grass. A fresh worm was soon fixed and
another trout followed ; and it was not without that grand delight
to a young sportsman that we saw, next morning, a large dish of
them beautifully cooked in oatmeal, the genuine Scotch style,
on the family breakfast-table. But though we have fished with
the worm since and made good baskets of trout, always fishing
up and letting our bait come tumbling down naturally, as if it
had come out of a spate-filled drain, or been washed off the
bank, we had, somehow, always a predilection when real bait was
used, and the water or the day did not suit the fly for the
minnow, the real live minnow which, ere our trouting days,
we fished out of the sun-lit pools.

Though all fishers have their ideas as to minnow-fishing
—and the worst thing, indeed, about fishing of all kinds is
the perpetuation of what cannot be dignified as theories, but
what may be called 'accidental notions'—we find that a very
simple tackle is best, knowing that the fish always make for
the head. Of course, as Mr. Pennell and other anglers have it,
trout sometimes hang off and 'fetch' their mark, short, as a sailor
would say, putting about hard for home again, and so body and
tail hooks, fixed according to the individual notions of the
fishers, in many cases get hold of a laggard. How to arrange
and fix these the angling reader will learn from Mr. Francis
Francis' *Book on Angling*, and other authorities on the subject,
the accompanying diagrams making everything easier to understand than a whole volume of letterpress. It is possible that
many young fishers will get perplexed over them, as indeed the
minnow tackle seems to be the *pons asinorum* of the art. Some
of the old school used, when fishing deep water, to have but a
single large hook inserted in the middle of the minnow, with the

bait protruding from the head, and part of the shank left to
steady the tail into which it was inserted. Fishing with a long
line and keeping well out of sight, they used to do much execution in deep water ; but few anglers would care now for trying
the single barb. Live minnows are not, however, to be procured
always handy, and with so many of the artificial kind now in
use fishing with them is anything but so common as it used
to be. The old school of village anglers, who fished all the
Saturday afternoon for their Sunday's breakfast, have been
forced off the waters by the rich men of the south, with their
fly-books full of lures, made to catch themselves intentionally in
the first place, and fish occasionally by accident. With them
have gone much that, though old-fashioned, was the result of
years' experience in the same water—not the casual experience
of a lessee during a single season or two—and was most effective.
Yet minnow-fishing is a branch of the art of angling so full of
pleasant varieties that one can always have a by-hour at it
when trout go off the fly-feeding, and less keen anglers take
to lunching, smoking, and looking on.

> ' I've fished wi' the flee, man, as lang as I'd see, man ;
>   When waters grew brown I jist on wi' the worm ;
> E'en too with the creeper I've ne'er been a sleeper,
>   But wheedled them out ilka ane fair and firm.
> But when waters were curly, and skies grey and gurly,
>   It's aye in my fishin' I made it a rule
> Just to throw 'gainst the win', oh ! a bonnie bit minnow,
>   The bonnie wee minnow that swam in the pool
>
> Some like their fishes laid out in nice dishes,
>   All peppered and salted and ready to eat.
> But I like them just leevin' with the line going scrievin' ;
>   He's no faith a fisher that's thinking o' meat.
> If rheumatics are risky, try a wee drop o' whiskey :
>   It warms ye betimes, betimes mak's you cool,
> When we make our trace spin, oh ! and birl our minnow,
>   The bonnie wee minnow that swam in the pool.'

But, while strongly in favour of minnow-fishing when the
water is just going off the flood, not that it is not deadly in
clear streams when the water is low, we must give in to fly-
fishing as the most sportsmanlike and the most popular form
of all.

> ' I've seen a child,' (says Joanna Baillie),
> ' On the edge of a clear stream hold out

His rod and baitless line from morn to noon;
Eyeing the spotted trout, that past his snare
A thousand times hath glided, till by force
His angry dame hath dragged him from his station:
Hope is of such a tough continuous nature.'

And hope is, too, of such a continuous nature with the fisher of more mature years. Fly-fishing, indeed, is the whist of angling, and though we have books and books about it, and books and books full of what are said to be the most deadly of flies, we have every day something to find out. It has been argued by some that the closer the natural fly is imitated the better; but possibly the old school-boy grace, 'Of rabbits tender, rabbits tough, we thank Thee, Lord, we have enough,' may explain the fact that trout will frequently refuse the natural fly when in the water, and seize that of the angler which does not in the least resemble it. Possibly, like the salmon, they take it with the view of returning it if found unpalatable, but, more impulsive, being used to striking at the natural flies, they get hooked. The strange fly, too, is not a weak deception: the imitation fly always is, and must sometimes be very easily detected. As every angler cannot be expected to tie his own flies, though it is an exceedingly nice pastime, he should always make a point of securing, on *the actual spot*, those 'from a native angler' whose work can be recommended. By so doing he will in time possess himself of a collection, of which in his way he may be as proud of as of a collection of blue china. Each fly may in time tell its own story, and when the day comes that the angler is no longer able to betake himself to the river-side raise its own pleasant memory. On one occasion, however, we were fairly beat, though using several 'casts' for a portion of a northern river which were said to be most deadly. Throwing, as we did, a long line and keeping well out of view we could make nothing of them, still an aged village weaver with an old-fashioned rod was pulling them out every now and then, and indeed making up a very nice basket. He was like his class, however, exceedingly uncommunicative, and a little selfish, doubtless from the fact that he gave away his fish to the butcher and the baker as a fair exchange for something more substantial. Let me get as close to him as I could he managed always to avoid letting me see his flies, and in answer to questions his replies were generally, 'Ay, ay, the watter is being clean spoiled, Mister, by the farmers using these guanos and artificial manures,'

or 'They'll be washin' the sheep the day, I'll wager ye, wi' some
of that new sheep-dip that kills lice and maggots, and, for the
matter o' that, good yellow trout tae.'

This was all very well from old Wabster, whose grey eyes
were twinkling from his Kilmarnock bonnet, round which were
twisted several casting-lines; but why did the guano and the
sheep-dip not cause the trout to refuse my flies as well as his
own? I tried him with the flask, but he only shook his head,
and a good half-pound trout at the same time being lifted
into his basket; I stuck my teeth together, and determined to
be even with him. Watching my chance I got alongside, and
threw my line right across his own with marked success, as
his remark with fierce glance and shining terrier teeth proclaimed: 'Ay, I might hae kent ye were an infernal haberdasher
frae the ell-wand-like style ye handle a rod.' Nothing daunted
I cleared my line, and saw that my flies could not possibly be
of use were his successful. I had not time to look at them,
but saw that I could find in my book what would suit, a
woodcock wing and hare's-foot body, with just a morsel of
tinsel; and with another much the same, only a corncrake wing
and a red hackle, I soon had a good turn at the game. At the
railway-station I met my Wabster acquaintance, who, being
wet with wading and the night being cold, thawed himself under
my flask. Buying his basket (I paid him in advance for some
flies he promised to tie and post me, and which he faithfully
did), we parted good friends, though I shall not readily forget his
face when I crossed his line. In leaving him I have to say that
he was not one of those totally imaginary men who sit down
on the bank of the river, after watching the natural fly, and
make an exact imitation of what they see before them. He
had certain fixed ideas as to certain waters and certain portions of waters, and the materials from which he made up
his flies were very few—the simple colours indeed of the old
black-and-red school.

It does not do, however, to linger long over trouting when
salmon are jumping in every pool. What deer-stalking is to
grouse-shooting, so salmon-fishing, as regards expense and everything, may be compared to trout-fishing. Yet possibly, of the
two, the former tests the patience and judgment the greatest,
though not the nerve and coolness in execution. Save on
Loch Tay, where the phantom has to be used, from the cramped
and unpoetical cobble (salmon, indeed, are fondest of the minnow

from March to June), in most streams the best of all sports to be
had with the monarch of the river is with the fly, or what indeed
might better be designated 'the feather lure,' since in no way
does it resemble any fly that ever flew. It used to be contended
that the salmon-fly was an imitation of the dragon-fly, but this
will not stand examination, as the salmon-fly is much more
brilliant in colour and very little like it in appearance. Whether
the salmon mistake the latter for some small tide-hanging fish
which they meet with on their autumn voyages along shore in
search of the river's mouth is difficult to determine, though the
merest tyro is always ready to advance a theory. Possibly from
the gingerly way they mouth it at times, like a horse afraid of
the bit getting back to its jaws, they wish to take it home, and
examine it, and digest it at leisure, if found to be a dainty
morsel, just as a dog would retire into a corner to gnaw a
bone. As regards flies, they have for a long time back been
becoming more gaudy and more showy—a fact as much to be
attributed to the supply of foreign feathers on tackle-makers'
hands as anything. Colour has possibly a good deal to do with
it, for one salmon-fly may suit only one particular river or portion
of a river at a particular season of the year ; and it is as essential
for an angler to know this as to know the favourite pools; and
it is well known that what may look as likely a pool as
another to a man is one which the fish have no notion of at
all, for reasons known to themselves. Then in modern days
artificial draining has to be considered, an upland shower
finding its way as quickly to the stream in one hour as in ten in
olden days, and thus darkening or discolouring the water when
the sky is comparatively clear or dull grey. It may be that the
farmer has to thresh in some place, and eight-horse power of
stored water is suddenly let loose from his dam, causing a change
which the angler has no means of readily detecting or ap-
preciating. O'ercast skies, o'erhanging banks, and other surroundings, have all to be studied, and the careful angler finds
always in doing so a delight. The salmon-fly must always be
sunk under the surface of the water, and many of the most expert
fishers of the day try to get it as deep down as possible. The
art of casting, or of striking, or of playing, cannot be learned
from books, though their perusal may give great assistance to the
young angler. Colquhoun's *Moor and the Loch* contains many
good descriptions of playing fish ; and there could not be a better
one than given to Mr. Brixey by Lord Malvern in *Tommiebeg's*

Shootings, save it be Christopher North's in one of his 'Sporting Jacket fyttes,' though no one possibly would get as excited over a fish as the renowned editor of *Maga.* We recollect an experience of just such a salmon-fight as Christopher North's, but which ended less successfully. A friend was playing what appeared to be a nice salmon, of from ten to twelve pounds, in a northern river on a nice autumn afternoon, and, *à la* Kit, was making the surrounding woodlands ring with his exclamations of 'Hoop, la!' Herr Salmonia, in his wonderful series of leaps and somersaults (*steady!*) 'over six bare-backed horses' (*woa! woa!*) 'and a feather-bed' (*birr, birr*), 'as performed before the Czar of Russia, the Pope of Rome, the Emperor of the French' (*splash!*).

'The Devil!' was the anti-climax, as, failing to free the mouth at an awkward somersault on the far-side, the line came back limp and slowly to his hand, and he walked back to a rock on the river's edge, where. seating himself, he buried his head in both hands. On going up to cheer him a little and tell him not to cry like a bairn over the loss of a salmon, he jumped up with the characteristically Scotch reply, ' Man, it's no the saumont, it's ma guid new half-crown flee am cryin' for.'

Salmon-fishing, in conclusion, may be classed as one of the most princely of pastimes, no matter where enjoyed—England, Ireland, Wales, or Norway. In Scotland it is perhaps more preferable from its scenic surroundings. Scarcely a Scottish song of river or lake that is played far from home fails to bring pleasant memories and tears to the eyes of a Northern-roving angler. Even ' Ye Banks and Braes ' brings to us a warm reminiscence of a day by Skeldon on the Bonnie Doon. The Carrick Hills are purple with heather, the woods have on the first of their autumnal tints ; low down hangs the ripening haze, like the grey frost-bloom on the sloe, and the water is purling away silently to the sea as the harvesters are busy getting in the corn. Carelessly we fling ourselves on a stook by the bank, and get our fly-book out. All alone. No! what are those glinting, mirror-like objects? They are the glittering cans of the little bramble-gatherers. It will not do to let them clamber along the banks with these dazzling objects in view of the fish, and they deserve their sport as well as we do,—nay, need its results more. There they are, shy and demure! We are discovered. Slowly they step forward as we beckon towards them with a shilling—little girls of about seven and nine years, moving slowly, for the weeest has on her

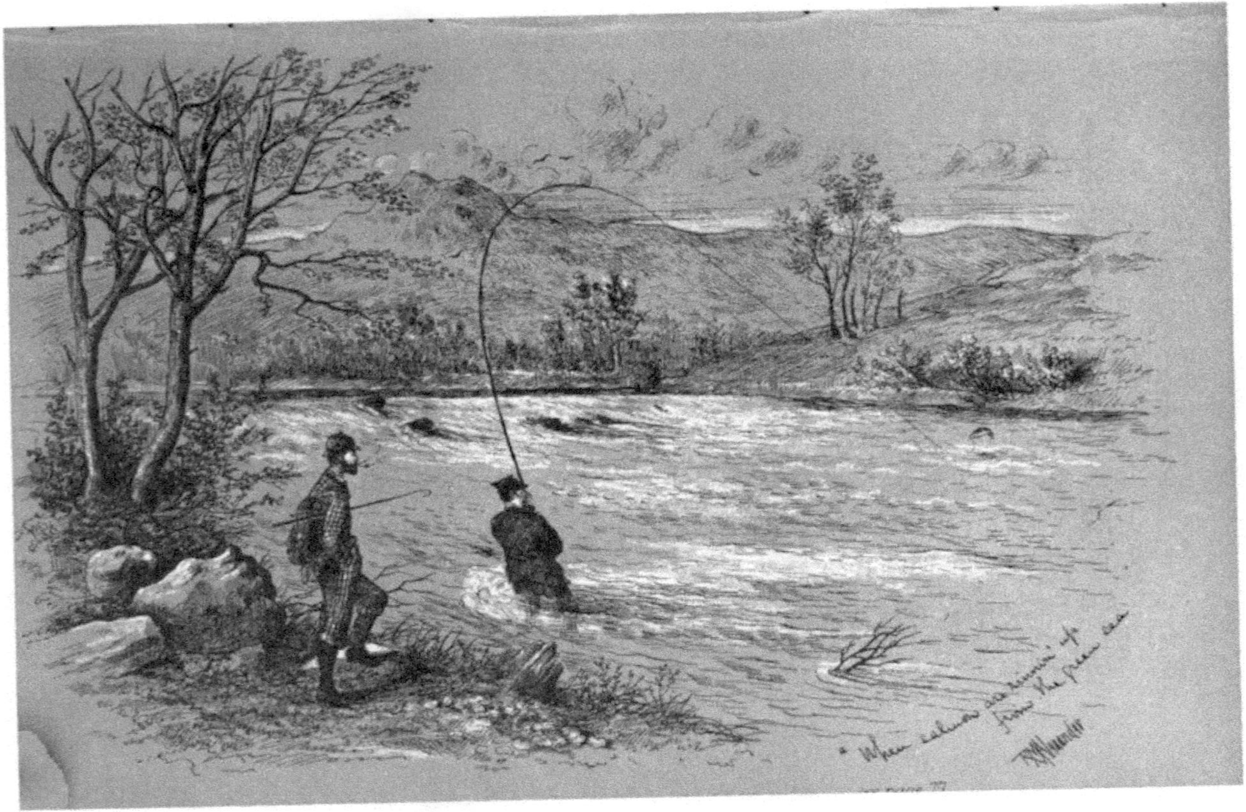
"When salmon are rinnin' up
from the green sea"

mother's shoon to protect her feet from the thorns and the
stubbles ; and—ha ! ha ! well, laugh—the wee feet of the eldest are
encased in the boots of her father, the ploughman, hob-nailed
and heavy. A bright new sixpence each—it would never do to
make their little hearts suspicious over worn ones—and they
reward us with some berries from their cans, and the promise to
keep off the banks. Off they rush to show the coins to their
father, who handles the pitchfork ; and as we dip down ready to
begin we see them, at the parent's request, clambering on to
their ' mither,' who is working in a different part of the field.
These are pleasant memories of the times

When Salmon are Rinnin' up from the Green Sea.

Oh ! scenes still we hallow, on lea, loam, and fallow,
   Where often we followed the keen-scenting hound :
And down to the railing our yacht we've been sailing,
   When harking to hear the winning gun sound.
But of all the gay sporting we've e'er been a-courting,
   By wood, wold, or wave, or 'neath the green tree,
There ne'er can be wrangling 'twas the gay sport of angling,
   When the salmon were rinnin' up from the green sea.

Oh ! sweet 'twas to ramble and pluck the ripe bramble,
   Where, blushing, the sloe nestled 'neath the black thorn ;
Where the water clear wimpled 'neath crab-apples dimpled,
   Or glided so gently amongst the ripe corn.
No sound but the cooing of cushats' gay wooing,
   Or the sough of soft winds on the daisy-pied lea ;
Oh ! ne'er such a pleasure can bought be by treasure,
   When salmon are rinnin' up from the green sea.

Where'er I am roaming, at morn, noon, or gloaming,
   My heart it goes back to the days of langsyne.
Oh ! forget will I never those hours by the river,
   When I wandered a youth with my rod and my line.
Under melodies waking I feel my heart breaking,
   And warm the tears trickle down from my e'e,
With memories mellow of cornfields yellow,
   When the salmon were rinnin' up from the green sea.

                           Rockwood.

'A DEAD HEAT.'

By A. HERON.

THERE is no doubt but that most of what is termed 'bad luck' is due to bad management of some kind or other; but still there are times when no amount of care or forethought is able to avert misfortune; and the worst luck which ever happened to me was ('goodness knows!') through no fault of my own. Since then many a year has passed over my head, and many a hair turned grey, but every detail of that time is as vividly present to my memory as if it occurred but yesterday, and, though nineteen years ago, it has ever been, as it ever will be, the cause of a deep regret to me.

We were all seated round the mess-table, as cheery a party as one could wish to see. It was a special guest-night, and we had several old officers of the regiment staying with us for 'our week,' as we called it, the chief feature of which was our race-meeting.

It was on the Monday night, and our races were on the Thursday. On Wednesday the County Hunt races were to take place, and on Friday we were to give a ball—a good programme, which we hoped fine weather would enable us to carry out successfully. Coffee had long since been handed round, and some of the younger members of our party were beginning to get restless, and wish for billiards; but the old Colonel sat on, as if he never intended to move, a broad grin on his handsome old face, as he listened from time to time to some good story, or the repetition of some occurrence, of former days, by one of his old comrades. We had, of course, been talking a good deal about the forthcoming races, and speculating as to who would win the several cups to be run for. Our races were a real institution, and no humbugging affair, made up of half-a-dozen horses, a band, and a big luncheon; we always had plenty of entries, and lots of sport. There were four cups run for annually, viz., 'The Regimental,' 'The Subalterns,' 'The Hunt,' and 'The Dragoon Cup.' The latter so called by reason of its having been given to the regiment by officers who had served in it when it was a Light Dragoon Regiment, and before its conver-

sion into Hussars.   The cups, except the Subalterns', were
open to competition by all the officers, and were on the table,
to figure a few days later at the race luncheon.

Of all the four, the one which invarably evoked the keenest
competition and interest was the Dragoon Cup for hunters,
the *bona fide* property of officers of the regiment, and which had
been in their possession for three months previously, and regularly hunted during the past season ; the distance four miles,
12 st. 7 lbs. each, with no winning penalties or allowances.
The conditions further enforced that at least five horses should
start : so it was always a good race.   I had won it myself the
year before, and hoped to do so again this year.   The added
money to this cup was further supplemented by an annual subscription from officers who had retired from the regiment, and it
was well worth winning, if from a pecuniary point of view only.

At last the old Colonel moved back his chair and rose from
the table, and a general adjournment was made to the billiard-
room, with the exception of a few of the more sedate of the
party, and himself, who preferred a quiet rubber to the inevitable
noise and scrimmage of ' black pool.'

' Are you coming to play, Dick ?' shouted out George Hudson
to me, as he saw me going down the stairs on his way to the
billiard-room.

' Yes,' I replied.   ' I shall be back in a few minutes ; I am only
going to the stables.   Like a good fellow, take a cue and play for
me till I return.'

' All right ! ' he replied, as he went whistling up the stairs ; and
I, taking my forage-cap and cloak off the peg in the lobby, went
off, as was my usual custom, to have a look at my horses.   As
the barrack stables were, as barrack stables so often are, bad and
insufficient, I had taken some stalls and a loose box just outside the barracks, and very good they were.   As I neared the
gate, and the sentry gave the usual challenge, ' Who goes there?'
I could hear the shouts and laughter from the billiard-room
in the clear night air, George Hudson's voice, as usual, above
the others, and I pitied the wretched sentry pacing to and fro,
and thought that he must wish that he too were an officer.

On arriving at the stables I proceeded to inspect the
horses in the stalls, and found them all right, and lying
down.   They were so used to my nightly visit that they
never attempted to rise ; and then I went to the box at the
end to look at the horse I hoped to win the Dragoon Cup

with. She was one of the very sweetest tempered and gamest
horses I ever owned ; a black-brown mare, with a rich tan
muzzle, about 15·3 and rising, six years old, as nearly thorough-
bred as she could be without being quite so, but with just
the taint of 'hunting blood' in her. To my mind she was
perfect in shape ; if there was a fault, it was that she was not
quite as close-coupled as some critics might wish, but which, if
not *too* light, I always considered the reverse of detrimental in a
hunter : long, clear shoulders, well thrown back, great depth in
the brisket, and a loin like a greyhound, powerful forearm and
quarters, and a skin like satin, which always reminded me of
poor Whyte Melville's lines, in which he so well describes a
well-bred hunter, viz. :—

> 'A head like a snake and a skin like a mouse,
>   An eye like a woman's, bright, gentle, and brown ;
> With loins and a back that would carry a house,
>   And quarters to lift him smack over a town.'

She was as clever as she was bold, and no matter how
fast hounds ran, or over what country, it was indeed a
wonder if she made a mistake. She could also gallop and
stay too. She had never run as yet ; and just now she looked,
if a little too high in flesh for racing, in perfect hunting
condition. She also was down when I entered her box, and
turned her head to take the apple I had brought her from the
dinner-table as usual. There was but one other horse entered
for the race which I at all feared, and that was the one I had
won with the previous year, a chestnut mare, named Brimstone,
a thoroughbred, not nearly as good a hunter as my mare Graceful,
but certainly faster, with, however, the most uncertain temper ;
the least thing set her wrong, and when upset she was 'the
very devil' to ride, though when it pleased her she was
equally pleasant. I had sold her to George Hudson after
the races the year before, and he had got used to her ways ;
but he and I were the only two who could manage her
at all. He was a horseman of no mean order, and though as
reckless and wild as a hawk, generally speaking, on a horse
he was a quiet, determined, powerful rider, and was made for
a horseman, with his long, light, sinewy frame, and could hold
his own to hounds against most men. He was a kind of *protégé*
of mine, for we lived near each other at home, and when he
joined the regiment some four years after I did I was asked to

look after him, and keep him straight, *if I could*. His father had commanded the regiment at one time, and at his death, which occurred a few years before George joined us, Mrs. Hudson was left comparatively poor; and it was only by careful management and screwing that she was able to place George in the old regiment, and I know it must have necessitated her and her daughter Grace denying themselves many a luxury to scrape together enough to do so; but as George had so set his heart on going into his father's regiment, she yielded unreluctantly to his wishes. No one could help liking George, he had the most charmingly frank manner, and was one of the handsomest young fellows I ever saw, but he had been dreadfully spoiled both at home and in the regiment; but I had known him from childhood, and would have done anything for him, both for his own sake as for that of his mother, and especially for Grace's, though the latter little knew how much. But he was well-nigh uncontrollable, and had got dreadfully selfish in his reckless extravagance, and latterly I had almost ceased to expostulate with him, as I feared by too constantly remonstrating I should lose the little remaining hold I had on him. He was very much in debt, and I often used to wonder how it would all end. His mother idolised him, and would not check him; Grace, it is true, did now and again drop a word or two on the subject of his extravagance, but it had very little effect.

George had always had a great hankering after the chestnut mare, and when I had won the cup with her the year before he had so plagued me to sell her to him that at last I very reluctantly yielded—reluctantly, because I knew he could not afford to add to his stable, and that he would wheedle the money out of his mother, who could so ill afford to give him the sums he was so continually applying for, and had I thought he would have accepted the mare I would gladly have given her to him, for I was not very fond of her, and as my own income was far more than I required, a horse more or less made little or no difference to me ; but I well knew he would not only refuse to take her as a present, but perhaps resent my offer, and so I let him have her at an almost nominal price.

On my return to the billiard-room there seemed to be little billiards going on, but a great deal of talking, and the majority were gathered round George and our senior Major, the former looking very excited with the champagne he had drunk at dinner and subsequent brandy and soda, and the latter lounging back on the sofa smoking a cigar, and looking the very reverse of George, and cool and sarcastic, as usual. As he plays a part in this story, I ought to have described him to you before this. He was a tall, dark, handsome man, with eyes which looked nowhere and everywhere. He *looked* a gentleman, but I don't know what it was, there was a something about him—a *je ne sais quoi* —which made one feel he was *not* one. Every regiment has its *bête noir*, I fancy, and he was ours. He had exchanged to us a year or two before from a Lancer regiment which was in India. It was *said* that his old regiment had *made* him exchange, but we never got at the rights of the story. From the Colonel down to the junior trumpeter we none of us liked him. He had, or assumed to have, the most insolently courteous manner, and I should say that he was a man who never had made more than one friend in his life, and that one, ' himself.' We disliked him in ' plain clothes,' but 'on duty' positively *hated* him. He seemed to have unlimited means, was always faultlessly turned out (too much so), rode thundering well, his horses were perfect and he had lots of them, and, had he been a good fellow, would have been an acquisition to the regiment, but as it was he was a brute, and was not, and never could be, ' one of us.' He and George were deadly enemies, and the latter took no pains to conceal his dis- like, and being very hot-tempered and unwise in his remarks, always fell an easy prey to ' De Lisle,' which was the name of our Major. I believe his real name was at one time Jones or Smith, or some such patronymic, but he had changed it to the higher-sounding one of ' De Lisle.' He had been at Eton and Cambridge, and all that sort of thing, and so should have been a better fellow than he was.

On my entering the room I heard him say, ' Thank you, Mr. Hudson, once is quite enough for me,' and he added (as George was moving away to play his stroke), ' That youngster requires a lesson or two, and is bound to get it sooner or later.'

On my inquiring what it was all about, they told me that George had been rather confidently asserting that the chestnut would win the Dragoon Cup, on which De Lisle had said, ' Perhaps she may, if you are man enough to ride her '—a rather unnecessary remark. This had at once roused George's anger, and he retorted, ' I'll bet you 3 to 1 she does,' and De Lisle said, ' All right, I'll take your three ponies to one, Mr. Hudson,' and George replied, ' Anything you like, and twice over if you wish,' and at that moment I came in. We were all rather disgusted at

De Lisle taking advantage of George's excitability and weak-mindedness. Some one or two of the older bystanders attempted to mildly remonstrate at such a stupid bet, but De Lisle said, ' No, it's a bet, and I shall most certainly stick to it; and if I win, as I probably shall, it will give that youngster a lesson not to brag. I don't want to win his money, and I will give it towards a new cup for the races next year.' To say anything to George just then would, I knew, be useless and unwise, and from what I knew of De Lisle I felt sure that he would not listen to anything in the way of a compromise. I only wished more sincerely than ever that I had never sold the mare to George.

Pool was resumed, and taking my cue I played for about an hour, when, seeing that the majority of the guests had had enough of billiards, I took the opportunity of going off to bed, as I wanted to be up early in the morning in order to give the brown mare her gallop before I had to go on parade ; but long after I had left I could hear George and one or two boon companions waking the echoes, and everything else too I should think, judging by the row they made. I did not see him on parade on the following morning, and on making inquiries I was told that he had insisted on trying to climb up into his room from outside by the gutter-pipe which ran near his window. He had done it once or twice before, and I had predicted he would come to grief some day, and on this occasion the pipe had given way when he was some distance up, and he had fallen on to the stones below, but, luckily, with no worse result than a dislocated wrist, which the doctor who had been called up had put right ; so after parade I went up to his room, and found him in bed looking very disconsolate, cursing his luck and the Government generally for putting up such rotten spouts, and added, ruefully, ' Of course I am "done for" for the races, and every one who would have a chance with the mare is riding for himself.'

I said 'What on earth, George, made you make such an ass of yourself with De Lisle last night? Why cannot you keep out of his way ? You know what a beast he is, and always scores off you ; besides, how the dickens are you going to pay him if you don't win ? I wish you would be a bit more thoughtful, if not for your own sake, at least for that of your people.'

He replied, ' He made me angry with his beastly sneering manner, and I did not care what I said, and I suppose I must pay him somehow or other.'

I well knew what 'somehow or other' meant. After a few

seconds' silence I said, 'Now look here, George; I will see you through this. I tell you what I will do. I will ride Brimstone, and young Boyle shall ride "the brown." He will be delighted at the chance of getting such a good mount; he does not ride badly, and she is not likely to put him down, and you may rest assured I will do my best to win for you.'

He replied, 'It's awfully good of you, old fellow, but I really could not allow such a thing for a moment.'

'Well,' I said, 'if I don't ride your mare I will not ride my own.'

After some little further remonstrance on his part he consented. Young Boyle was overjoyed, and so the matter was settled, and I hoped satisfactorily. I little thought what the result would be.

Thursday dawned as bright a day as we could wish. We drove over to the course in the coach, George (with his arm in a sling) being of the party. There were six races on the card : our own four races, a match, and a cup we had given the farmers to run for; the Dragoon Cup being the last race. The preceding races had all been very successful, and amongst them one or two very close finishes. The course, a good one, being all grass and nearly all natural fences, was in capital going order, and now every one was all anxiety to witness 'the race of the day.' Eleven horses 'weighed out' for it, the betting being as follows: Even on Brimstone; 2 to 1 against Graceful; 3 to 1 against any others.

On the way to post I had time to caution Boyle to take care of himself and the mare, and ride her steadily. When, seeing George on the look-out for me, I stopped and said, 'I hope it will be all right, old boy; anyhow you can rely on me!'

We got away to a capital start—'at the first attempt,' as the reporters call it. For the first field or two Brimstone shook her head a good bit, and tried to get 'out of hand,' but after crossing the water, which was a few fences further on, we came past the stand the first time; and, as the pace was getting too hot to last, I managed to get a good pull at her. To my surprise Boyle, who had been riding alongside of me, immediately followed suit ; the rest were then a good field ahead of us, and I let them go for nearly the next mile and a half, when I had the satisfaction of seeing them coming back to me, and I eased the mare still further. During the next mile three of them were disposed of, being done, and 'out of it,' and one other horse badly lamed

The Dragoon Cafe
at Mule Cave, on the

Frederic Remington

apparently. Boyle all this time stuck in close attendance on me, copying everything I did, and altogether riding a devilish sight too well to please me. Rather more than three-quarters of a mile from home I let the mare 'out,' and she quickly ran up and through her horses. She was going wonderfully well, steadily, and fencing perfectly. Two fences from home Graceful nearly came down, and Boyle lost some ground, but directly after he came racing up alongside of my girths, with his reins slack, and both he and Graceful beginning to 'show signs;' for we had been latterly, and still were, going 'a cracker.' We took the last fence side by side, the brown mare pecking a bit on landing, and nearly unshipping poor little Boyle, who was beginning to roll about in his saddle, being all unused to going the pace. However he righted himself, and then I thought it prudent to draw away. This was too much for him; and thinking, I suppose, that it was the correct thing to do, he began flogging. At the first sound of his whip Brimstone swerved away to the left. Despite all my efforts I could not keep her straight in the course, nor could I 'let her out,' and there was young Boyle on my right whacking away as hard as he could, and making her worse. I had pulled her head almost round to my knee, in the hopes of keeping her off the rails, and as a last resource I took up my whip in my left hand, and tried to keep her straight with it. Nearer and nearer we drew to the winning-post, and nearer and nearer we got to the side-rails. The crowd were shouting. 'Graceful wins!' I just managed to steer clear of the post opposite the judge's box by a miracle, when smash we went head-over-heels, into the side-rails and the crowd. I knew no more, excepting that I was picked up by some one or other, luckily none the worse beyond being a bit dazed. On my coming to I was conscious of the crowd, in a very excited state, collecting round something near me; and just then one of our men ran past, looking very white and scared. I called out to him to stop, and asked what it was. He said, 'Mr. Hudson's killed, sir.' '*What?*' I exclaimed, and forcing my way through the people, regardless of everything else. There was poor George lying on the ground, with one of our officers, who was with him at the time, holding his head; but it was but too evident that he was dead. Our doctor came up a second or two after, and confirmed our fears. He said he must have been killed instantly. There was the mark of a blow on his temple, which had evidently been done by the mare's foot as she smashed into the rails.

It was a terrible shock to us all—of course to me doubly so, and I shall never forget it. The day which had dawned so brightly for us all closed sadly indeed. I dreaded to think what the effect of the news would be on poor Mrs. Hudson and Grace. I saw them at the funeral, but have never set eyes on them since, for they immediately after went to live abroad, and I went with my regiment to India during the following year; but in a letter I had some time after from Grace she said her mother had never recovered the shock, and feared never would do so.

    •   •   •   •   •   •

It was indeed strange that, after all, the race was declared to be 'A DEAD HEAT.' Aptly so, indeed!

PAST AND PRESENT COACHING.

By SEPT. BERDMORE ('NIMSHIVICH').

OACHING has become such an institution, as a summer pastime, that the man getting on in years not unwillingly recalls his introduction to it in far-off times, and congratulates the present generation that they have not experienced that ghastly blank between 1850 and 1870, when almost every vehicle in the shape of a coach was run off the road. Now-a-days any one with time and money may get a taste of it throughout the summer, and, for the matter of that, during the winter too: for does not the famous 'Old Times' take us down to Oatlands Park?

For myself I might well be excused were I a little prolix in my recollections, so persistently from childhood have I taken any route in travelling that would bring me in contact with my favourite mode of locomotion.

I think it must have been in 1836 that, between Exeter and Bristol, we pulled up to change at four cross-roads, and I recall my childish wonder as to how it was possible for the coachmen to remember the right road on such a long route as that which was before me! From the Midlands up to school and back again gave me plenty of coach travelling between 1838 and '41, but it was when, in 1842, I was sent to a private tutor's near Sherborne that I first had the full enjoyment of a coach drive; and in this, as in other cases, I trust that these recollections may

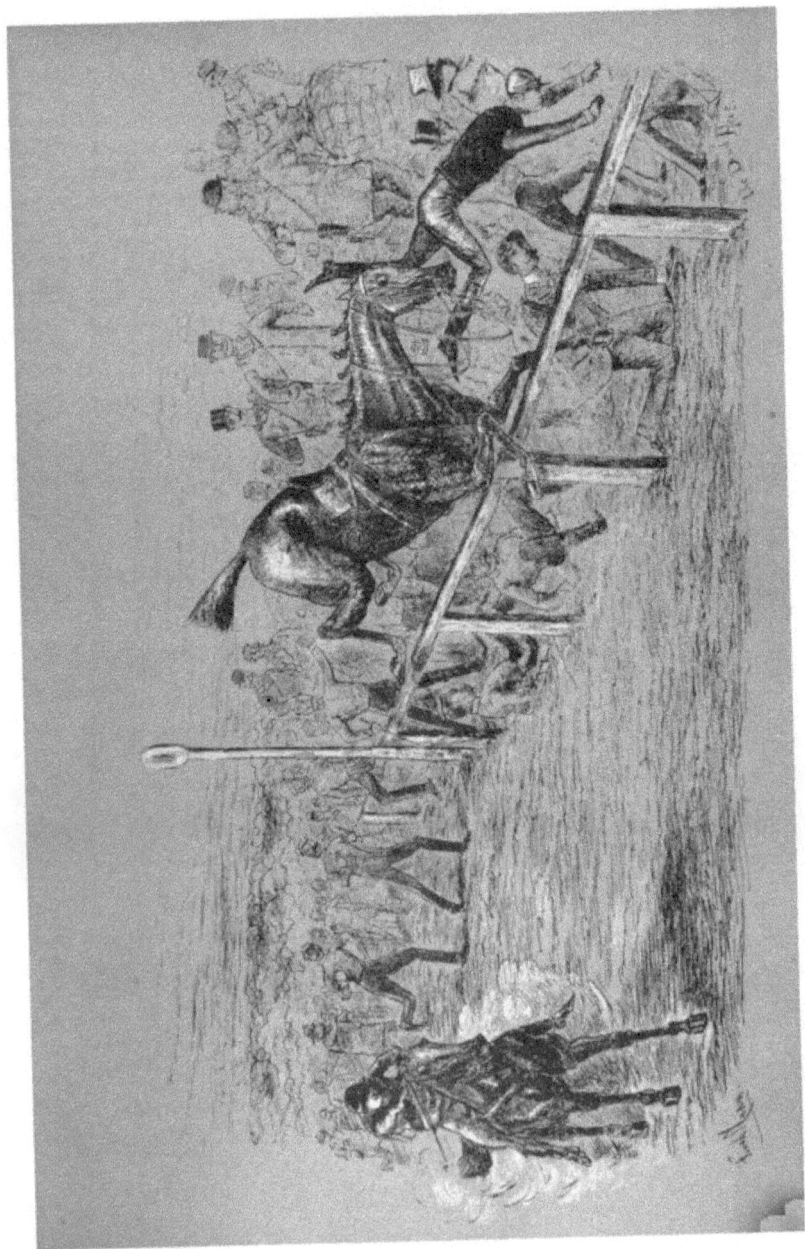

be of some use to those who contemplate one of those driving
tours which cannot become too fashionable, for they enable those
who indulge in them to learn something of the beauties of their
own country, and, here and there, of the capability of our
landlords and their ladies to cater for man and beast.

I went down on this occasion, one fine June day, by train to
Southampton, and mounting the box-seat of one of Matcham's
coaches, sped away merrily by Ringwood, Wimborne Minster,
and Blandford, to the pretty little town with the famous minster
with its flying buttresses. The return journey was not made
under quite such happy auspices. It was late in the autumn,
and my tutor had driven me into Sherborne, hoping to find a
seat for me on the Exeter and Southampton coach, which was
due at the latter town about midnight; but it was full. A friend
of his was also disappointed, and proposed that we should take
a chaise and catch the night coach at Wincanton, which passed
over Salisbury Plain and landed its passengers at Basingstoke.
This we did, and secured outside seats. I fancy my parents had
scarcely provided me with great-coat or wraps, for never shall
I forget that cold in the early morning going over Salisbury
Plain. Nor is this a route that I should commend to the
driving tourist. I think it was somewhere about this period of
my life that I first got four reins between my fingers, a feat for
which they were always itching. It is true it was only a 'pickaxe
team,' but how proud one was to boast to one's schoolfellows of
even having driven that !

During holiday time I had great experience of the Dorking
coaches when visiting my people on that road, but they were
none of them fast. Hayes' morning coach out of London, from
the Golden Cross, was about the best of them ; for Broad,
who went up to the City in the morning, had wonderfully fat,
heavy cattle. I remember one morning giving up the box-seat
on his coach to General Shubrick, who owned Brocardo, rather
a favourite for the Derby, but also a bit full in flesh—so they
told me. The best-horsed coach, and the fastest on this road,
was the Horsham ; and the coachman, a little man, was a very
noted whip. The intelligent writer of the notices on old inns, that
appeared some time ago in the *Licensed Victuallers' Gazette*,
picked up a good deal of gossip about this man when he was
collecting materials for one of the most noted of these Horsham
posting-houses, but I have myself forgotten his name. I have
mentioned elsewhere that Hayes' coach was the last that left

the Golden Cross Hotel for any place in the country, for he kept
on the Dorking road after Broad's and the other West - end
morning coach, which used also to enter the Golden Cross yard,
had ceased running.   Still, long after even Hayes had left us,
we had a coach every other day through Mickleham in the shape
of Clarke's Brighton Coach, which used to start from some
stables in the Edgware Road, go down Oxford Street, Regent
Street, and through Tichborne Street, turn round to pull up at
a booking-office on the site of what is now the Criterion, and
then crept along Piccadilly to Kew Bridge, Richmond, Peters-
ham, Kingston, across Ashstead Common to Leatherhead, and
so by Dorking, Horsham, and Henfield, to Brighton. I have
been particular about describing the route, as I have heard it
incorrectly given. I have also repeated the word 'crept,' because
it was not, and never pretended to be, a fast coach. They had
four horses for the first stage out of London, but on most of the
others only three, and these for very long stages. I need only
instance that from Brighton to Henfield, and another from
Henfield to Horsham.

I wonder what Captain Blyth on the 'Defiance,' or Selby
with his Virginia Water coach, would say if they were asked to
go their pace with such means! No! Clarke's coach is noteworthy for being the connecting link in the South between the
good old times and the modern coaching revival. I lost sight
of him about 1852, but I have heard that Mr. Eden, who afterwards horsed the Wycombe coach, took him up, and that it was
better horsed than when I knew it. Anyway, Clarke was a civil,
good coachman, who had to make ends meet by picking up
intermediate passengers and old ladies who wanted to get to
Brighton from the different points on the very pretty route he
selected. Indeed, so pretty is it that I have always been surprised that none of our modern Jehus have taken it up, for there
is undeniable good catering at Dorking for the down, and at
Horsham for the up journey.

Amongst coaching anecdotes that have been revived, I do
not remember having seen that one about the Brighton coach-
dog. This intelligent animal, which had attached itself to the
coach, did not see the point of accompanying it on its pilgrimage
from the stables in Edgware Road round to Regent Circus, so
it used to trot across Hyde Park and wait at the Corner till the
coach came by. Sometimes they would hoist it up to give it
a rest ; but this proved fatal, for it jumped off one day and got

run over. Clarke, by the way, always had a guard, with, I think, a key bugle or cornet.

I think it was in 1846 that I made my last trip to and from Exeter and Plymouth, by a morning coach for the down journey that passed through Newton and Totness, and by the renowned 'Quicksilver,' that took the direct road through Ashburton, and made light work of the hill out of Chudleigh to the top of Haldon, whence she used to descend with skid on at no gentle pace if the guard called out that we were a minute behind-hand.

About 1847 some affairs took me down to Portland Roads, to assist in the parliamentary surveys for what has since become an important harbour of refuge. My coaching experience on that occasion made such an impression on me that some year or two after I made it a subject for my first appearance in print by contributing some notes of it to the *New Sporting Magazine.* The route is certainly one of the very best adapted for any one desirous of beginning a driving tour to the Westward. We left Southampton at about 10 or 11 a.m., and arrived at Weymouth about 6 p.m.

At first our route was *via* Lyndhurst, through the New Forest, and as the second stage was long and very sandy we had three leaders attached to a long centre and two small side-bars. With a sight of the sea at Bournemouth, then absolutely without a house, the long tidal estuaries by Poole, the inland beauties of the country to Dorchester, and then the rapid drive down hill to Weymouth, where all the world (for it was August) were on the promenade ; this made an enjoyable bit of coaching.

Taking up the burden of my song at Dorchester, and allowing some seven or eight years to pass over my head, I recall with pleasure a drive from Dorchester to Exeter in (about) 1855. Never since I was a boy have I failed to go out of my way to catch a coach to arrive at my destination. I happened that autumn to be on a visit to some friends near Esher, and my destination on quitting them being Exeter, it was obvious that the easy and reasonable way for conventional mortals was to take the train to Waterloo, a cab to Paddington, and the express to the capital of my beloved Devon. But this would not suit me. There was a railway to Southampton and Dorchester. Between the latter town and Exeter the gap must surely be filled up by some coach or other. So to Southampton and Dorchester I sped. Nor was I disappointed. About midday I

found a coach whose route was through Bridport, Axminster,
and Honiton ; and, barring the first stage or two, a pleasanter
trip I never made.   It was just late enough in the autumn to
require lamps for the last stage or two, when we seemed, as one
does in night travelling, to fly along faster.   So another cigar is
lit, whilst—

> 'Silently one by one, in the infinite heaven of space,
> Blossom the lovely stars, the forget-me-nots of the angels.'

And then we pulled up at the 'New London,' and reflected that
we had been in the last coach that that renowned inn would
welcome to its doors.

How the carpet people had cheered us at Axminster!   How
the lace-makers smiled on us at Honiton !   'Only a coach !' the
cynic says.   Yes; but, somehow, they don't cheer or smile at
trains!

In the years 1848-50 I took a practical part in coaching in
the North of England.   Being on the staff of a West Riding
railway, I found lodgings, by chance, in the house of one of the
first whips of his day.   Tom Madeley had been for years coachman to the London and Glasgow mail, working it chiefly from
Newark in the south to Greta Bridge in the north.   In the
southern portion of his district he frequently had Mr. Foljambe
to take the reins : I mean the squire of that name, who afterwards lost his eyesight.   To the north, between Ferrybridge and
Wetherby, Mr. Lane Fox would be at his lodge gates in the
middle of the night to drive the Glasgow mail northward or
southward, as the case might be.   Madeley told me that in all
his experience he had never met any amateur to come near
Mr. Fox.   Under my new friend's tuition I soon placed myself,
for in summer time there was a three-horse affair to York, and I
knew that, once passed through his hands, the coachmen of the
Leeds mail (evening) and Leeds coach (morning) would give me
the reins.   So it turned out.   The mail used to go out at 4.30,
and I used to drive it to Harewood, where the day coach
from Leeds changed horses, and this I drove back.   We had the
queerest of cattle ; for the mail proprietors, Littlewood and Co.
of Leeds, did not receive much mileage, and the traffic was not
great ; but Michael Robinson, their coachman and guard, had a
method of talking to blind ones, and bolters, and jibbers, that
made them somehow get through the work and up the long hills
that prevail on that route.   One day, I recollect, I stuck fast with

a peculiarly nasty jibber half way up a hill; but Michael came
to the rescue, turned the coach back to the bottom of the hill,
and took care there was no time to shirk before we arrived at the
top. Queer as were the teams, they were fine lessons in driving.
Soon afterwards Downes, who married Miss Sturdy, daughter of
the landlord of the 'Harewood Arms,' and had done a bit of
coaching in his day (I believe he was originally in a lawyer's
office) with a Sheffield coach, and again on the London and
Stroud mail, took a fancy for horsing a short five-miles stage
from Spacey Houses to Harewood; and then we had some real
clinkers. The leaders were generally a couple of hunters or
steeple-chasers, on whom there was no occasion to throw the
point of the thong under the bar as we wound up the steep hill
near Harewood Park. That stage was a treat to drive. This
Downes had a great mania for clipping or shaving instead of clipping or
singeing his horses. I gave an account of this in the *Live-Stock
Journal* some years ago. His plan was, after shaving, to lubri-
cate the horse with lard, and cover it with a sheet, which was not
removed for three days. The result was that in a fortnight, and
for the rest of the autumn and winter, the horse had the fine,
soft, silky coat of the thorough-bred, with a perfect natural
colour. I should observe that this was done not later than the
middle of September.

Mrs. Pearson, who horsed the day coach, had fairish cattle,
and her son, Tom Pearson, used to drive. 'The last of the
Mohicans!' was his cry as he used to tear up the hill into the
little borough. I suppose I must have had the confidence of
the professionals pretty well in that day, for I remember I was
once sent home at night in charge of the coach alone. There
was one old lady inside, and it has been an everlasting source of
regret to me that I did not 'kick' for a fee when I pulled up at
'The Crown.' She did not volunteer it. In winter the work
was mostly night work, which I always enjoyed even more than
the day coaching. One winter's night I drove into Leeds with
Michael. There had been snow, and a thaw, and a frost, and
the roads were one sheet of ice, and the cattle were not roughed.
I remember we kept time to the minute; but I wonder now
how I ever accomplished it. I did not want much outer covering
for that work. I was quite warm with my work when I got to
Leeds.

Apart from this home work there were several coaching
drives in which I indulged in other parts, in some of which I

took my place as coachman. As those most noteworthy from the driving tourist's point of view, I may mention the Leeds and Ripon—all fine scenery ; the Sheffield and Newark, through Eckington, Worksop, and Alfreton—this route from Worksop to Newark abounds in the perfection of forest scenery, past Welbeck Abbey, Clumber, &c. The Sheffield and Nottingham, through Chesterfield and Mansfield, was another favourite route of mine, and I generally drove most of the way.

Away up in Lincolnshire I struck on a mine of the decaying pastime, on coaches from Lincoln to Horncastle, Louth, and Grimsby ; and there was another famous coach to Barton, opposite Hull.

Touring up in Scotland, of course I tried the Perth and Inverness fast coach, whilst above Inverness I met with one or two teams, the quality of which I have never yet seen equalled out of a private coach.

In Ireland, too, I remember driving a night-coach from Londonderry to Coleraine, and stopping for a drop of the 'creetur' at a cabin on the top of a tolerably high plateau in the early hours of the morning. Down Limerick way I found a man who was driving his eighty miles a-day, and that not on a fast coach. As a distance this feat has been much excelled in England by Thorowgood of the Norwich 'Times,' and others; but with better pace the number of hours on the box would not be so great, and consequently the residue left for repose would be greater.

A couple of decades, or rather more, brings me down to the revival of coaching, which has become one of our summer pastimes in the last quarter of the nineteenth century.

Let us never forget the names of those to whom we are indebted for this,—Angell, Beaufort, Clitheroe, Eden, Londesborough, Meek, and Pole, not forgetting Bear! These may be said to have been the pioneers—and some of them, alas! have gone—but, sturdily supporting the new movement with purse and action, the names of Lord Aveling, Blyth, Barnett, Bailey, Dickson, Hargreaves, C. Hoare, Kane, Lowther, Lord Arthur Somerset, Colonel Somerset, Seager Hunt, Secker, Shoolbred, Wilson, and others, may be mentioned.

Assisting them professionally there have been many good coachmen and excellent guards. Of these my friend Finch Mason is giving an illustration of that well-known whip who still horses his own coach, the 'Old Times,' in a fashion

Finch Mason

BRIGHTON COA

OLD TIMES.

FARES

SINGLE

RETURN

FARES

RETURN

Now then, who's for the Old Times?

see page 92.

that will bear comparison with the best of those in days gone by.

A great judge of a horse-keeper's duty (one of the first requisites in a coach proprietor), a good judge of pace, and an advocate for short stages, Selby, has made for himself a well-deserved reputation. He had a good schooling when he worked the Tunbridge Wells coach with Mr. Hoare, and others; and it is much to be regretted that this road should have become vacant the last few years.

Referring to other professionals of the present day, we may say that by the Thorowgoods we are linked to the greater generation of coachmen, for they are nephews of the famous Thorowgood of the Norwich 'Times,' but in Cracknell and both the Wards we have the last representatives of an epoch when 'finish' was far more insisted on than it is to-day. That, to my mind, is the distinction in point of 'artistic merit' (to use a modern phrase) between the old and the new school of coachmen; but there is the brilliant exception in the elder Fownes, who, if not dating as far back as those I have named, has inherited from early association with the old school all the best traditions of the road. You can no more define 'finish' in driving than you can the excellence of some great master in painting, and, reflecting over the past, it may seem odd that one can recall it, as practised by Tom Madeley, who was mostly driving a night mail, and find it wanting in many who now pass through the glare of Piccadilly. But such is the fact, and it is with just reason that the Wards, Fownes, and Cracknell, are esteemed for this quality of 'finish,' as well as for their personal merits. C. S. Ward still coaches the rising generation in the use of whip and reins, and we have seen his brother not so long ago on the Sevenoaks coach during its short career.

As modern guards, Edwin Spencer, that past-master on the horn, should have a word from us; and Perrin, formerly on the Tunbridge Wells, now works efficiently with Mr. Sheather on the Dorking 'Perseverance.'

The road flourishes, and the 'White Horse Cellars' have been rebuilt! May Messrs. Banks continue to book plenty of fair women and brave men for this pleasant summer pastime!

A DAY'S SHOOTING IN THE PYRENEES.

By the Author of 'The Tommiebeg Shootings.'

O to what department of France you may, there will be found in it about as many shooters as there are hares and partridges; but for all that you will rarely, if ever, stumble upon a sportsman, in our acceptation of the word. There will, nevertheless, be found in every town, every village almost, some *one* individual who is the *chasseur par excellence*—who has a reputation—who is quoted as the great authority in all matters pertaining to woodcraft. This individual is generally some official, an *employé* in one of the infinite number of *bureaux*, which are spread like a net over the country—a net which is worked by the great 'head centre' at Paris. He not unfrequently has a bit of faded red ribbon at his button-hole : in his own idea he is no insignificant atom in the public administration ; and this, setting aside the faith he has in his own personal merits, justifies him in thinking no *vin ordinaire* of himself—we should say in England, 'small beer.'

In a former chapter, as an introduction to another 'Day's Shooting in the Pyrenees,' I took occasion to narrate how it came to pass that Fred Somers and myself were travelling in that part of France at a season when all the tourists had long since deserted it ; and how we had brought with us our guns, on the chance of getting an occasional day's shooting.

We had no dogs with us, and even if we had possessed them it would not have rendered us independent. I had on former occasions shot too much in France not to be aware that the law of trespass, good as it is in principle—far better and more equitable than our absurd game-laws—is an absolute bar to a stranger enjoying anything of pleasure or comfort in shooting, unless accompanied by some one who is authorised to give him a free range, or who knows exactly the boundaries of the little holdings into which the country is parcelled out.

Through the agency of the postmaster, or the landlord of our inn, we contrived always to become acquainted with this mighty Nimrod—the great *chasseur* of the district—the sort of individual we have described ; and let me say, *en passant*, that

in the course of our journey we never failed to meet with the
utmost courtesy and the most ready aid from every one. Of
course we met with a great variety of character. The gun
and the fishing-rod carry one to many a beautiful spot, unknown
to those who travel by rule of 'Murray,' and bring one in contact
with so many strangers, that I suspect we learned a good deal
more about the country and the people, of their habits and
manners and peculiarities, than if we had followed the beaten
track of travellers.

We arrived late in the evening of the 8th of November
at Argellez, which we had passed through some days previously,
merely to change horses, on our road to Luz and Cauterets. It
looked more like shooting than almost any neighbourhood we
had hitherto seen, and the landlord of the hôtel had then
promised us that he would, on our return—for we must
necessarily pass through the place again on the post-road to Pau
—put things *en train* for us.

We had already killed a few woodcocks in a desultory sort of
way—it was enough to show us that there was a flight of them in
the country—and if we were to believe the florid account given
us by our informant of the abundance of the bird, we might not
unreasonably calculate on getting, at least, one day's good sport.
Besides, it was to be our last expedition of the kind : our next
halt was to be at Pau, where we were to get rid of our old
carriage, to which we were indebted for so much wild adventure,
and relapse into civilisation and railroads.

Our host had been, he informed us, as good as his word, and
while we were preparing for dinner he went himself to inform
the Monsieur, who was to be our patron on the morrow, of our
arrival. We were presently introduced to a very decent fellow,
who held some office in the district, and who expressed himself
delighted at the prospect of joining us in an expedition to a
famous covert for cocks some two to three leagues off. He
was, as he expressed it, *passionné pour la chasse*, and was the
happy proprietor of a brace of pointers, which were to be of the
party on the morrow. One of these, a tall, ungainly-looking
dog, he brought with him, and we invited both master and dog
to be of our dinner-party.

Azor, our guest, was his favourite, and to give us an idea
of his cleverness—and qualifications as a *sporting* dog—he put
him, in the course of the evening, through his wonderful tricks.
Now, as it was the first and last time we ever saw one of his

race trained to the accomplishments of the *salon*, we consider
the exhibition worth recording.

.' *Tenez, Messieurs,*' he said, ' *vous allez voir !*' I'll show you
something ! Ah ! he is a miraculous dog, is Azor ! You shall
judge. ' *Allons! Azor! mon brave! Debout !*' (we should say
in English, ' Beg !') Poor Azor retreated into a corner, and
lifting himself slowly and clumsily, with his back to the wall,
raised himself on his hind legs, and looked as miserable a dog
as can well be imagined. ' *C'est bien ! c'est très bien !*'—capital !
said his delighted master, looking to us triumphantly for
approbation. He then threw a bit of biscuit to the other end
of the room—'*Apporte !*'—Go fetch ! was the command, and
Azor, obedient, made a dash at the morsel and devoured it on
the spot, then waited meekly for what was coming next.

' *A présent,*' said his master, ' *couches-toi !*' Azor sat down
upon his tail—' *A terre ! entends-tu ?*' This was said in a stern
tone. Azor rolled himself up comfortably on the floor. ' *Fort
bien ! Excellent !*' was the approving verdict, in which we were
invited to join. ' Ah ! now, Messieurs, you shall see something
vraiment merveilleux—something worth seeing. ' *Azor!*' he said
in a sepulchral voice, ' *fais la mort !*' Azor stretched himself
out at full length in the fashion of defunct dogs.

It is impossible to imagine anything more ludicrous than the
exhibition of a grave, sedate-looking pointer, apeing the poodle.
To us it seemed but cruel fun ; to the master it was a triumphant
proof of his own educational powers, or skill in dog-breaking, as
well as of the brilliant qualities of poor Azor. We bore, of
course, willing testimony to our four-footed friend's sagacity, and
devoutly hoped that so much time and training had not been
devoted to these lessons of ' deportment' and social accomplishments to the neglect of the cultivation of the more solid and
more profitable talents we naturally look for in a dog of *business.*
I must say I had my doubts on the subject.

We had been favoured with a month of the most glorious
weather, and I may remark that there is no better season of the
year for mountain excursions than the month of October, the
only drawback being the shortened days and the rather more
than freshness of the mornings and evenings. The last few days,
however, had given us warning to leave the high lands—that
winter was setting in—and our anticipations for the morrow
were somewhat damped by finding, on taking leave of our friends
at the inn-door, that some rain had fallen ; the clouds were

drifting in heavy masses across the moon, which ever and anon shone out and lighted up fitfully the glorious expanse of the rich vale of Lavedan, in which Argellez is so delightfully situated.

We were on foot at daybreak the next morning, and were presently joined by our brother-sportsman, who brought with him our talented acquaintance Azor, and his comrade Médore, as well as a stout lad to carry the goodly bag of provender, for we had a long day before us. We set off at a good round pace, as the air was keen and searching, and in a short quarter of an hour left the high road and began the ascent of a stiff hill-side clothed with orchards, and groves of oak and beech, and chestnut and walnut, with farm-houses dotted about here and there and giving life to the landscape. This brought us to a wide *plateau*, or level tract of rich pasture, and here Azor and Médore distinguished themselves by running into a small covey of gray partridges, out of which Fred and I secured a bird each; and I have no doubt Monsieur Adolphe would have done as much if his gun had not been slung across his back. Fancying we had marked the remainder of the covey down at a spot some fifty yards above us, which was covered with straggling patches of brushwood, Adolphe, who was now vehemently excited, and had unslung his weapon, dashed off almost at a run, followed by Fred, who was about as wild as himself, while I remained below, and having lighted a cigar, looked on at their proceedings. There were, I knew, but three birds left for their four barrels, and these only the common English partridge; the odds, too, I fancied, were greatly in favour of the birds, for Azor and Médore were scampering backwards and forwards in high glee.

I watched the gunners for some time; they did not seem inclined to give the thing up, and higher and higher they kept working. Adolphe took the lead, and communicated with Fred by telegraphic signs, for the latter did not understand what he said. Presently I saw the former crouch down, and Fred, following suit, put himself also in form. It was to be a stalk, it appeared; and with some interest I marked their movements. Onward they crept from bush to bush, peering out cautiously from behind the cover, till I lost sight of them except at intervals. The dogs, too, had been brought to heel; there must be something up, and I began to regret not being of the party. Half-an-hour must have been thus employed, when I heard the report of two barrels, and I caught a glimpse of Adolphe rushing frantically forwards with Fred close after him. '*Tirez!*

Tirez donc !' I now heard called out in imploring accent. '*La voilà ! Monsieur Fraide ! Tirez !'*

And now, to my great surprise, I observed Fred retracing his steps at a quick, resolute pace, which soon brought him down to me. He was boiling over with indignation. 'Confound the fellow !' he angrily exclaimed, as he took off his cap, and began mopping his forehead with his handkerchief.

'What's the matter, Fred ?' I inquired.

'To think,' he replied, in a reproachful tone, 'of a fellow being made such a fool of !'

'But what is it ?' (I began to have an idea.)

'Oh, hang it ! you know, you were up to it all the time ; and I must say I don't think it treating a fellow fairly.'

'But tell me, what did you shoot ?'

'What did *I* shoot, indeed !' he answered, in a most contemptuous accent. (I saw it all now.)

'But what has our friend bagged, then ?'

'Bagged !—he missed it clean !'

'What ? You have not told me what ?'

'Why, an infernal blackbird ! and I *do* say, if this is to be the sort of thing, you know—if this French fellow —— '

' Hush, Fred ! here he is. Now don't look so glum over it— above all, don't let him see you are put out about it. With him it is "all fish that comes to net." He is really a very good fellow, and I should be sorry to see him affronted. Besides, it is, if you will only look at it in its proper light, rather fun. Fancy stalking a blackbird !'

'Oh, yes ! capital fun for you, I dare say, looking on and getting time for a quiet cigar,' said Fred, half laughing, half angry. 'But, I say, do just conceive his wanting *me* to shoot it !'

By this time our friend arrived, hot and angry, too—angry, as he told me, because *ce jeune Monsieur* did not choose to *tirer sur une belle merle*—to shoot at a noble blackbird—actually sitting on the top of the bush ! Ah ! if *his* gun had only been loaded !

Now, it is likely enough Adolphe, if he had been alone, would have spent half a day with that lively songster ; and it would have afforded him intense excitement and amusement. There is some philosophy in it, after all. One goes out shooting for amusement's sake, and if a French *chasseur* really takes pleasure in the pursuit of a thrush or blackbird, it may be questioned whether he has not the best of it, and is not, in fact, rather to be envied.

After this little episode we continued our march through a beautiful little valley covered with the greenest of pasture, through which a rivulet, now swollen with the last night's rain, was dashing along rather angrily and noisily, forming tiny cascades and miniature pools and eddies.

In the narrow path along its banks we were rather unexpectedly brought to bay by the hostile demonstrations of three monstrous tawny dogs, which might have passed for gigantic wolves. Azor and Médore fell into the rear without being told, and the brutes, with furious bark, were bearing down upon us in close order.

'*N'ayez pas peur*—Never mind the curs!' exclaimed our friend, valiantly; '*chien qui aboie ne mord pas!*' For which we have a Scotch proverb to match, 'Great barkers are nae biters.'

'*Aha! coquins!*' followed up the speaker, picking up a big stone, and making a bad shot, which was immediately remedied by Fred, who, laying down his gun, proceeded to choose a big boulder, and throwing himself into frame for bowling. 'Now, just look here!' he said. 'Here goes at the middle stump!' and, delivering his ball, he knocked one of the dogs over and over, and his howl put to flight at once the other two, but brought out from a hovel the other side of the stream a couple of savage-looking men, who, after making some very uncomfortable remarks relative to things in general, and to chasseurs in particular, in rather uncourtly language, called off their pets, the vanquished hero limping dismally after his comrades, and too much disabled to leap the brook. I have often come across these huge sheep-dogs, and, however ferocious and threatening their demonstrations, I have never known them hesitate to turn tail if I stooped down to pick up, or to make pretence of picking up, a stone. Their duty is to protect the sheep from four-footed marauders—wolves and bears—who, in hard times, are driven down from the mountains to seek what they may devour.

Azor and Médore enlivened our walk presently by a glorious course, over a beautiful bit of open country, after a hare, which Monsieur Adolphe, I am certain, missed clean, and which Fred— I fancy on the principle of taking a wild shot at anything which has been shot at—as evidently hit. The delight of their master was intense as he cheered the dogs on, and it was heart-rending to hear his cry of anguish when the poor animal, doubling, threw out its clumsy pursuers ; but his exclamations of triumph ought to be told in French to be appreciated, when the dogs ran into the poor hare, and, after roughly tearing at her for some time, and quarrelling over the dead body, proceeded to carry it between them, growling and snarling all the way, to their exulting proprietor. There was, we found, one shot in the shoulder.

It was some time before our friend was calmed down, but this was brought about by our coming upon a piece of marshy, sedgy ground, at the burn-side, on which we flushed first one snipe, which got up too wide, and where we eventually succeeded in getting two couple between us.

We had now a bit of rather severe walking, and then came upon another extensive level, or wide glade, between two hills, and here we found, to our great disgust, that there was a coating of snow on the ground—what had been rain with us below had fallen in flakes at this elevation. 'There!' said Monsieur Adophe, pointing to a hill-side about a mile from us, 'There we begin our *chasse aux bécasses*.' The hill was completely clothed with a thicket of low oak underwood, uniformly about six or seven feet high; not a leaf had fallen, and the snow, which had come down lightly, had only made a dense white cover to the trees, leaving the ground underneath comparatively clear. It did not look promising.

We were skirting the outside when we flushed two cocks, both of which we knocked down, but only bagged one, for the other had lodged somewhere in the foliage of snow; and it was quite hopeless, we discovered, attempting to penetrate into the covert, for each movement brought down an avalanche, which filled our pockets, covered our guns, and insinuated its particles very uncomfortably down our necks. We now thought it best to couple up the dogs and keep the edge of the wood till we could find an opening, where the brushwood was thinner. As we went on the woodcocks kept getting up before us, one after another, and we were pretty lucky in picking up those we shot—four got up together in one place, and we gave a very good account of them. Whenever we shot we put up birds all over the cover out of reach of us; they took but a short flight, however, and generally settled down in the wood.

Having looked in vain for anything like an open spot in the whole expanse of the hill-side, we resolved upon walking round the covert; but having tried the upper level, and put up nothing, finding it, moreover, bad travelling, we came down again to the track we had followed, and determined to let the dogs go.

Finch Mason

"Azor and Medoc returning for Home"

I have heard stories of cock-shooting in Albania, but I scarcely think it possible that even there one could see often in a day's shooting more woodcocks than we saw on that hill-side —the place was alive with them. The birds, I imagine, were collected for migrating; they had perhaps been surprised by the snow, and did not care to leave their quarters so long as the ground remained open under the oak-trees.

We stationed ourselves at intervals (while Azor and Médore disported themselves at pleasure out of sight) in such positions as best commanded the top of the wood, and waited thus the chance of a bird coming within range. In this way we picked up a few, as well as a hare, which nearly ran against me as it was hotly pursued by those first-rate harriers, Azor and Médore. But, finding the cocks got wilder, we took up the dogs, and having chosen a convenient spot under the lee of the wood, we determined to eat our lunch, during which the birds, we hoped, would have time to recover from their alarm.

The temperature was much too wintry to invite us to make a lengthened *siesta*, so, having lighted our cigars, we made another attempt at getting the birds up by letting the dogs run. It was positively heartbreaking to see the cocks moving all over the wood, where it was hopeless attempting to follow them.

Our united efforts enabled us, with some difficulty, to make up a bag of nineteen woodcocks ; we tried hard to make up the ten couple, but a heavy sleet began to fall towards three o'clock, and driven, as it was, straight into our eyes by a cutting wind, it compelled us reluctantly to give in, and abandon the field. Adolphe was in perfect ecstasies at the result of our day, and insisted on putting all the birds into his *carnassière*, asseverating that he would with pleasure have carried ten times the weight of *bécasses*. The hare we consigned to the boy, who had been lightened of his load by our onslaught on the good things and the bottles of wine our host had provided for us.

We met with nothing worth recording on our homeward march, save that I could not resist a long shot at a big hawk by way of discharging a barrel ; this proved to be a buzzard, and, having looked it over, we left it on the ground. The boy, I observed, however, stopped behind, and I saw him slip it into his bag. On asking him what he intended doing with it, he said, '*J' d'mande pardon, M'sieu! elle sera bonne pour la soupe !*'

I have never tasted buzzard soup, but I dare say it is very good, and it pleased me to see my bird was not wasted.

Our old enemies, the wolf-dogs, contented themselves with giving us a salute of furious barking as we passed their domicile, but they thought it prudent to keep the brook between us. We arrived at our quarters pretty well drenched with rain, and were not sorry to find ourselves comfortably seated, in due time, at our dinner, to which, of course, we had invited Adolphe; and you may imagine how we talked over our day's adventures. It was agreed *nem. con.* that if—those ifs!—*if* it had not been for the snow, we should have been obliged to send a horse and man to fetch the woodcocks we *must* have killed, and we were all equally unanimous that it was not our fault we had not done so.

It was our last day's gunning in the Pyrenees, and Fred and myself voted it was not a bad wind-up to our season.

YOUNG NIMROD AT ETON.

HE GOES TO ASCOT.

By FINCH MASON.

'When we were boys, merry, merry boys ;
When we were boys together.'
Popular Ballad.

SAY, Nobs,' said young Nimrod, to his friend and schoolfellow, Neville of Hardistys, as they sat together one hot Tuesday morning in June on the wall at Eton, discussing a pottle of strawberries a-piece, obtained on tick from the confiding Joby, and criticising the passers-by, of whom on that particular morning there were more than usual, for it was the first day of Ascot races,—' I say, Nobs, I wish we were going to Ascot—don't you ?'

'Yes, I do,' replied Master Neville, taking a damaged strawberry from his pottle and shying it at Tottleby minor, who was walking by, with such good aim that it landed with a splash on that youth's brand new hat, obtained only that morning from Saunders's.

'Yes, I *do*,' replied he, pleasantly ignoring the muttered blessing bestowed on him by the injured possessor of the damaged beaver. 'Look!' he exclaimed ; 'there goes another drag! and here's a break and four posters! It's quite aggravating, ain't it, to sit here and watch 'em all go by ?'

'Why don't yer goo, then ?' observed old Joby, who was

standing near. 'Tom Cannon, up at Windsor, he'll let you have some hosses in a minnit, I know, if you ask 'im.'

'By Jove! do you think he would?' said Nimrod, catching at the idea.

'Why o' *corse* he would,' replied the good old man, confidently. 'A ride to Ascot, now,' continued he; 'that 'ud be worth bein' swished for: better than shying o' strawberries at the Queen's carriage, like you did last week. *Too* bad, that was.'

The escapade alluded to by Joby was this. About a week before the conversation just related Nimrod was, as now, seated on the wall, discussing a pottle of strawberries, when he was suddenly aware of the approach of one of the royal carriages; which carriage had come down from Windsor to fetch little 'Baby Bunting,' who was one of the Queen's pages, to the Castle, where some state ceremonial was taking place. The Baby, figged out in all his finery, was inside, and being what Mrs. Gamp would call 'an imperent young sparrer,' could not resist, as he drove swiftly by, popping his curly head out of window and what is vulgarly called 'taking a sight' in a derisive manner at his friend Nimrod; in return for which attention Nimrod felt it incumbent upon him to immediately hurl his half-emptied basket of fruit at the Baby's head, hitting that young gentleman on the nose, and sending the strawberries flying all over the carriage. Unfortunately, one of the Masters passing by was a witness of the daring deed, and accordingly that same afternoon Nimrod found himself in the bill. In short, that hero was never out of mischief, much to the annoyance of his tutor and the proportionate delight of his father, who, as we related in a former chapter, took the liveliest interest in all his hopeful son's escapades.*

The advent of the strawberry season was the means too, almost on the same day, of procuring his friend Neville an interview with the Head Master in the library. Now, Neville, going into three o'clock school and not knowing a word of his Horace, bethought him of a plan by which he could not only avoid being called up, but escape school altogether. Placing then a large strawberry in his pocket-handkerchief and crumpling it well up, he marched boldly into school with his fellows. Shortly before his turn came, out came the handkerchief, and a cough, accompanied by an appealing look at the Master, soon had the desired effect of attracting that worthy man's attention.

* *Vide* 'Young Nimrod at Eton.' No. I. of *Sporting Notes and Sketches.*

'What's the matter, Neville? Ah! I see. Nose bleeding, eh?
You'd better go away.'

It was a masterly stroke of business had it been properly
carried out; but, unfortunately, Master Neville could not resist,
on leaving the room, the temptation of removing the handkerchief for a second, just to show his admiring friends what a
clever boy he was. At that very moment the Master looked up.
'Come here, Neville. Have the goodness to remove your
handkerchief, if you please. I thought so—*dirty* little beast!
—a gross piece of deception. And now go on. Ha! I guessed
as much. You don't know a word of it, Sir—not a single word.
Præpostor, take this to the Head Master at once.'

But to return to our mutton, or rather our Ascot. Nimrod
was so struck by Joby's proposition that he made up his mind
on the spot that pay a visit to the Royal heath he would. His
friend Neville, otherwise Nobs, also jumped at the notion, and
whilst they were discussing the affair, who should come slouching
up, with his trousers turned up and his hat on one side as usual,
but their young friend, Billy Ballynasloe, most sporting of Irishmen, who no sooner heard of the proposed expedition than he
expressed his desire to go too; and he, as luck would have it,
being personally acquainted with Mr. Thomas Cannon, it was
forthwith arranged that after four that same afternoon they
would all three repair up town to see that worthy, and arrange
with him to provide some horses to take them to Ascot on the
following Thursday—the Cup day.

Who that was at Eton twenty years ago does not remember
Billy Ballynasloe? Certainly the most widely known and perhaps the most popular boy of his time. When, during the wars
with savage nations that have taken place so frequently of late
years, we have taken up our newspaper and read therein 'Our
Special Correspondent's' account of the terrific feats of valour
performed by that most dashing of *sabreurs*, 'Lord William
Ballynasloe;' how, one day, he is spitting Zulus by the score,
just like larks on a skewer; how, another, he is knocking
Afghans over in a cavalry charge like so many ninepins, in fact
behaving himself like a Paladin of old; our thoughts *will* wander
back to the good old days—what days they were!—and once
again, to all intents and purposes, we are an Eton boy. What
am I doing, and where am I? Sitting in front of the fire in my
room in London and smoking a cigar, do you say? Not a bit
of it! You're quite mistaken, I assure you. At this moment I

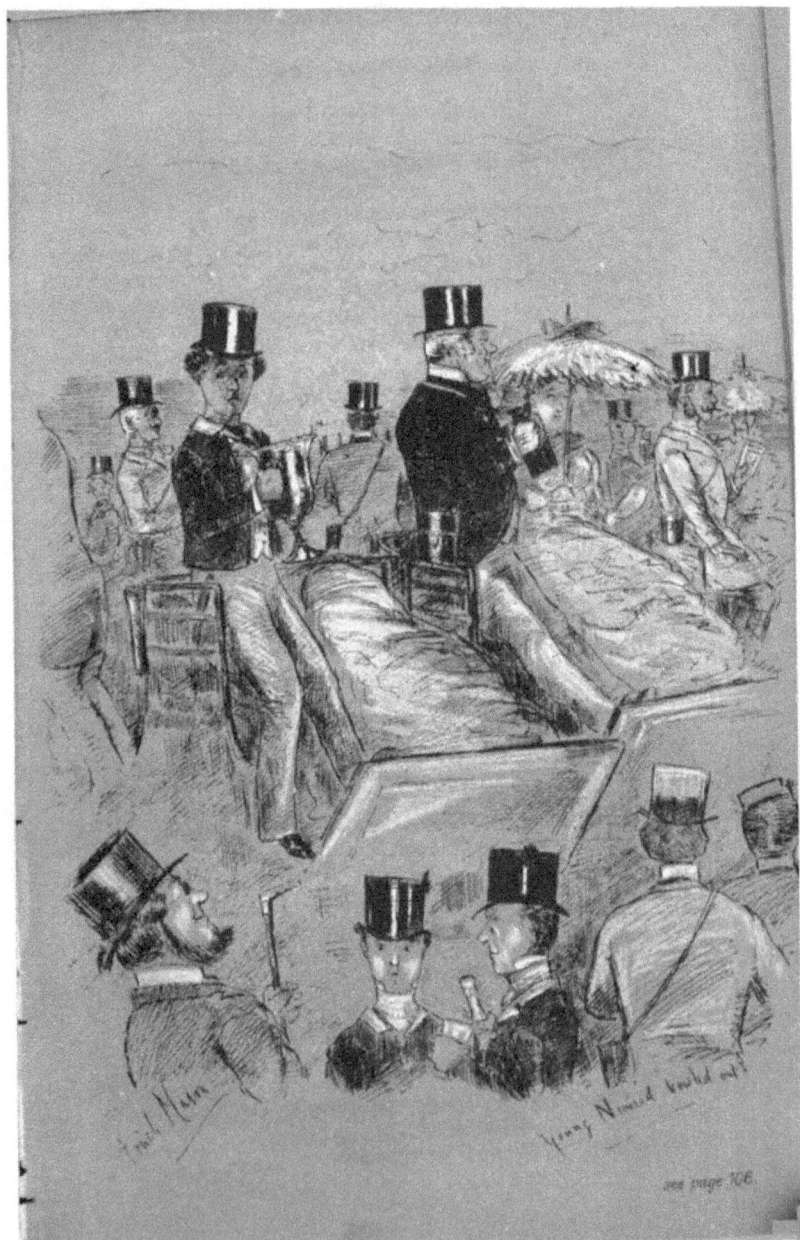

Emil Maler

Young Nimrod bowled out!

see page 106.

am at Eton. It is the last day of the half, and I have just come out of five-o'clock school and am forming one of a lot of boys assembled round one of Charlie Wise's flies, and bidding somebody therein farewell; which somebody is none other than Billy Ballynasloe, who, with his three bulldogs inside and his luggage out, is just taking his merry self off to the station, *en route* to Ireland for the holidays.*

The Cup day arrived in due course, and on that day, just as the clocks of the royal borough were striking half-past one o'clock, our three young friends, who had contrived to shirk their respective dinners and had left instructions with their præpostors not to mark them down as absent from chapel, might have been seen in a heated state hurrying up Windsor Hill at their very best pace. In such a hurry, indeed, were they, that they did not even drop in to Layton's. At the entrance to the 'Long Walk' were two hacks and a pony being led about by two stablemen; these being the quadrupeds sent by Tom Cannon to convey our heroes to Ascot. There being some demur as to who was to have the pony, the ostler sagaciously suggested that the 'littlest on 'em' should take him; which being considered fair, he was forthwith mounted by Neville, who chanced to be the smallest of the party, and without more ado off they started at a gallop, to the great admiration of the ostler and his attendant satellite.

What a jolly ride it was! and how they laughed and chaffed as they sent Tom Cannon's quads along at their very best pace! Soon after they had started a little additional excitement was caused by the sight of Nimrod's tutor, 'Johnny Old,' coming along on his old gray about a mile behind them. Johnny, as he was irreverently called, was quite a sporting character in his way, and always rode over to Ascot on one of the days. This happened to be his day; but even if he saw our three sportsmen, which is doubtful, he was too far off to be dangerous in any way.

Ascot was at length reached, and confiding their now smoking nags to the care of three out-at-elbow looking worthies, our young friends rushed off to find the drag belonging to Neville's brother; which haven of refuge they reached just as the horses were coming out for the Gold Cup. It was Buckstone's year, so it may be imagined what a state of excitement the Etonians were in when he and Tim Whiffler ran their famous dead heat.

---

* Boys living in Scotland or Ireland always left for the holidays the night before the others.

After the race the occupants of the drag all went off to the stand, leaving the three boys in possession ; and very good use they made of the opportunity.   Going without their dinner, and their ride combined, had given them a splendid appetite for the lobster-salad and other good things ; added to which, the heat of the weather made the fiz go down uncommon slippy, as Neville remarked with a grin ; and altogether they all agreed that it was the jolliest lark they had ever had.

•   •   •   •   •

The sun was at its hottest, the fun of the fair was at its height, when Nimrod on the top of the drag, with his countenance hidden in the depths of a huge silver cup filled with champagne, suddenly felt a gentle pull at his leg, which dangled easily over the side of the coach.

'Shut up, you ass!' shouted he, not taking the trouble to look down, for he thought it was Ballynasloe.   'Shut up! confound you! can't you see I'm drinking?' exclaimed he, still louder, as he felt another pull at his leg.   This time our friend condescended to remove his somewhat wine-flushed face from the tankard, and look down, and—it wasn't Ballynasloe, nor was it Neville, but it was the gig-lamped countenance of the Reverend Russell Nox, one of the Eton masters, that met his horrified gaze, and it was the insinuating voice of that gentleman that was now saying, in the pleasantest manner imaginable—

'I'm *extremely* sorry to spoil sport, my young friend, but I am *afraid* I must trouble you for your name, and that of your tutor.'

•   •   •   •   •

SETTLING DAY.

SCENE—*Eleven o'clock school at Eton.*

Enter PRÆPOSTOR OF THE DAY, *armed with a slip of paper.*

PRÆPOSTOR (*loq.*).   'Please, Sir, is Nimrod in this division ?'
MASTER (*loq.*).   'Yes.'
PRÆPOSTOR.   'He's to stay.'

PERILS ABOUND ON EVERY SIDE!

THE

Railway Passengers Assurance Company,

No. 64, CORNHILL,

INSURES AGAINST

ACCIDENTS OF ALL KINDS,

ON LAND OR WATER,

AND HAS

THE LARGEST INVESTED CAPITAL,

THE LARGEST INCOME,

AND PAYS YEARLY THE

LARGEST AMOUNT OF COMPENSATION

Of any Accidental Assurance Company.

Chairman   -   **HARVIE M. FARQUHAR**, Esq.

Apply to the Clerks at the Railway Stations,

the Local Agents, or

WEST END OFFICE,

8, GRAND HOTEL BUILDINGS, CHARING CROSS;

OR AT THE

Head Office, 64, CORNHILL, LONDON, E.C.

WILLIAM J. VIAN, *Secretary.*

TWO SHILLINGS

FORES's SPORTING NOTES &

Sketches.

Nº 3. OCTOBER 1884.

Contents.

EIGHT TINTED FULL PAGE ILLUSTRATIONS,
By FINCH MASON
& R. M. ALEXANDER.

PUBLISHED QUARTERLY BY
MESSRS FORES' 41 PICCADILLY, LONDON.
SIMPKIN, MARSHALL & Cº.

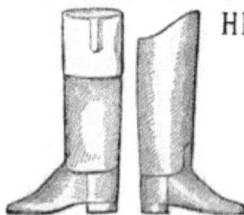

1

MESSRS. FORES'S
SPORTING & FINE ART PUBLICATIONS,
41 PICCADILLY, LONDON
(Corner of Sackville Street).

SUSPENSE, by Cecil Boult. A model 'Whip,' neat, muscular, and well dressed, mounted on a good stamp of 'Whip's horse,' at the corner of a covert where 'Charley' is likely to break. The natural and easy seat of a perfect horseman is well represented as he turns in his saddle and listens eagerly to the music of the Hounds in cover. Altogether it is one of the most sporting bits this artist has produced.
Coloured, 16 by 12 inches, £2 2s.

HIS FIRST AUDIENCE, by A. Harvey Moore. A Fisher Lad, leaning against the stern of a boat, intently playing on a pipe; three donkeys standing near appearing absorbed by the musical strains.
Coloured, 14½ by 8½ inches, £2 2s.

FOX-HUNTING, by Cecil Boult. A Set of 4 Upright.
1. A FAVOURITE MEET. | 3. IN THE FOREMOST FLIGHT.
2. THROWING THEM IN. | 4. 'BREAK HIM UP, BEAUTIES!'
Ladies, as well as gentlemen, are here introduced in the varied incidents of the chase. The treatment is sportsmanlike and unconventional, the shape is elegant, and the size convenient for hanging.
Coloured, 21½ by 9 inches, £8 8s. the set of Four.

ON THE ROAD TO GRETNA, by C. Cooper Hender-son. Shows that historical vehicle, an old 'Po Chay' and four, going at speed, with a gentleman leaning out of the window offering a purse to the Post Boys—pursuers in the distance. The stamp of Horses and character of Post Boys are admirably given by the above unrivalled painter of Coaching and Road Scenes.
Coloured, 17½ by 11 inches, £2 2s.

FORES'S HUNTING SKETCHES, by Cecil Boult.
PLATE 7.—IN A GOOD PLACE.
A Lady following Hounds out of Cover, with Huntsman in the Distance.
PLATE 8.—A PROMISING YOUNG ONE.
Flying a Brook in first-rate style, ridden and handled by a workman.
PLATE 9.—GOING TO THE MEET.
Two Ladies driving in a well-appointed Pony-trap.
PLATE 10.—HOME AGAIN AFTER A HARD DAY.
A Lady on a 'pumped out' Bay arriving in sight of home.
Coloured, 15 by 10½ inches. 10s. 6d. each.

'LOST AND FOUND,' by Stanley Berkley.
'Weary, and worn, and sad,
By the lamp's cold gleam I stand,
Waiting and watching, sighing and sighing,
For that loved and long-lost hand.'

A large Dog which has been stolen, having broken the rope which held him (a part being still round his neck), regains the door of his old home, and waits eagerly and anxiously on the doorstep in pelting rain for 'that loved and long-lost hand.' Coloured, 10½ by 8½ inches, £1 5s. Plain, 10s. 6d.

ANGELS EVER BRIGHT AND FAIR, by E. George. Represents in the Firmament two lovely Female Heads (dark and fair), with flowing gauze drapery : one gazes eagerly and intently upwards, the other 'casts a longing, lingering look' below. Coloured, 11½ inches circle, £2 2s.

8

FORES'S HUNTING CASUALTIES, that may Occur

WITH HOUNDS. After H. ALKEN, Sen. Six Plates, price £1 5s.

1. A TURN OF SPEED OVER THE FLAT.
2. A STRANGE COUNTRY.
3. DESPATCHED TO HEAD QUARTERS.
4. UP TO SIXTEEN STONE.
5. A RARE SORT FOR THE DOWNS.
6. A MUTUAL DETERMINATION.

FORES'S STEEPLE-CHASE SCENES. After H.

ALKEN, Sen. Six Plates, price £3 3s.

1. THE STARTING FIELD.
2. WATTLE FENCE WITH A DEEP DROP.
3. IN AND OUT OF THE LANE.
4. THE WARREN WALL.
5. THE BROOK.
6. THE RUN IN.

FORES'S HUNTING SKETCHES. (The Right and

WRONG SORT.) Showing a Good and Bad Style of going across Country. After
H. ALKEN, Sen. Six Plates, price £3 3s.

1. HEADS UP AND STERNS DOWN.
2. A GOOD HOLD OF HIS HEAD.
3. A CUT AT THE BROOK.
4. CLERICAL AND LAY.
5. A CUSTOMER, AND HOW TO GET RID OF HIM.
6. THE FARMER'S FIELD OF GLORY.

FORES'S SERIES OF THE MOTHERS. After J. F.

HERRING, Sen. Price 7s. 6d. each.

1. HACK MARE AND FOAL.
2. CART MARE AND FOAL.
3. DUCK AND DUCKLINGS.
4. HEN AND CHICKENS.
5. SOW AND PIGS.
6. THOROUGH-BRED MARE AND FOAL.
7. DRAUGHT MARE AND FOAL.
8. COW AND CALF.
9. HUNTING MARE AND FOAL.

FORES'S RACING SCENES. After J. F. Herring, Sen.

Price 21s. each.

1. ASCOT.—The Emperor, Faugh-a-Ballagh, and Alice Hawthorn, Running for the Emperor's Plate, value 500 sovs.
2. YORK.—The Flying Dutchman and Voltigeur Running the Great Match for 1000 sovs. a-side.

FORES'S CELEBRATED WINNERS. After J. F.

HERRING, Sen., and others. Price 21s. each.

1. THE HERO, with John Day, Sen., and Alfred Day.
2. THE FLYING DUTCHMAN, with J. Fobert and C. Marlow.
3. TEDDINGTON, with A. Taylor and Job Marson.
4. BRUNETTE, the celebrated Steeple-Chase Mare.

FORES'S COACHING INCIDENTS. After C. C. Hen-

DERSON. Price £4 10s. the set of Six.

1. KNEE DEEP.
2. STUCK FAST.
3. FLOODED.
4. THE ROAD v. THE RAIL.
5. IN TIME FOR THE COACH.
6. LATE FOR THE MAIL.

FORES'S COACHINGS. After J. W. Shayer. Price

21s. each. UP HILL—Springing 'em. DOWN HILL—The Skid.

FORES'S ROAD SCENES. (Going to a Fair.) After

C. C. HENDERSON. Price 15s. each.

1. HUNTERS AND HACKS.
2. CART HORSES.

LEFT AT HOME. After R. B. Davis. Price £1 11s. 6d.

Represents a fine stamp of Hunter, and Hounds of perfect form, excited by the sound of the huntsman's horn.

LONDON: PUBLISHED BY MESSRS. FORES, 41 PICCADILLY, W.

SHIPPERS SUPPLIED UPON LIBERAL TERMS.

ESTABLISHED 1838.

GILBERT KEMP,

Contracting AUCTIONEER and Mortgage BROKER,

57 & 58 CHANCERY LANE, LONDON, W.C.

GILBERT KEMP begs to inform Merchants, Shippers, and others, that his

NEW Spacious PREMISES at the COMMERCIAL DOCKS

will shortly be Open for the Assignment of all kinds of Goods for Auction or Private Sale.

ESTIMATES

sent by Return of Post for holding Auction Sales in any part of the United Kingdom.

FORES'S
SPORTING NOTES & SKETCHES.

A QUARTERLY MAGAZINE.

No. 3. OCTOBER 1884. PRICE 2s.

CONTENTS.

LONDON :
PUBLISHED BY MESSRS. FORES, 41 PICCADILLY.

SIMPKIN, MARSHALL, & CO.

9

FORES'S SPORTING NOTES AND SKETCHES.

Opinions of the Press.

'FORES'S SPORTING NOTES AND SKETCHES, a new quarterly magazine, published by Messrs. Fores of Piccadilly, is brightly written by experts in the several divisions of outdoor sport—hunting, shooting, fishing, and cricket; but the charm of the first number is in the spirited, life-like pencillings by that chief of graphic sportsmen, Finch Mason. Seven characteristic designs from his hand, as sure of catching a likeness as his namesake Finch of wicket-keeping fame was of catching a ball that came in his way, illustrate four of the half-dozen literary contributions, one of which, the last, is the artist's own. His cross-country sketches go without saying. The two which embellish Mr. Heron's paper, "A Long Way to Covert," are as good as anything that John Leech ever turned out. The caricature—for such it is, though within the limits of becoming mirth—which represents Monsieur Alphonse equipped for a bear-hunt in the Pyrenees, is irresistible. In "A Famous Match" the likenesses "all over" of Archer and Cannon, with various thumb-nail portraits thrown in, are superlatively true to form, feature, and expression. But finest of all is the character sketch of old Joby, dealer in buns and jam, and umpire at cricket. "Young Nimrod at Eton," written and illustrated by the same hand, is a fresh and lively contribution, full of animal spirits and shrewd reminiscences. Mr. R. M. Alexander, in his illustration to the article on "Thames Trout-Fishing," shows himself well up in his theme. Altogether, the magazine starts with a fair breeze on the sea of public favour.'—DAILY TELEGRAPH.

'MESSRS. FORES, of Piccadilly, have just issued a new quarterly sporting magazine, which they have designated *Sporting Notes and Sketches*, and the opening number fully bears out their title. Hunting, fishing, shooting, racing, are all treated in what may be called a bright, taking way, and, in addition, each article is illustrated by some really clever and characteristic full-page sketches, which are for the most part spirited and realistic. No less than seven of the sketches are from the hand of Mr. Finch Mason, who also supplies a very amusing story of, shall we say, pre-university life, called "Young Nimrod at Eton." The sketch of the college umpire given with this story is really excellent, and decidedly one of the best in the magazine. Mr. Mason has given us "Joby," as he is called, to the life. To our mind the really best sketch in this number is the single one supplied by Mr. R. M. Alexander to "Thames Trout-Fishing," written by that well-known fisherman, Mr. J. P. Wheeldon, a supplier of piscatorial literature to many papers and magazines of the present day. Mr. Watson tells the story of the meeting of those two equine wonders, Bend Or and Robert the Devil, in what he may certainly call their "Famous Match." "Orange Blossom," the celebrated poetic tipster of *Bell's Life*, contributes some racing lore, which he terms "Full Forty Years Ago." A humorous account of "A Day's Shooting in the Pyrenees," by a couple of *voyageurs* on their way back from the East, is not at all dull reading; and the hunting article is from the pen of Mr. A. Heron, and is entitled "A Long Way to Covert"—capital reading for a railway journey.'—THE FIELD.

'SPORTING NOTES AND SKETCHES, published quarterly, by Messrs. Fores of 41 Piccadilly, is to hand. This well-designed and got-up little book, and the eight illustrations by Finch Mason and R. M. Alexander, are most admirable, and remind us forcibly of Leech and Doyle. Finch Mason's horses in particular are horses, and one seems to know instinctively how they are going to "negotiate" their next fence. We can only say that in the story, "A Day's Shooting in the Pyrenees," we have had an almost similar experience ourselves; and the figure in the foreground is an old acquaintance of ours, and by no means overdrawn. We heartily commend the book.'—UNITED SERVICE GAZETTE.

'FORES'S SPORTING NOTES AND SKETCHES.—This is a new venture, which seems likely to be a successful one, an illustrated sporting magazine to be published quarterly by Messrs. Fores, 41 Picca-dilly. The contents of No. 1 include a hunting sketch by Mr. A. Heron, called "A Long Way to Covert," with two pictures tinted, full pages, by Mr. Finch Mason, who, indeed, has done all the illustrations except one fishing picture by Mr. R. M. Alexander. "A Day's Shooting in the Pyrenees" forms an excuse for the introduction of the conventional French "sportsman." "Orange Blossom" gossips very pleasantly of the Turf "Full Forty Years Ago." Mr. Wheeldon contributes a fishing paper, and Mr. Alfred E. T. Watson, in an article called "A Famous Match," compares the careers of Bend Or and Robert the Devil, including a description of their race for the Epsom Gold Cup. Mr. Watson does not seem to be quite satisfied yet that Bend Or is Bend Or. In hitting off the likenesses of well-known racing men Mr. Finch Mason has been singularly successful, in spite of the smallness of his sketches. A very cheery sketch, "Young Nimrod at Eton," by Mr. Finch Mason, concludes an excellent number.'—ILLUSTRATED SPORTING AND DRAMATIC NEWS.

'FORES'S SPORTING NOTES AND SKETCHES.—Seldom has a candidate for public favour made such a good first appearance as this new quarterly magazine, published by Messrs. Fores, the well-known sporting printsellers of 41 Piccadilly. There is not a dull line between the two covers, and the illus-trations by Mr. Finch Mason are quite beyond the sporting pictures which are usually to be found in pages meant for sportsmen. Indeed we may say that few artists in black and white can compete with Mr. Mason in the delineation of the horse, and the spirit with which he contrives to invest his animals while in movement reminds us of the drawings of John Leech, whose humour he also seems to have caught. The literary merits of the magazine are of a high order, as may be guessed by a mere reference to the title-page, for we have contributions from Mr. Alfred E. T. Watson, Mr. J. P. Wheeldon, Mr. A. Heron, the author of "The Tommiebeg Shootings," Mr. Finch Mason, and "Orange Blossom," who gives us one of those pleasantly written chatty articles on sporting lore that almost compel one to become *laudator temporis acti*. The merits of the new magazine are undoubted, and if Messrs. Fores will but keep to the standard shown in the first number, *Sporting Notes and Sketches* should be a great and permanent success.'—BELL'S LIFE.

'JUST on going to press we received an advance copy of the first number of *Fores's Sporting Notes and Sketches*. Of the sporting tales and essays by Messrs. A. E. T. Watson, Heron, Finch Mason, "Orange Blossom," and others, we will not say anything till next week; but we will remark that the illustrations, of which there are eight, all by Mr. Finch Mason, are amongst the best pictures from the field that have been issued for many a long day. These drawings, which abound in portraits of well-known sporting men, are quite stirring. They are reproduced in black and white by a most effective method, and for the sake of these pictorial sketches alone the number is worth more than the florin asked for it.'—COUNTY GENTLEMAN.

' FORES'S SPORTING NOTES AND SKETCHES.—We have received the first number of Messrs. Fores's, the well-known sporting-print publishers of Piccadilly, new quarterly sporting magazine, which contains some spirited articles, the first of which is "A Long Way to Covert," by A. Heron, which is certainly amusing. "A Day's Shooting in the Pyrenees," by the author of "The Tommiebeg Shootings," is in the style which may be expected. "Thames Trout-Fishing," by J. P. Wheeldon, beautifully illustrated by R. M. Alexander, is a very good article. "A Famous Match," by Alfred E. T. Watson, on which subject the author is quite at home, is cleverly written, and so is the last article, "Young Nimrod at Eton," by Finch Mason, who is as good with his pen as he is with his pencil. This number contains several full-page sketches by him in his well-known and characteristic style. The present number is certainly what the proprietors claim for it, the first instalment of a high-class magazine.'—LAND AND WATER.

' FORES'S SPORTING NOTES AND SKETCHES.—Messrs. Fores, of 41 Piccadilly, have issued the first number of their new quarterly magazine. It is excellently printed and illustrated by several charming sketches by Finch Mason, which are alone worth the value of the number. The contributors include Messrs. A. Heron, J. P. Wheeldon, A. E. T. Watson, Finch Mason, and the author of "The Tommiebeg Shootings." The articles are all well written, and there is not a dull page in the magazine.'—THE SPORTSMAN.

' A VERY high-class magazine, called *Fores's Sporting Notes and Sketches*, is being published quarterly by Messrs. Fores, of Piccadilly. The illustrations by Finch Mason are on a scale not often attempted in this class of work, whilst the names of "Orange Blossom," J. P. Wheeldon, and Alfred Watson, signed to articles in the first number, which is now before us, speak for the literary merit of the publication.'—SPORTING TIMES.

' FORES'S SPORTING NOTES AND SKETCHES.—This new magazine, to be published quarterly, has made its first appearance, and bids fair to form a valuable and welcome addition to high-class sporting literature. Finch Mason has so ably proved himself a master of the sketching art, that his name needs only to be mentioned in proof of the excellence and originality of the illustrations. Hunting, racing, fishing, shooting, and cricket, have capitally written stories devoted to them, and A. Heron, Alfred E. T. Watson, J. P. Wheeldon, and "Orange Blossom," are names which will guarantee the respective subjects being done justice to. We heartily wish *Fores's Sporting Notes and Sketches* the success to which it is entitled.'—SPORTING LIFE.

' FORES'S SPORTING NOTES AND SKETCHES is the title of a new quarterly magazine, published by Messrs. Fores, the well-known sporting printsellers of 41 Piccadilly, London. The calibre of the contributions to this new candidate for popular favour may be easily inferred from the names of the contributors. A. Heron furnishes an excellent paper, entitled "A Long Way to Covert;" the author of "The Tommiebeg Shootings" supplies "A Day's Shooting in the Pyrenees," and the accomplished "Orange Blossom" discourses on things that happened "Full Forty Years Ago," telling us in that pure English prose for which he is as famous as for the gracefulness of his verse, how he just missed "tipping" Caller Ou in *Bell's Life* for the St. Leger she won, and thereby rendering himself famous—at least for a day. J. P. Wheeldon is always at home in describing feats of piscatorial skill, and the votaries of the rod and reel will find him at his best here, discoursing of "Thames Trout-Fishing." "A Famous Match," by E. T. Watson, is a graphic description of the grand race between Bend Or and Robert the Devil for the Epsom Cup of 1881, introduced by an allusion to the great race the two horses made for the Derby of the previous year, and the sensational objection to the winner which followed. It is astonishing how many people still believe that Bend Or was the son of Clemence, and not of Rouge Rose at all; and their argument certainly derives some force from the fact that Garb Or, who ought to be own brother to Bend Or, is not the least like him, but is the model of Tadcaster, who was credited to Clemence, but was said to be the real son of Rouge Rose. Nobody supposes for a moment that the Duke of Westminster's servants, much less the Duke himself, wilfully lent themselves to a fraud that could not benefit them in the slightest degree; nevertheless, there is a strong suspicion abroad that there may be some truth in the statements of the discharged groom, and that the colts may have got "mixed up" somehow either in the stable or the paddock. "Young Nimrod at Eton" is a very amusing paper by Finch Mason, whose facile pencil also furnishes the eight full-page illustrations with which the number is embellished. These are all spiritedly drawn in the style which "Phiz" made familiar to the last generation of sportsmen in his *Racing and Chasing*, and the tone of the paper on which they are printed—a yellowish sage-green—gives them a very attractive appearance. Judging by this initial number, we can honestly say that the new sporting quarterly is full of promise, and we heartily wish it every success.'—SPORTING CHRONICLE, MANCHESTER.

' FORES'S ILLUSTRATED SPORTING MAGAZINE is a new candidate for public favour, and we venture to predict that it will be extremely popular. R. M. Alexander, the name of one of the artists, is new to us, but a man who can draw so well, and whose touch is so delicate, and yet so full of vigour, is sure to make his mark. The American magazines are so far ahead of us in the matter of illustrations that we gladly welcome a sketch as spirited and as graceful as that of Mr. Alexander.'—SOCIETY.

' FORES'S SPORTING NOTES. (Messrs. Fores, 41 Piccadilly.)—This interesting magazine is to hand, and we have nothing but the very highest praise to award to it. The letterpress is very good throughout, and the eight tinted full-page illustrations by Finch Mason are, of course, admirable. There ought to be a very brilliant future for this new magazine.'—SHOOTING TIMES.

11

MESSRS. FORES'S

SPORTING & FINE ART PUBLICATIONS.

THE NIGHT TEAM, by C. Cooper Henderson, forms
Plate 6 of the celebrated Series of Fores's Coaching Recollections, and shows the
night 'Screws' being 'put to,' the duck-toed Coachman looking to the harness,
whilst the Guard affixes the lamps. This is replete with 'character,' and one of
the best of the Series.
Coloured Engraving, 26½ by 17½ inches, £1 1s.

THE FIRST DAY OF THE SEASON, by Cecil Boult,
introduces us to a charming young lady on a well-bred chestnut, preceded by
her father on a clipped bay, who is opening a gate into a lane in which are the
Huntsman, Whips, and Hounds.
Coloured, 19½ by 8½ inches, £2 2s.

THE END OF A LONG RUN, by Basil Nightingale,
Companion to above, presents us with the ultimate of the Noble Sport, 'The
Death of the Fox,' who has just been rescued from the Pack with Brush, Pads,
and Mask intact, the former doubtless intended for the Lady on the well-bred
Chestnut, which forms the centre of the picture. The Huntsman's Bay and
Hounds possess quality and character.
Coloured, 19½ by 8½ inches, £2 2s.

THE SPORTSMAN'S DREAM, by R. M. Alexander,
represents a tired and sleeping Sportsman reclining in his easy-chair before a
comfortable fire, dreaming of the following Sports, which are cleverly depicted in
the wreaths arising from his half-smoked pipe, viz., Hunting, Yachting, Coaching,
Pigeon Shooting, Billiards, Golf, Deer Stalking, Grouse Shooting, Steeple
Chasing, Salmon Fishing, Boxing, Racing, Polo, and Cards.
Coloured, 14 by 11 inches, £1 1s.

SALMON FISHING, by W. Brackett, in four subjects,
entitled 'The Rise,' 'The Leap,' 'The Struggle,' 'Landed,' are clearly the work
of a Salmon Fisher, and being replete with artistic finish, will surely commend
themselves to lovers of the sport.
Coloured, 11 by 8 inches, £1 1s. each, or £3 13s. 6d. the Set of Four

SHOOTING, by Basil Bradley, in four subjects, viz.
Partridge, Grouse, Wild Duck, and Woodcock, will prove acceptable to all
'gunners.' Dogs, game, and sportsmen are thoroughly well delineated by one
who is evidently master of the 'business.'
Coloured Engravings, 23⅝ by 14¾ inches, £1 1s. each, or £3 3s. the Set of Four.

'DOLCE CON ESPRESSIONE,'

By J. WATSON NICOL,

Is in this Artist's happiest vein of humour. Two Court Jesters in
motley garb, with cap and bells, are beguiling the tedium of their ordinary avocations with a vocal and instrumental duet, and the admirable
soul-wrapt expression of their faces is inimitably given as they are discoursing a passage 'dolce con espressione.'
COLOURED, 17 by 12 inches, £3 3s.; UNCOLOURED, 15s.

PUBLISHED BY MESSRS. FORES, 41 PICCADILLY, LONDON, W.
12

see page 110.

FORES'S
SPORTING NOTES AND SKETCHES.

A REMINISCENCE OF THE DEVON AND SOMERSET STAG-HOUNDS.

By H. H.

HERE is the man, who, having enjoyed stag-hunting, does not look back upon the days spent amongst the spreading heaths and coombes of Exmoor with pleasure, and revel in the remembrance of the glorious sport he has seen with the wild red deer? Novelists have sought therefrom incident and subject, and it has furnished at least one poet with a theme for some of his most charming verses.

Now that the glorious bright autumn days have come again, let me (although no longer able to be there in person) endeavour to recall some incidents of the chase that have roused my blood and made my pulse beat quicker in years gone by. Let us take a clear but fresh morning in September, and station ourselves on Cloutsham Ball, where we shall find many a well-known face, come not merely to look on, but to participate in the glorious sport as long as they possibly can. What a scene is before us as we stand on the Ball itself, and look across the deep Horner Woods to Leigh Hill on the one side and the North Hill on the other, beyond Hollow Coombe, where the woods of Holnicote and Selworthy (there, by the way, a good deer is said to harbour) as well as Bratton Ball are half-hidden by filmy mist, which, driven by a slight east wind, is sweeping towards Porlock Bay, and for a time settling over the Severn Sea, leaving us canopied by the clear blue sky, dotted here and there with soft, fleecy clouds, to light up the nearer landscape of

> 'Promontories, gleaming bays,
> A universe of Nature's fairest forms,
> Proudly revealed, with instantaneous burst,
> Magnificent, and beautiful, and gay.'

While, if we turn our heads, behind us is the bold outline of
Dunkery Beacon, towering seventeen hundred feet above the
sea level, where blazed the signal fires of the dreaded Doons
of Badgeworthy, whose haunts we are presently to explore.
Below it lies the thick gorse covert of Sweet Tree, beloved of
hinds and their calves; and a good sportsman, who knows all
their haunts, has told us as many as twenty of them may probably be harbouring in it at one time. Close in our rear is the
farm of Cloutsham, where Mr. Bermingham (steward to Sir
Thomas Dyke Acland, who preserves the deer so strictly in
these parts) dispenses hospitality to all, while the tufters are
at work and the pack kennelled in his out-buildings. How
many a well-known form, as we look round in fancy, graces
the scene! some dismounting to stable their horses ere making
their way to test the quality of Sir Thomas's bread and cheese
and cider, others mounting stout cobs and ponies to take part
in the 'tufting,' or chatting with the fair ones of the West, some
merely in carriages to watch proceedings; but there are others
who can show us the way across the moor if hounds run.
Alas that so many can only be seen in fancy, for the happy
hunting-grounds of this world shall know them no more!

Make way there at the gate in the corner! Here comes
'Little Jack Babbage' on his old chestnut, with the tufters and
Arthur Heal, keenest and most energetic of whips, to help him
rouse the old stag that Blackmore has harboured in the Hollow
Coombe below. Best of servants and most civil of huntsmen is
Jack Babbage, who never was the worse for liquor, or wore
trowsers but once in his life, and who, while he hunted the
Devon and Somerset, was never known to beat his horse in
the longest day or hardest run. We see away in the left
corner of the field the stalwart figure of Mr. Fenwick Bissett
(who may fairly be termed the saviour of stag-hunting,
so much did he do for it during his five-and-twenty years'
mastership), standing on the left bank, glass in hand, to view
a warrantable deer away. Better not to speak to him now,
kind and genial as he is at other times; his whole soul is con-
centrated on the chase as soon as the 'tufters' are at work,
and he likes not interruption at such times. When the pack
are laid on, welter weight as he is, you will see Sunbeam,
Chanticleer, or Digby Grand, taking him along well in the van.
Alas that such a man should ever die and be written of as
one who was! About a hundred yards from him comes within

our range of vision *the* best sportsman of his day in broad England—a fact none will deny when we name the Rev. Jack Russell,
beloved alike by prince and peasant. Talking with him are three
fair sisters, who know their way across the moor as well as
any one, and old stag-hunters will at once recognise them as
the Misses Taylor of those days. Miss Kingslake, dismounted,
is chatting with the merry and kind-hearted 'Peter' Dene on
one side and Whyte Melville on the other, while hard by are
Mr. Granville Somerset, Mrs. Somerset, also Miss Leslie, and
other ladies. Mr. Williams of Barnstaple, as good an agri-
culturist as he is sportsman, as he holds his Blair Athole
chestnut in hand, is probably exchanging notes with Mr. Halse,
one of the keenest farmers in the country, on either farming
or sport, while you may lay your life that J. Joyce, Para-
more, and Snow of Oare, are talking far more of deer than
sheep ; and the first-named soon leaves his companion and trots
away down the Ball with Mr. Froude Bellew, to join in the
work of 'tufting.' Mr. Warren, the Hon. Secretary, is talking
to a youth who some day is to be Master (Lord Ebrington) ;
and Dr. Collyns, of Dulverton, has his grey hard by that
carriage-full of ladies, and is making as good use of the time
spent in tufting as any one. Mr. Knight of Simonsbath, to
whom Exmoor belongs, comes up late on something that looks
like galloping, you may be sure, and we wonder whether it has
any of the old 'Dongola' blood in its veins or not.

By Jove! they have found already, and the tufters are
rattling away up the coombe to a right merry tune. No more
time to see who is present, for one and all are making a rush
for their horses. Small need for it as yet though, for there goes
a beautiful hind across the heather to our right, and already
Mr. Bellew and John Joyce are galloping their hardest to stop
and cut off the tufters. A tough job they have, too, for that
lemon-and-white bitch is wondrous keen on the line, and takes
a deal of rating before she will give it up and go to draw
again. But Arthur Heal has now joined the others, and getting
the three couple in hand, takes them back at what looks like
a very break-neck pace down that steep path to join Jack
Babbage and the couple which did not come away in Horner
Wood. Another half hour is devoted to cigars and gossip.
Mr. Bissett's countenance wears a more serious expression than
before, although Blackmore assures him there is a right heavy
deer in the wood, and is trying to point out the very place in

which he harboured him. He might perchance get a somewhat
energetic answer, did not a burst of hound music at the moment
tell us that another deer was roused ; and Arthur Heal's 'view
halloo!' as he views him lets us know that a warrantable deer is
on his legs at last. A short ring or two in covert, and then
' There he goes!' bursts from the assembled multitude, as a
deer is seen on the sky-line crossing Leigh Hill. The Master
brings his glass to bear on him in a moment, and shouts with a
voice that can be heard across the coombe,' A young male deer !'

Arthur luckily gets to their heads before the hounds break
covert, Babbage's horn brings them back like lightning, and in
a few seconds 'the old stag,' who has roused the young deer
and lain down in his place, is on his legs once more and
speeding over the open. Mr. Bissett is the first to view him,
and this time he shuts up his glasses, muttering, ' All his rights!
brow, bay, and tray, two upon top one side and three the other,'
as he turns to mount his horse. Arthur is already far away
with the tufters, and Babbage comes up the hill as hard as he
can rattle for the pack. Soon he is on a fresh horse, and the
great five-and-twenty inch hounds, all anxious for the fray,
swarming round him, and away he goes, through fields and
narrow lanes, in the direction of Stoke Pero, to 'lay on,' with
the impatient field making all the haste they can after him.

When Stoke Pero Common is reached, Arthur is seen there
awaiting our coming with the tufters. In a moment he has exchanged his tired horse for a fresh one. The eager pack on
being let go swoop down upon the line, and the next moment
every one is racing across heather up to their horses' knees,
scattering the rosy blossoms in a shower around them as they
go. Who has time to think of either heath or blossom now,
or aught else for that matter, save to keep as near the
fleeting vision of hounds before them as they can ?   No
slight task is it, for how gradually, if silently, they steal
away ; the lengthening file of itself tells the pace they are
going, did not the quick stroke of the thorough-bred one under
you, as he lays down to his work, show that it is no mere
exercise canter he is taking, and you feel that you would have
to ask him a serious question to range up alongside those
leading hounds, who on their part have no time for talking.
Thus the chase progresses for a mile or two, when, as the pack
are sweeping down into the coverts in the bottom, a brace of
deer are seen climbing the ascent of the other side and setting

their heads straight for the moor—one our hunted deer, who
had there waited for us when the tufters were stopped, and
another nearly as good, who, being disturbed by the tumult of
the advancing chase, has joined him. It is such a sight as is
seldom seen, and not likely to be soon forgotten by those who
are lucky enough to witness it. Wild hills all around, purple
with heather, the woods, down the midst of which a brawling
stream ran, just putting on their beauteous autumn garb, the
black game rising from every holt and hollow, hounds and
horsemen in the foreground, and on the opposite hill the two
wild red deer in all the pride of their full rights, not contending,
as is their wont at this time of the year, in direful battle, but
speeding side by side, like brothers in difficulties, from a
common foe. Away on the sky-line shaggy ponies, almost
as wild as the deer themselves, hastening from the strangers
who interrupted these vast solitudes ' with hark, and whoop, and
wild halloo,' the whole scene strangely recalling Sir Walter
Scott's beautiful description in *The Lady of the Lake.* Quick
as thought Arthur Heal is round the pack to stop them, and a
few who are with the Master on the other side of the coombe
make a vain endeavour to separate the deer. It is useless, however, and a good sportsman on our right says, ' There are twelve
miles certain before we take either one or the other, and
probably before we view them again,' as they disappear over the
crest of the hill, and those who had endeavoured to separate
them draw rein in despair. Soon the signal is given to lay on once
more, and away go the pack across the old camp at Nutskull,
which tradition asserts to have been the stronghold of a tribe of
ancient Britons, or some of those old-world gentry who made a
coat of paint serve instead of broadcloth ; at least, that is how
we understood the gentleman who volunteered some information
on the subject. But with hounds running on abreast, high scent,
there is little time to attend to archæological conversations, and
we must plead guilty to caring more for getting a front place at
the moment than for all the camps in the universe, and those
who made or inhabited them into the bargain. What a wilder-
ness of hill and heath opens before us as we press forward on
the line in the direction of Aldermans Barrow, and vividly we
realise Charles Kingsley's description of such a scene, where he
says, ' Nay, I never rode with those stag-hounds, and yet I can
fill up his outline for him wherever the stag was roused. Do
you think he never marked how the panting cavalcade rose and

fell on the huge mile-long waves of that vast heather sea; how one long brown hill after another sunk down greyer and greyer behind them; and how the sandstone rattled often beneath their feet as the great horses, like Homer's of old, "devoured up the plain," and how they struggled down the hill-side through bushes and rocks, and broad, slipping, rattling sheets of screes, and saw beneath them stag and pack galloping down the glittering, the shallow, glittering, river-bed, throwing up the shingle, striking out the water in large glistening sheets?'

The remembrance of this passage enhanced the pleasure of that wild chase in one bosom at least amongst the 'panting cavalcade.' As each hill was reached and mounted, a short Parthian glance revealed two lengthening lines, far back as the eye could reach, and extending like a telescope. Luckily for us our mount is a good one, and we espy just before us a guide in whose knowledge we trust reliantly; for, believe us, Exmoor is not for the novice to traverse unpiloted if he would escape grief and disaster, and sleep safe in his own bed at night. There he goes! That tall, slim man, who gallops so confidently o'er heath and rock, is no other than the owner of Exmoor, and we may well trust our fate to his guidance. Lucky, indeed, that we do so, for a bog soon intervenes between our division and the pack as they sweep away to the right, at such a pace that the Rev. Jack Russell, who is about the last man in the country to despair, exclaims, in anything but hopeful accents, 'They'll run right away from us! we shall never see them again to-day!' And even Jack Babbage, who is out of luck like the rest of us, is fain to take unusual liberties with his chestnut not to lose sight of them altogether. How we envy those who are stretching away for the dread-looking range of hills in the distance, and fancy we can recognise their outlines, and see who they are! Fancy, indeed, it is; though, as Nimrod says, 'we could name them all.' Arthur Heal is as surely to the front as the sun sets in the west; Froude Bellew comes hard on his track; and we could wager our birthright that John Joyce on Tufter, Chorley on the game old brown mare, and Halse on the chestnut, are well within hail. Neither are the Misses Taylor, Miss Kingslake, or the Dulverton Doctor, out of the hunt. But where is the Master? Reader, trouble not your head for him; in spite of the twenty-stone handicap in the saddle, one of the cracks we have named will turn up with him in the right place at the right moment, just when his guiding hand is most wanted.

'Surely the Parson is right, and they will run away from us, and the others as well!' we eventually exclaim ; ' for no men and horses can cross those hills and live with hounds.' Still, on they go ; horseman after horseman appears on the sky-line, and fades from view—where ? into the valley of the Doons ; that is, Badge-worthy, before us. Forward goes our pilot, confident, as if treading the walks of his own garden ; and probably he knows the ground quite as well. Up a steep incline, down the face of a hill like the side of a house, twisting and turning, through boulders, holes, precipices, and beds of scree we go, galloping, sliding, all but falling at times, yet ever following, as it appears, madly in the track of our pilot. Not a hound to be seen, not a halloo to be heard. Short through a bridle-gate in a stone wall he leads us ; down a still more desperate path, and into the bed of a rushing mountain torrent, sometimes shoulder deep, anon barely covering our horses' hoofs, perspiring, breathless, yet never doubting, we go ; up the opposite bank, through more bridle-gates, past a white shepherd's house ; and then he pulls up suddenly under the shelter of a wood on the steep hill-side, and raises his hand for silence. We are all ears in a moment. Yes! surely it must be the baying of hounds that is borne faintly on the breeze. That surely was a view halloo! We are not out of it yet.

' He has taken to soil ; they have just fresh found him, and are bringing him down the water,' quietly observes our guide. ' They will be here in a few minutes ; pray keep quiet, and don't blanch him.' We quickly place ourselves well out of view behind an angle of the covert, and in such a position as not to give the deer our 'wind,' and find, ere waiting many minutes, that Mr. Knight's prophecy is realised. The music of the pack draws nearer and nearer, and then, within a hundred yards of our hiding-place, the two deer break once more into the open. Sharp as has been the burst, they do not so far seem to be very much distressed, but as they started from Stoke Pero so they go away from the home of the Doons side by side like horses in a chariot, and with that long, slinging gallop, which looks so slow, but is in reality so fast. What a turn of luck for us ! We, who had been somewhat out of it at first, were suddenly placed, as the Irish-man would say, ' at the head of the hunt.' And what a country to ride over ! As the deer headed away for Brendon—no fear of bogs there—Whyte Melville (and no man understood the sub-ject better) says, ' Choose a pilot, then—Mr. Granville Somerset

we will say, or one of the gentlemen I have already named—'and
stick to him religiously, till the heather is brushing your stirrup
irons once more. On Brendon you may ride for yourself with
perfect confidence, but on Exmoor you need not be ashamed to
play "follow my leader," only give him room enough to fall.'
Happily Brendon, and not Exmoor, is now before us, and the
leading hounds already straining across the heath, with, if possible, an improved scent, while our nags, thanks to that lucky
nick, are fresher than those which laid close to hounds during
the early part of the run. Yes, we may take a liberty now,
although

> 'Acre on acre the moorland is spread,
> And acre on acre fleets under his tread.'

We know nearly how far it is to Waters Meet, or the sea, and
for one point or the other our deer are certain to make. To be
one of the few who can get and keep a lead anywhere is exciting
enough, and makes most men ride as they will not do at other
times ; but to get a lead over such a country as this, where
there seems no mark, no bound, save the horizon, is exhilarating
indeed when your mount is full of go. Then we feel

> 'The exalting sense, the pulse's maddening play,
> That thrills the wanderer of that trackless way,'

in its full force ; even as does the mariner when his vessel is
going free before the freshening breeze, with not a sign of land
for hundreds of miles. We *are* going now ; the very hounds
themselves begin to string and tail more than is their wont, and
a long half mile or more separates the beautiful Belvoir tan three-
seasoned hound, who has held the pride of place ever since we
left Badgeworthy, from old Nestor, whose sagacity put them
right down the water. 'Never mind, old boy, there shall be
more checks and difficulties yet ere this stag is "set up to bay,"
and your turn will come again.' Ah ! the gay tan has to feather
and swing round for the line at last, and as he does so, three
couple more dash through the gate which Mr. Knight opens in
the boundary fence between one common and another, and are
away before him, while a dozen or so of the first-flight men have
come such a pace as to go through the same opening almost as
soon as we do. Our deer have turned to the left, and gone for
the deep-wooded coombes which surround Waters Meet, so that
for a mile or two we follow them far more by ear than eyesight.
What scenes of beauty they take us through, and how the

sound of hound music reverberates under the arched canopy of
foliage that overhangs every glade! But now we are on the hill-
side once more, where green tracks of short and elastic turf lead
us amidst boulders of grey rock, beds of bracken, and acres of
gorse. Luckily for us it is slow hunting, and only where the
deer have crossed the turf or run a track are the hounds able to
press them as heretofore. Besides, how their numbers have
diminished since they dived into the woodland shades!

'The deer divided at the water,' says a man on a pony, who,
by his appearance, has rather met the chase than followed it.
'Arthur Heal is gone to stop the other lot; the stag you are
on is making for the sea, and you had better get down to
Lynmouth as quickly as you can.' The advice seems good,
as the hounds have disappeared down a hill-side where we certainly cannot essay to follow them. In vain we look round for
our leader, who also has vanished; so, putting the old mare's
head somewhat in the direction of Countisbury, we ride in faith
on the line pointed out to us, and, after much perturbation of
spirit, come to the high road from Porlock to Lynmouth, where
we fall in with other unfortunates, who, like ourselves, have been
thrown out.

They have heard a rumour that the deer is gone to sea, and
that a boat has already been sent out from Lynmouth to capture
and bring him in; and we soon find that the rumour is correct, for
already sturdy arms have brought a boat alongside the swimming deer, captured him, and are fast towing him to shore,
where a small band of sportsmen are waiting at the end
of a run sixteen miles in length, and rather more than an hour
and a half in duration. All those I have named are there to see
him brought in, even the ladies, though many amongst them
bear marks which plainly tell that a run with the Devon and
Somerset is not to be ridden through from end to end without
falls. 'But where are the rest?' we ask; and echo answers,
'Where?' On many a heathy hill, in many a wooded coombe,
will the stragglers and beaten ones be found wending their way
slowly, perhaps sorrowfully, homewards. Let us hope no Exmoor bog holds struggling horse or hapless rider in its tenacious
grip. 'Here they come!' is shouted, as the boat tops wave
after wave as it rushes on to the beach, and, ere many seconds,
he who

'The fate of each element eager to dare,
Had clove through the sea as he clove through the air,'

is ready for the death-stroke. It shall not be dealt, however. He is not a warrantable deer; fair lips plead for his life, and although his hounds deserve him, and he knows after such a run he will do no good in future, but only spoil sport, the gallant Master relents against his better judgment, and orders him to be taken to the forest and turned out again. We then set our horses' heads homewards, and ere our distant hearth is reached the hunter's moon rises bright and clear over the hills, the owls hoot and call to each other across the valleys, and the otter plunges in the mountain stream that brawls down the gorge on our left.

Again, and yet again, over the evening pipe in the autumn twilight we linger in memory on this our first real good run with the Devon and Somerset stag-hounds, and as the reminiscence of it pleases us, it may, perchance, also amuse our readers.

THE OLD CUTTER'S LAST RACE.

By 'AN OLD CORINTHIAN.'

UTTER ahoy!'

There was no response to this hail from off the pierhead at Lamlash, in the island of Arran, on the Frith of Clyde, and the gentleman who had shouted so lustily turned round to his friend (the writer) with the remark, 'There's nobody on board ; but, brown sails or not, I could swear to her amongst a thousand, and she's my old boat the *Peggy!* There's no mistaking that old cock-up stern of hers, like a sea-gull's when riding over the top of a comber.'

'Did you wish to go on board that boat, sir?' was the remark made in a deep bass voice, which startled us somewhat, as it was not that of the piermaster, whom we knew.

The speaker was a tall, broad-chested fellow, fully six feet in height, clad in jersey-blue pilot-cloth trowsers, and had top-boots up to his knees. His beard was short, thick, and like the brent on the sea-shore toughened from long exposure to the driven spray. Above his eye-lashes, which hung down like reef-points, there shone through the windows of his soul an honest, undimmed light, which let you know that he was a good, manly fellow, with little churlishness about him—all straight, indeed, and above-board.

'Well, no,' was the reply from the first speaker, who was the owner of a schooner which lay just ahead of the vessel he hailed, the latter having come in while we were off on a drive to the other side of the island ; 'but I could have sworn that that was an old cutter named the *Peggy*, which belonged to me about six years ago.'

Laying down a stone water-jar which he carried under his left arm, and rubbing his loof as if to clean it on his jersey, the new-comer stepped up smiling, and ' How do you do, sir ? Do I see you well ?' he asked, holding out his hand. 'You don't remember me, sir ?'

' How do you do ?' was the reply, given with as cordial a shake. 'Why, you're the man I sold her to! And it is the *Peggy*, after all !'

'And so you knew the old girl, did you ? though she's given up her gold stripe and her white muslin, and is only a bit fisher lassie. Well, I'm glad of that !'

' Knew her ?' was the reply. ' Bless you, I'll never forget her, sir ! Why, my sister Peg named her ! I sailed in her first race—ay, and sailed in her last one.'

' Not her last one! Excuse me ; not her last one !'

' Well, I dare say you've been trying her against some of these old fishing-smacks, with foresail boomed out on a boat-hook, and all that kind of thing ; but a real right spin round the mark boats and home to Commodore—why, look what her mainsail is like, with a big patch in it, too, and ——'

' That patch could tell a story better than any of your old cups the *Peg* won. No, sir ; she won a good and true race, and put more in our locker in one go than ever she did in your day. But would you mind goin' aboard, sir, for old times ? She's not so well 'off for stores, maybe, as in your time, but there's a spare mug and a pipe.'

My friend was only thirsting for the invitation, for he saw in his old vessel, in which he had spent many of the happiest days of his young life, an old sweetheart. It was indeed, as he expressed it to me afterwards, like renewing after long foreign service an acquaintance with an old flame in widow's weeds that he had once had a flirtation with when she was a sprightly young barmaid.

Sending the dingy, which had been waiting, off to the

schooner—not, however, before whispering some instructions to
be given to the steward, and which we saw were obeyed to the
letter within a few minutes after we had boarded the *Peggy*—
we entered the stranger's boat. Jumping on deck, we waited
till the Grimsby fish-dealer and fisherman—for such he was—
made fast his punt at the stern, and then followed him down
the small companion into what once was a luxuriously fitted
cabin, but was now a kind of sail-hatch and net-locker. The
upper net-railings still remained, as in the old times, though
the cabin seats had all been removed, as well as the locker
arrangements—the yacht, indeed, having been gutted out to
suit her new requirements. The ladies' cabin aft still remained,
but gutted out also, though the shelves for the berth to starboard showed that the owner and captain still retained that
part as his sleeping-place.

'You'll scarce know her so well below,' he said, with a
laugh; 'but velvet cushions, swing tables, and the like, take
too much room for my work—though I put 'em on board yet,
sometimes, and give the missus a sail when trade is slack.'

'Oh, yes, I would know her,' was the reply; 'I would know
every plank of her. Many a night I've sat there in that corner
after a hard-sailed race at Belfast, Kingstown, or Cowes, and
smoked a pipe with good old yachting friends, who have gone
God knows where; but the sight of the old corners makes my
heart quite full. Ay, ay, how time flies, to be sure! I'd rather
sleep on board her here to-night than in the schooner if I
thought somehow to-morrow I was going to race her against
the old boys; but that can never be! What about that last
race of hers, though?'

The skipper, who had produced a small square bottle of rum
from a corner, was about to apologise for having but one glass
on board the ship, when a boat bumped on the side, and in a
few seconds a luncheon-basket, containing bottles, glasses, and
many good things, were handed down, my friend apologising
for taking this liberty, with the explanation, 'Stores are not
too plentiful ashore, I know, and we are well victualled in the
schooner. I know, too, you would have done the same for me.'

'Well, you want to know about the last race the *Peg*
sailed, so I'll just fill up my pipe and then fire away.'

So saying, he flung himself on a bunch of nets in the corner.

'When I bought the *Peggy* from you that day, you will
recollect that I said her racing days were over, and that her

spinnaker and other of her balloon canvas wouldn't be of much
use to me. So I thought ; but I kept them on board, with good
luck, and sent all her fittings ashore. It was the herring business we were after, and herring scales don't improve a vessel's
furniture nohow. The ballast we kept in as it was, though we
had to trim it a little afterwards, and with a little overhauling
she was as staunch a vessel as ever carried a pilot. We unbent
her sails, however, and browned them with " kutch " in regular
fisherman style—not that, as you will say, that does much good ;
but for the class of work we had in view we did not want sails
that would shine in the moonlight.'

'Trawling ?' was the query of *Peggy's* old owner.

The speaker simply nodded.

'Yes. I dare say there were plenty about to tell you as
much at the time ; and some of 'em weren't slow of carrying
the news up to Greenock, to the captain of the gunboat which
was cruising about there, to see what they called " fair fishing,"
as if all herring fishing was not fair so long as you filled your
boat. Well, all sorts of things were said about us. I was " an
ugly unhung East-Coast man, who had to flee for my life for
murdering apprentices," they said, and the *Peggy* was a
" rakish-looking, piratical craft, which had the devil's own luck
in getting the best of a breeze." They never would own to her
superior speed, they were a bit too conceited for that, though
we could leave the best of them hull down in a twenty-mile
stretch.'

'And that she could, with the wind just aft of the quarter.
Oh, I know what she can do !'

The skipper nodded assent and continued :—

'Yes, with a quarter-wind with a whole mainsail there are
few boats will look at her yet. But to get to my story. The
close time came on for herring, and set in, as luck would have
it, when herrings were selling at three prices in the south ; for
the fishing except on the west coast of Scotland, had been
rather a failure that year. No sooner, however, had the close
time set in there—it's abolished now, thank Heaven !—than the
whole Frith was filled with shoals of fish. The sea was, indeed,
almost solid with them from Ailsa Craig up to Inverary ; and as
you may well guess, I was anxious to have as much of them as
I could get. It was a stupid old law was that, for it only applied
to Scotland ; and if a man could get his fish all landed and across
the border at Carlisle, he could defy it and all the Fishery

Board officials in the world. You may guess, therefore, that I kept the *Peggy* pretty busy, and many a hard race we had for it with the cabin full to the skylight of trawled herrings, which we sent off to be cured in the southern market. But the gunboat men had their eyes on us, we knew, for there were always plenty of men to tell them about our movements — lazy drift-net fellows, who were always raising a noise about the effects of trawling, and such-like, and volunteering their evidence to Frank Buckland and the big authorities up in London. However, the old girl had paid her price more than twice over, and I thought I could afford to risk a lot, so we kept at it. Well, we were lying in Black Farland Bay in the Kyles of Bute one late night in autumn; one of our crew had gone done to Rothesay for letters and telegrams by the steamer, and we had to wait for him in that snuggest of snug anchorages on the whole of the Clyde. You see we had to keep ourselves posted up in the gunboat's movements, as well as give the fishermen a hint or two: besides, we didn't know where we might want railway-trucks, or when. About seven o'clock that night we heard a call of "Ahoy!" from the Bute side of the shore amongst the rocks, our man having come overland from Rothesay, laden as he was with provisions. The letters I looked at first, and telegrams and all were to the same effect—markets still rising, and any amount of demand for herrings.

'" And what about Her Majesty's ship *Provider*, Bill? See anything of her?" I said to my man.

'" Well, no; but I heard something," he said; "and I've got something here as I can show you."

'He pulled out one of the little papers of the place, and directed my attention to a little bit of news about what was called "The County Ball." There was not much except that My Lord and My Lady Somebody or other were to be there, and that invitations had been issued amongst others to "the officers of H. M. S. *Provider.*"

'" Ahem! Is she in the Bay, Bill?" I asked.

'" No; but she's expected. Those young figure-head looking fellows, the man as gave me the paper told me, wouldn't be long away; they liked picnicing and dancing better than hunting herrin'-fishers, he said."

'As the ball was fixed for the next night, I lost no time in getting the boat under way. We ran up the loch with a freshening breeze off the land, and next night, with a lot of Tarbert men, were hard at the trawling. There was a young moon in the sky that night, and stars shone out very brightly where there were no clouds. Altogether it wasn't a bad night for the work, more especially seeing that the gunboat-men were all no doubt dancing gaily with the Rothesay lasses. The loch was a kind of big jelly-fish of herrings, and with the phosphorus all shining lovely, it was a fine sight as we hauled the nets in to the *Peggy's* side. We had just sunk her well down, when one of the Tarbert men in Gaelic spoke to one of his mates, and at the same time pointed with his hand. And there, steaming hard and coaling up, was Her Majesty's ship *Provider*, which we had made certain would be lying snugly off Rothesay pier. The trawlers cut adrift, and with our brown mainsail half hoisted we were soon slipping through the water at a nice rate to a strong breeze which was coming off the east shore. Banks of cloud cast a thick shadow over us, and we were in hopes that we would get away with our fish, and leave the Government men to tackle the fellows in the smacks. The moon, however, burst through for a moment, and we were discovered. Round they came after us; and I knew that if ever the old *Peggy* would have to travel it would be that night. The *Provider*, we knew, was anything but fast; in fact, she was about the slowest thing that ever burned coal or turned a paddle: so with plenty of wind, and none of it ahead till we got right out of the loch and into the Sound of Bute, where we could make it fair any way we chose, we were all right. Well, down the land we went, with the boom always having to be eased over a bit to starboard, for somehow the wind was getting more aft as we travelled; and going a fearful pace, with the lee scuppers full foaming and hissing, and behind us the old *Provider*, puffing and thumping away at the water like an old porpoise, and the smoke drifting away to leeward, thick enough to show you that the stokers weren't saving any coal for the picnics.

'" Go on, old girl!" says I to the *Peggy*, "and I'll stand you a new jib."

'And you maybe wouldn't believe me, gen'lemen, but she knew every word I said, just as when I had promised my old woman a bit of head-gear. Down did she lay her shoulder to it like a champion swimmer doing his winning spurt, and the water was hissing away in the scuppers to a rare tune. But all the time it was getting more aft, and I saw that abreast of Skate Island there would be no help for it.

' "Get ready the spinnaker forward there," I shouted ; "and be ready to lower the boom, for we've got to give old Black Smoke the slip."

'The wind at the same time came a little bit more off the land ; so I hauled in through the Sound between the Skate and the mainland, almost scraping the rocks on the little island, which is just big enough to graze a couple of sheep, and no more. Like an idiot the sailing-master of the steamer followed us ; and I can tell you I prayed hard that he would stick the old boat ashore, as they had been closing the least thing on us. They slowed a bit, however, their pilot being afraid ; and so, squaring away the boom to the rigging, we ran out our spinnaker on the port side, and to make certain that it would sit, Old Bill, the heaviest man of my crew, creeps out to the boom end. It was rough work steering her, I tell you, 'twixt watching for a gybe in the puffs, which came aft at times hard enough to give Bill a swing as high as the masthead, and threaten to pitch him over the rigging, and at the same time keep an eye on the old *Provider*. Still we were travelling fast, and, bar accidents, bound to save our bloaters, if not our bacon. The moon was shining out bright at the time, and no doubt giving a splendid view of us running double-winged to our opponents ; and all idea of running up the Kyles and fogging them somehow about Loch Ridun, as I had thought, was out of the question, and in a long channel chase they were bound to catch us. Worst of it, too, the wind was heading ; and Bill was just walking along the boom to the deck, when *whissh* went a lot of spray all over us, and the boat's head swung up just as if the helm had been put hard down. Two seconds and up came a crack from the steamer ; and on looking at the mainsail we saw that a shot had just struck close astern and ricochetted through—a close shave for the old cutter ; good practice and fine work for Charleston in the old blockade-running days, but rather too hot for Clyde. With the sudden swing the spinnaker came in ; and worse, the boom snapped. But the powder had raised our blood, and we were not to be taken. To get the spinnaker on to the bowsprit was not very difficult ; and as we had been going rather off the land to get it draw, we found it sat well. Heading in for Inchmarnoch Island, the *Provider*, which had sent a couple of more shots after us, made certain we were for the Kyles of Bute, and steamed to cross us ; which was all I wanted, for I got hold of a land breeze off the Bute shore which carried me to the Garroch

O dear Jem ! its the old Cobre.

see page 122.

Head, the bold bluff which marks the north entrance to the Clyde. Hauling our wind there, we made for the Tan Sound, which divides the Greater from the Little Cumbrae, and just gybed under the gloomy bluffs of the former when we saw the smoke-drift of the steamer coming round the Garroch.

'"Well, boys," I said, "we've one chance; they'll make after us for Greenock, and we've a leading wind, and a good one for Ardrossan, where we can truck our fish in an hour on the very quay. Shall it be Ardrossan?"

'"Ay, ay, sir; Ardrossan!" was the cry from all.

'And away we went down through Fairlie Roads, past Fife's Yard, where many a smart boat has been built, and round Portincross into Ardrossan.

'Well, sir, to make a long story short, we got to Ardrossan, trucked our cargo, and we were lying sleeping under the quay-walls, with the mainsail drying, when the steamer comes and sends a boat aboard, only to find us without so much as a single herring for breakfast. The young lieutenant chap who was in charge did not say much, but he looked very savage, and couldn't keep his eye off the hole in the mainsail.

'"What did that?" he said, looking at me sharply.

'"Ran herself against a bowsprit," I said.

'"A little too clean for that," was his reply. Then, as he stepped into his boat, "I'm sorry that ball missed you."

'"I'm sorry you missed that ball, Captain," says I; "it would have been nicer dancing with those Rothesay lasses than getting your old steamer licked by a piratical old fishin'-smack.'

'"Let fall," was his call.

'And I heard him mutter something like an oath as he pulled off to the *Provider.*

'Well, sir, I cleared 120*l.* off that night's work; and I don't think, sir, you can say now that you sailed in the old *Peg's* last race.'

The *Peg's* old owner nodded acquiescence, and we rose and were pulled on board the schooner. Next morning, on going on deck, we saw the *Peggy* with a free sheet scudding out of the Sound.

'Good-bye, old girl; good-bye!' was the almost affectionate farewell of the schooner's owner, as he watched her disappear behind Holy Island. 'I shan't see you again; but I cannot forget how my old cutter won her last race.'

A DAY WITH 'JOCK' TROTTER IN MEATH.

By 'Triviator.'

THE simple Saxon who would measure Ireland by the delegates she sends to what Lord Macaulay termed the most aristocratic assemblage in the world—our House of Commons—and conceived that the Pandemonium created by 'the Patriots'—'paid' Patriots *bien entendu*—was a sample of the normal state of society in the 'Green Isle,' would greatly err in his estimate. Even Mr. Trevelyan (who, by-the-by, may in youth have represented his uncle's sapient schoolboy of precocious proficiency), the baited and badgered by day, the tortured and 'questioned' by night, could answer for the brighter side of the gloomy national picture ; and it is to one of the brightest bits of colour and animation in the social life of Ireland I would beg to call the reader's attention,—to a Goshen green and gladsome in the midst of a plague-stricken land of Egypt,—to a bright and cheery oasis, refreshing the heart and senses of the wayfarers through sandy saharas, scorched by the hot breath of the sirocco,—to a pastoral Paradise dedicated to the pursuit of the fox, where Irishmen are really united and the visitor of venatic sympathies is heartily welcomed — where sport is supreme, and the days of King Arthur and his knights, *minus* Launcelot and Queen Guinevere, are in a fashion revived. Let us cross the Meath marches and enter upon this goodly inheritance, for the land is *ours* if our hearts and horses be good enough to take possession of it and master its difficulties ; not, perhaps, to hold in fee or by lease, but to gallop over and cross in the tumult and excitement of the chase.

Before we attempt to give a sketch of a day in Meath with the county hounds it may be advisable to devote a few paragraphs to a description of the country, and to take its bearings as the sailors say ; and we may remark on the threshold that the Meath hunting territory extends far beyond the boundaries of the shire of that name, running up northwards into Cavan and Monaghan, being practically limitless in this direction ; while on the east it joins hands with Dublin and Louth, on the south it stretches

its frontiers into Kildare ; while Western Meath, which formed a
portion of the original palatinate of Hugh de Lacy, the first Suze-
rain of Meath after Strongbow's invasion, and was only separated
from it in the reign of Henry the Eighth, limits it on the west.
The accepted pronunciation of the county might be expressed
phonetically as *Meeth*, but those whose dialect is more Doric than
suits the caste of Vere de Vere, call it *Maith;* and as 'maith' in
the vernacular signifies a level tract of country unaccentuated
by hills or mountains, this word was probably assigned by custom
or conqueror to this rich stretch of eastern prairie land, which
may be described generally as a huge cattle-ranche, whose area
covers nearly a million of statute acres, through which are interspersed, at rather wide intervals, a few towns, a few villages
and hamlets, and a certain number of stately parks and
pleasaunces, where dwell the lords of this rich soil ; this bovine
Bœotia, where the ox is almost as great a fetish as he is still
among the mild Hindoos, though for very different reasons and
with widely differing consequences to man and beast.

The historic Boyne, fed by innumerable becks and brooks,
cuts this huge grazing privilege into two unequal parts; and
it is a moot point whether the Trans-Boyne (or the northern)
hemisphere be or be not superior as a hunting county to the
Cis-Boyne, or southern section. The former is certainly larger
and wilder, but the fields do not cover the same area as on the
Dublin side ; while the fences, if smaller, are naturally far more
numerous, more trappy, and '*intricate.*' The question of merit
and natural advantages will probably remain a very open one
till the end of time, and men will answer it according to their
ideas of hunting, riding, and indeed, to a certain extent, according to the class of hunters they may possess at the time :
for whereas cleverness and handiness are the great desiderata
in the former, boldness, dash, and galloping capacity, are the
characteristics most in request for the latter. Certain it is that
the Dublin side is much the best known, and that its chief
fox haunts are classical in what Byron calls

> ' The court, the camp, the vessel, and the mart.'

A word now about the fences which separate these broad
pastures from each other, and which must be jumped by all
who would fain follow in the wake or by the side of the 'Meath
Minstrels,' for gates are an institution very imperfectly understood here, and as a rule are either stapled up or secured by

bolts and chains (for they are only opened at rare intervals in the year), while their height makes them unjumpable, and *gaps* in a cattle county would be wholly inadmissible.   As a rule, the fences in all Meath are very large.' Timber being scarce and dear, posts and rails are only found near gentlemen's residences and parks ; and public opinion, and a sense that *la chasse oblige*, has vetoed the appearance of wire save in a very few spots ; hence earthworks must be thrown up, and the form they take is that of a huge embankment, with ditches generally brimful of water on *both* sides, or an embankment with a single fosse.   But these ditches are occasionally eight or nine feet in width, and generally deep : the former are known as 'doubles,' the latter as 'singles.' Quickset thorns may or may not render 'the great divide' more repulsive and difficult : on many farms, happily, they do not appear.   Another very common barrier is the rhene, which, unlike its prototype in Somersetshire and Gloucestershire, is almost invariably margined by a small bank, which necessitates that rapid 'changing the feet,' which is the characteristic cleverness of *the* accomplished Hibernian hunter.

In Upper Meath walls and stone-faced banks diversify the jumping programme ; in Lower Meath such barriers are exceptional. Brook-jumping is a necessary accomplishment in a Meath hunter, for the land might be almost christened a land of springs, like Jamaica (Xamaica).

Having said our little say about the county, let us add a paragraph or two about the hounds and their history. Curiously enough, Meath, which combines all the attractions of 'the shires' of England, *minus* their notorious drawbacks and deficiencies, and *plus* ampler extent and a wider horizon, is a comparatively *new* fox-hunting country, hardly fifty years old.   To be sure, there were fox-hounds in Meath, but they were the appanage of a few families, and they could not be called a county institution. Sam Rennell, the Meynell of Ireland, saw the capabilities of this great county, and set to work vigorously to organize its resources, dotting the land with gorse and stick coverts.   For more than twenty-five years he presided over the venatic destinies of Meath, well backed by his countrymen and by all the strangers within his golden gates—by no one, perhaps, more thoroughly than by Lord Spencer and his A.D.C.'s, especially by Bay Middleton and poor 'Chicken' Hartopp. When Mr. Rennell resigned the horn of office Mr. Waller accepted the post of M. F. H., and with Frank Goodall as huntsman the hounds, who had hitherto been anything rather than a high-class pack in appearance, becam greatly improved.   After a few years Mr. Trotter, who, after leaving the 5th Dragoons, settled at Brownstown, near Navan, was invited by the voice of the county to assume the management of the pack which Mr. Waller wished to give up.   He accepted the onerous, if honourable, office ; and after seven years of devotion to the task he may claim the distinction of being at the head of the premier pack of hounds in the world.   Not that half-a-dozen packs in England could not rival them (possibly beat them) for evenness, colour, symmetry, and substance, but they lack opportunity and arena (comparatively), while the hunt-horses of Meath are generally considered to be unrivalled, and the establishment to have approached perfection.

Now for a dash *in medias res*, or a coign of vantage in Dunshaughlin village, about ten minutes to eleven o'clock a.m., for here is the Meath meet, and already there are signs of its being a *monster* one.

Dunshaughlin, a single-street village some eighteen miles from Dublin, is one of several hunting centres, or dépôts (we do not profess mathematical exactness), where men of all nationalities stable their hunters.   The hound-van, a present from Lord Howth, may be seen opposite Julia Murphy's* little hostelry, and precise in their punctuality the M. F. H., with his staff and their A. D. C.'s, a corps of ten men and lads, mounted on well-bred 14-stone hunters (there are no *servants'* horses in the Meath establishment), are close by; in five minutes more the street is ablaze with scarlet, and the coffee-house matinée has begun. Let us glance at a few of the units of this converging hunting host.   On the box of the Killeen drag is the Earl of Fingal, whose grey leaders might be, and probably are, good hunters. His Countess has a hunting-hat on, so she evidently means ' pursuit ' to-day ; and so do the Ladies Plunkett.   Those roving rancheros, the Hon. Horace Plunkett and Alexis Roche, with Mr. and Mrs. de Burgh, fill an ' outsider.'   Major-General Fraser and the Rokeby roans never miss such a tryst with this pack. Kildare has sent a strong contingent, and among them Lord and Lady Kildare, the Ladies Fitzgerald, Captain the Hon. Maurice Bourke, R.N., and the Ladies Bourke, Lord Clonmell, and his brother-in-law, Mr. Percy La Touche.   Sir Thomas and

---

* Alas ! since writing this paragraph that most excellent hostess and kind heart has joined the majority.

Lady Hesketh, Lord and Lady Donoughmore, Mr. and Mrs. Hope-Johnston, may be termed *single-season* hunters; but they have entered to Meath right well.   Lord Cork has eschewed the stag to-day, and turned to fox instead ; and Lord Dungarvan has forsaken Wiltshire for 'Royal Meath,' while Count Zborowski, though the sole representative of the stars and stripes, is a host in himself.   The Guards form a strong detachment, with the Messrs. Luke and Harry White, 'invincibles' over a county ; and Colonel Inigo Jones, Sir Thomas Baker, Major Eardley Wilmot, and two or three more, represent the *état major* of Dublin.   Lord Langford has driven over a party from Summer- hill.   Major and Mrs. Bunbury and Mrs. Stewart Duckett are the Carlow delegates.   Captain Macneil has brought Lord Willoughby de Broke to the meet, and Lord Cole 'has sunk a heat' in Cheshire to take his pleasure, and possibly pick up a hunter or two, in Royal Meath.   Lord Headfort generally keeps to the Trans-Boyne country, but he is here to-day,

> 'Agnosco crines incanaque menta
> Regis Medensis.'

And with him his daughter, Lady Adelaide Taylour.   From Black Castle comes Lord Donoughmore, intent on the 'dramatic illustration' of the gay scene, and with him Lady Donoughmore, brightest star of the Southern Cross galaxy ; while Lady Mow- bray and Stourton and the Misses Preston survey the scene from a waggonette.   There are a couple of Home Rule M.P.'s out, a light weight and a heavy weight ; and the latter's mount, though a very good one, possibly makes more noise in the world than his rider.   'The Royals,' with Mr. Burn Murdoch, are in force ; and so are the 18th Hussars, the 21st, the 5th, and 16th Lancers, represented by Messrs. Orr-Ewing Chetwynd, Brown, and Lord St. Vincent.   The Hon. G. B. Bryan is the sole champion of the 10th Hussars, while the Royal Rifles, the Gunners, and the Line, swell the glad throng, and point the fact that a very fair share of 'the flower of British chivalry' is in the field.   'Man the hermit sighed till woman smiled,' says the bard, and the hermit need not sigh here at any rate, for lovely woman smiles all around, and so devoted to hunting I trow, that possibly not a few of the spinsters would compound for ordinary honeymoon Elysium if given unlimited hunters, a grass county, and the man of their heart for perennial pilot.

Just as the column of march has been formed, Lord Spencer's blue roan team appears on the scene: he has left his cavalry escort a few miles off, and his bodyguard consists only of his staff and personal friends. In another five minutes the collectors of half-crowns have finished their work—the exchequer has gained 18*l.* odd—and a tortuous lane has led some 400 sportsmen and women to a series of large pasture-fields surrounding the famous Poor-house Gorse. It is waving like a troubled sea, and two foxes break away, one heading towards Lagore; the second, the chosen of the pack, points in the same direction; then, bending towards the Poor-house, crosses that *cloaca maxima* the ' Poor-house drain,' which is a sort of 'bottom' with sloping banks. Very deep it is, and some fourteen or fifteen feet wide. It has to be done generally at a stand.

> ' Of the three hundred grant but three
> To make a new Thermopylæ.'

Thirty or forty get over, but only three close to the hounds, and almost on their backs; and these three only saw ' Rantipole' pin poor Reynard as he was jumping the last ditch into Pellattstown Gorse, a mile and a half further to the southward. Ten minutes, and the pace as good as fox, hounds, and horses could make it; 'and who were the three' I will forbear, like the Speaker, from 'naming' on this occasion. The tinta-marre of the chase has driven three foxes fugitives from their furzy fortress of Pellattstown Gorse (Lord Howth's), hence there is no use trying here. So a diminished host pushes on to Rowanstown Gorse, a couple of miles to the southward: it is drawn blank, so, following the hounds and staff, some 200 set off for ' a school' over a decidedly large country, till a very famous gorse (Harry Bourke's) is reached. The hounds, who know it well, rush into it at Press's signal, as if they were already charging a foe. The Freemasons' motto, *'Audi, vide, tace,'* is now the legend of the field, who were full of chatter and chaff ten minutes ago, for music has begun, and in an instant fifty men are jumping simultaneously a small bank and ditch to see the pack streaming away a field in front of them. Two fields, crossed, a meandering little trout-stream now in full spate, arrests attention. It has overflowed its banks, and, save in a corner where the banks are higher, the taking off is somewhat undistinguishable. ' Timber slow, water fast,' is a riding axiom, but not always a wise one, as some thirty or forty realised when struggling in the rapid current. Companions of the Bath now, the Knights of the Garter and other orders mingled in the turbid torrent. Presently, in another mile, the brace of foxes, who had kept close together, separated for strategic reasons, and divided the pack and the field. The Master and First Whip, and a few more, 'followed' one lot, through Hamwood and Ballymacoll to the verge of Carton, the Duke of Leinster's park, where hounds checked, and horses were so dead beat that no aid could be given. The remainder of the pack crossed the Meath line near Dunboyne, and with some fifteen men on good terms with them, fairly wore down their fox beyond Ashbourne, after crossing eight miles of steeple-chase country—Irish miles, too.

The hounds had divided, as we saw just now, and both sections had given good gallops. They met at some cross-road on the route homewards, and very near ' Harry Bourke's ' happy haven for foxes. There was nothing else near, and though it is tying a gorse very high to draw it twice on one day, the occasion was exceptional, the stranger element was unusually large, and not a few had been 'disappointed' in the first two runs, failing to get *off* and succeeding in getting *in.* So with a following reduced to some seventy, of whom a few were on *third* horses, the good gorse was again investigated, and again successfully. Once more brook land is approached, but this time the beck is *not* charged in line, and the result is far more satisfactory to all concerned. Then came a sort of Mesopotamian mile, over which hounds flew as if *coursing* their quarry ; then, *of course,* came a turn, for the pace was too good for even a greyhound fox ; but with the turn no check or pause, as Wood Park was skirted and the Porterstown uplands, where Lord Spencer's viceregal chases are held, were galloped over ; then a swing to the right brings a straggling squadron over the *Fairy House Fields,* well known to all chasing men, and in twenty minutes more seven panting and heaving hunters find themselves jumping or creeping into the Kilrue Lane in time to see Mr. Trotter and Press coming back, for the hounds have run their fox to subterranean safety. *Fifty-eight minutes* by the watch ; but—

> ' Who to sober measurement
>   Time's happy swiftness brings,
> When birds of Paradise have lent
>   Their plumage to his wings ?'

Such is a sample of sport in Royal Meath, a county of

see page 130.

magnificent sport and magnificent distances. And a happy man
was Harry Bourke, for *his* gorse had done its *devoir*, 'and he
was there to see.'

BLACK-GAME SHOOTING ON EXMOOR.

By ' HELWR.'

RCHARD is a gentleman-farmer, young, and not
badly off in respect of this world's goods, and an
enthusiastic sportsman. When he wrote in the last
week of August asking me to come to his place,
Belle Église, on the borders of Exmoor, for a fortnight's trout-
fishing and 'poult-shooting,' I at once resolved to tear myself
away from the all-engrossing pleasure and business of town—to
'leave the busy haunts of men,' and to avail myself of the opportunity of enjoying wild sport such as is, alas! fast becoming
rare in England. I reached the nearest railway-station on the
evening of the 28th of August, and found a dog-cart awaiting
me. The man said that his master could not come, for 'he was
'most mazed wi' villin' catridges.' He further observed that
'' twas only a matter o' vowerteen mile, and us would zune be
theer.' The road lay for the most part over moors—indeed, as
a rule, there was no road at all; but we really did spin along,
and 'us was zune theer,' as he would have said.

I was much impressed by my first view of these moors at
night, while a moon, nearly at the full, illuminated everything
with a light, pleasing yet weird, bright yet shadowy. One could
hardly describe the moors at noon, with a blazing sun in a
cloudless sky shining overhead, and the purple heather, fresh
green bracken, and dark bog patches, all giving forth a vaporous
heat, stretching away far as the eye can see. The varied scents,
the air laden with a suspicion of sea-breeze, the thoughts and
feelings—sad, gay, and tender—called up thereby are known to
many; but they are put into words duly portraying and expressing them by none! Who, then, shall essay to convey, through
the poor medium of written words, the effect produced upon
one's eyes, mind, and heart, by what I saw that night?

After a loud and cordial welcome from my friend the Squire
I was taken into the house, where I was at once struck with the
magnificent oak-panelled walls and roof of the hall—and by
Miss Urchard. I apologise for introducing this young lady into

an account of Black-Game Shooting, although she is pretty
enough to 'make a man throw stones at his grandmother' (as
poor Browne once said) ; but she was so deeply interested in
the sportsmen's comfort and the commissariat, so prolific and
imaginative in preparing lunches, under no matter what difficulties of weather or situation, and, withal, so original and
piquant in her remarks upon sporting topics, that I feel that to
leave her out of my story would be like omitting Falstaff from
the play of *Henry IV.* I do not consider it necessary to describe Miss Urchard's personal appearance and charms. She
has a nose, chin, and a pair of lovely blue eyes, as so many
of our sweet countrywomen have ; but she has, what *all* British
maidens have not, a gay manner, a true and tender heart, an
expression ever varying yet ever charming. (N.B.—I feel it
due to myself, and to her, to state that she is seventeen, and
that the writer's hair and beard have long been grey—moreover,
there are 'incumbrances.') She is, in fine, an exceedingly se-
ductive little maid, and vastly sympathetic with sport and
sportsmen.

The few remaining days of August were devoted to trout-
fishing. On this alluring sport, which my soul loveth right well,
I will not now hold forth ; suffice it to say, that trout figured
on the breakfast-table for several successive mornings, and they
were not groped, netted, nor inveigled in any way other than
by displaying before them certain artificial flies—to wit, the
coachman, red-spinner, and blue upright.

At last the evening before the great day arrived ; and after
dinner Urchard and I smoked on the lawn, watching the sun
setting behind the moors, and sinking to his rest in Barnstaple
Bay, whilst Miss Urchard officiated with the claret-jug in her
usual inimitable manner. The Squire all at once said, 'To-
morrow all England will be shooting partridges. You and I
must make shift with the "poults."' I assured him that I
hankered not after the birds, but considered myself a man to be
envied in my prospects of wild sport with him. 'Early to bed
and early to rise,' was the order. *Very* early I called it ; for we
were to have breakfast at the uncouth hour of four o'clock.
Miss Urchard was far too good a housekeeper not to be at the
breakfast-table to see her 'guns' properly fed and started for
the day's work. She appeared, looking very attractive in a
riding-habit, which caused her brother to exclaim, in his usual
loud, quick way, 'What's that toggery for ? You ain't goin'

shootin', you know, or I shall have you and Helwr gabbling
about music and poetry, Lord Vere de Vere and Beathoven (so
he pronounced it), and frightening all the "poults" out of the
district.' She replied, 'Indeed, I am going; and Mr. Helwr and
I are much too good *sportsmen* to be gabbling about *Beathoven*,
as you call it, when business is on hand.'

We had no distance to walk in order to commence the day's
sport, for the moors surrounded the house and its grounds—
indeed, I could see 'poults' from my bedroom windows.

In the courtyard were assembled about a dozen men, keepers
and beaters, most of the latter being yokels pressed for the
occasion. The 'guns' were four in number, viz., Squire Urchard
and Mr. Helwr, on the premises, and Mr. Twister and Captain
Pole, just arrived on horseback.

We were all good shots, good walkers, and keen sportsmen,
except Twister, who was neither. His fat impeded his walking;
his want of practice rendered him a most poor shot; his early
life and training were not calculated to make him a sportsman.
He had been, in fact, a pig-dealer (Urchard called it pig-*jobber*);
but this humble occupation had been so skilfully and *sharply*
carried on that he was now rich, and owned some extensive
moors adjoining Urchard's. This was the reason why we were
to have the pleasure of his company; for we were to shoot over
the moors of Twister and Urchard. It must be added that the
attraction that drew Twister into company that he knew secretly
derided him, and which induced him to take part in what to him
was tantamount to a spell on the treadmill, was our fair young
hostess.

The 'guns' and attendants now set out in a line nearly a
quarter of a mile in length, with Miss Urchard on her pony in
the rear. We were not to shoot over dogs, but the head-keeper
had two retrievers in leash. I suppose the tract of land we were
going to beat was three or four miles long. It was not divided
in any way that I could see, though Urchard and his men had a
name for every few hundred acres of it. Thus, we were to open
the ball on 'Witty Moor.' A very steep ascent, thickly clothed
with old, tough heather, stared us in the face; and up we
charged in a pretty accurate line. It was exceedingly hard work
thrusting through the stiff, unbending stems of this old 'yeth'
(so the keeper called it), the great heat and abrupt incline not at
all mitigating the labour. I was on the extreme right of the line,
'well forward and bringing round,' according to orders received.

Just before the brow of the hill was reached a great noise of flapping and whirring brought my heart into my mouth and my gun to my shoulder simultaneously. Fifteen birds came back right over us; a quick glance showed that there were only six cocks; we were to 'ware hen.' I fired at the bird I deemed my lawful quarry, and, not making good business of it the first time, I gave him No. 2, which caused him to tower in a manner suggestive of sudden death. I did not hear the others shoot; but on glancing along the line I noticed that every gun was smoking, and, as the 'trievers were let go, I hazarded the supposition that they had not smoked in vain. The head-keeper was saying to Twister, on the extreme of the line—but, owing to the clear air and high elevation, quite audibly to me—' I zaid to 'ee "'ware hen," and yet I zeed 'ee vire at a hen just as if 'ee zingled her out a purpose. Dont'ee du it, zur!' Fortunately the grey hen had gone away unscathed, and so Twister's sin was overlooked. Although my cock had had such a satisfying dose yet he managed to carry over the deep valley behind us, and dropped in the heather halfway up on the opposite slope, probably half-a-mile distant. Before Mr. Keeper had finished admonishing Twister, as above, Beau was splashing through the stream and its adjoining marshy border, and was racing up the slope. His colleague and *uxorcula*, Belle, was in hot pursuit of a winged bird in our immediate front. Soon returned both Beau and Belle, almost at the same time, and each carrying proudly and tenderly a mass of black feathers enclosing the body of a *Tetrao tetrix*. The dogs then took a short journey together, and returned laden as before. Two brace of blackcock for the 'first blaze' and to four 'guns'—one of whom was known to have fired a mere complimentary volley, or *feu de joie*—was not a bad start. Some one must have killed his brace; Mr. Keeper said that honour belonged to his master. It may or it may not have been so, but I do not consider the man's evidence conclusive.

'Forward! forward!' A few minutes' struggling and panting and the ridge is reached. What a prospect presents itself! All seemed inclined to stay a few minutes and 'admire the scenery;' to look across the heathery hills, green slopes, dark, boggy goyals, and rest the eyes upon Barnstaple Bay gleaming in the west, whilst the roar of the ground-swell upon the bar at Appledore was heard, in imagination, suggestively cool. The day's work was hardly commenced, but Twister had had

I zeed it too sd a hu fust au of sr zight the nd a fortune

see page 134

enough ; the eminent ex-dealer in swine, like our dear, dear friend Sir John Falstaff, knight, is 'fat and grows old ;' his valour and endurance (and, indeed, his appearance, habits, and manners) are akin to Sir John's. If he had now spoken some of the well-known words that the 'fat knight' speaks to all the world, he would very aptly have described his position : ' I am as hot as molten lead, and as heavy, too. . . . give me leave to breathe awhile. . . . If I travel but four foot by the *Squire* further afoot, I shall break my wind. . . . Eight yards of uneven ground is threescore and ten miles afoot with me ; and the stony-hearted villains know it well enough. . . . I need no more weight than mine own *internal arrangements.*' (For the last quotation *vide Paraphrased Edition of the Works of the 'Immortal Bard,' for the Use of Dames' Schools,* by J. R. Helwr, Esquire.)

Miss Urchard charitably suggested that the weary sportsman should stay with her, whilst we descended the next slope, floundered through a bog, and then repeated the process we had just concluded. He was only too happy to enjoy her delightful society, and to escape the company of the ' stony-hearted villains,' his male companions: so it was settled that he was to remain with the lady until luncheon time, and help her to arrange that meal in a convenient situation not far away.

Now that we had got rid of the fat man we did not force the pace quite so much ; for it must be confessed that Pole and I had maliciously jumped off at the start at a rate we had no idea of maintaining throughout the day : this we did for Twister's benefit ; the Squire, to whom four, five, or six miles an hour is equally indifferent, of course, kept up. We reached the bottom, called very appropriately ' Soggy Moor,' without moving fur or feather, and were treading gingerly on the edge of the bog, looking carefully for tussocks of rushes, which are always safe footholds, when a sharp cry of ' Mark Duck!' woke us all up most effectually. A mallard rose about thirty yards in front, capping the rushes with his broad, strong wings ; and almost as soon as he was well up, a duck sailed swiftly in his wake. We were standing all in a heap, seeking the firmest ground for our passage of the black, slimy sea, and so no etiquette forbade any of us to shoot. Urchard did not stand on ceremony, but cut the old mallard from sky to bog in very quick style ; and just as I was levelling at the duck, I heard a crack close to my ear, and saw her reeling from the effect of a message from Pole. The mallard was dead, and lay high and dry on a moss-heap ;

but the duck gave Beau and Belle a pretty bit of sport before
she was brought to hand.

We soon got among the 'poults' again; but the wary old
cocks seemed to be away from the pack. At last, just as we
reached a ridge overlooking the trout-stream, to which I have
alluded before, ten or a dozen cocks got up at very long range.
They were, probably, fifty yards away, but did not fly straight
from us. Very considerately, whilst maintaining their distance,
they flew across the line, and we saluted them with six barrels,
and had the satisfaction of seeing a brace and a half fall dead,
whilst one bird got away very hard hit. This bird, upon being
struck, turned outwards from us, and went across the water
towards a moor, which was 'off our beat.' It was very high and
craggy, and the cock seemed as if he would go to the top and
explore the interior beyond. The keeper kept him covered with
the glass, and finally declared that he had dropped 'into a patch
of *yeth* (*i. e.*, heather), but, my dear heart! a mort of a long way
off!' We all sat down and watched him make his way across
the bottom, where he waded through the brook, there being no
bridge near (he called it *burge*), accompanied by his two curly-
coated allies; and, ere long, we saw him struggling up the
opposite rocky steep. The dogs now began to draw, and he
followed them no farther. Very soon Beau appeared with the
bird in his mouth, struggling and flapping violently, and Belle
trotting admiringly beside him. I am not sure whether Belle
most admired his exquisite personal appearance or his accomplishments; but, certainly, she did seem to consider him a
canine phenomenon.

A flag waved, and a shrill whistle blown a long way in our
rear told us that it was luncheon-time; and we had also internal
promptings that feeding-time had arrived. We found Miss
Urchard, a maid-servant, and our plump friend, under the shade
of a tall, overhanging rock, crowned with a few mountain-ash
trees. It was eleven o'clock, and flaming hot, so this shelter
was agreeable in the extreme. A cloth was laid upon the short,
dry turf, and on it were meats, pies, salad, and many other
solids; but our young hostess drew especial attention to her
junkets and clotted cream. We all ate some of the junket, as it
was made by herself, and swore that we liked it. I know I
didn't, and I strongly suspect Captain Pole of a 'stretcher.' Of
course Urchard, being her brother, was free to declare that he
'cared for none of these things.' Our thoughtful little lady had

not forgotten the liquids : this was very important. She had a
great stone jar of ale, ditto of cider, plenty of claret, and all
these *in ice !* What does the sporting reader, who has followed
us from four o'clock until after eleven, in the hottest weather,
through stiff and unyielding heather, pleasantly interspersed
with bogs, swamps, fir-plantations, ascents like the side of a
house, and turf-pits treacherously concealed beneath grass and
moss, think of her for a caterer ? It will be understood that
Miss Urchard's fresh, pretty face, and gay, sweet voice, did not
in any way make our repast less enjoyable. The situation was
splendid ; we were, probably, at least a thousand feet above the
sea-level : in front a deep valley, clothed on either side with
heather, bracken, and many sorts of mosses, having also here
and there clumps of ash and fir, stretched away for some miles ;
away to the south, the long ridges of Dartmoor walled in the
smiling plains of South Devon.

Just as pipes were lighted and we had commenced the short
ten minutes' grace that divided us from our next labours, Miss
Urchard was asked by one of the party to favour us with a few
of her views upon the sport. ' First of all,' she said, ' I can't see
why you do not shoot the hens, as you meet with them more
easily and frequently than the cocks. They are just as good
to eat.'

This was explained to her by the one who ' drew her out.'
' Then,' she continued, ' why don't you let Pook and Charlie
(the keepers) carry guns ? I am sure they shoot much better
than any of you, except my brother.'

' Ah, but we want the sport !' was the reply.

' I call it sport to get a good bag. You really ought to have
some assistance ; the shooting has not been good. As for Mr.
Twister, I don't believe he can hit anything !'

To this sally there was no direct reply, though poor Twister
ventured to point out to his dear tormentor that the walking
was half the fun.

' Fun ?' she cried ; ' it did not seem very funny, except to
the others, when you were struggling up Witty Moor !'

Twister declined the combat and gave her a languishing
look, which made her, and, indeed, all of us, laugh considerably.

Urchard knocked the ashes from his pipe in a resolute
manner, sprang suddenly to his feet, and called out ' Come on !'
And so Scene II. is about to be enacted. Not far from the
spot which will always be associated in my mind with our

pleasant picnic, two small fields made an oasis in the midst of
the moors. One was a field of turnips, and the other a field of
oats. As we descended the slope in order to drop down upon
these little patches, a covey of birds whirred up with that
startling noise so peculiar to them. Several shots were fired,
and two brace fell. We found, to our great satisfaction, that
the old birds were numbered with the slain. The covey now
consisted of about ten birds, and they dropped in the turnips
in a very separated manner. We confidently expected pretty
shooting. The men halted, and the 'guns' walked quietly in
line through the turnips. Twister was with us again, gun in
hand; he was kept well forward, and we did not expect him
in *that position* to kill anything. Had he been in the rear of
the party he *might* have bagged somebody. Soon after entering
the field, they began to rise, one by one, here and there. Each
man had several shots, and each several times brought down a
fluttering heap of feathers—except Twister, and, as far as I
remember, nine dead bodies were picked up. We decided
that the tenth must have got into the adjacent barley, and I
volunteered to go alone and murder it whilst the others sat
down and wiped away the superfluous perspiration from their
heads and faces. I soon flushed my bird, and rolled it over in
my usual clean manner, when horror! up got another covey,
and went away to moor! I managed by dividing the contents
of the second barrel indiscriminately among them—very wrong,
I know—to stop a brace; but what would have happened if
my two colleagues had been with me?

'No use crying over what might have been,' was the Squire's
philosophical remark, when I told him. He declined to go after
the birds, as we were out to kill 'poults,' and not partridges
(unless they foolishly came in our way), and we made another
start. It was now three o'clock, and so hot and glaring that I
feared some of the men, whose heads were not protected so well
as mine (I wore a topee), would have *un coup de soleil;* but
Urchard said that it would be physically impossible for any
amount of sun to get at their brains, and that we must 'stick to
it.' We came to a sort of table-land—a lofty plateau, about a
hundred acres in extent, covered with bracken and heather, and
under the heather the inevitable 'wort' bushes. This part was
called 'Red Ford,' because there was no ford, and because the
only colours that anywhere met the eyes were the green below
and the intense blue above. This was looked upon as the *piece*

de résistance. We formed our old lengthy line, and prepared to take it in two beats. Twister was placed on the extreme left, and again well forward—the reason being obvious to every one but himself. Very soon they began to get up all over the place —some within range, some far beyond. We had been told that here we might kill a few hens; as for Twister, he was given no instructions, but let off his gun whenever he felt inclined. There was a great fusillade, some even loading and firing a second volley. In this ' Red Ford' six cocks and three hens were killed. All at once Twister, who had been doing a lot of shooting, roared out, ' I've done it, by Gad!' and lo! by the unanimous verdict of the men, he had indeed killed ' right and left.' Who shall describe his joy and exultation? He had expended thousands of cartridges in the last few seasons, but, according to his own keeper's report, he had never yet drawn blood. He at once gave Pook a ' fiver' for the men to drink his health with at night : Urchard prophesied the result. The money was all spent at the Poult Inn (and more added to it by Pole and myself) ; and next day we suffered much inconvenience from the debauched state of our attendants.

Shall I describe the next day ? I think not ; space forbids. We took a fresh beat—rougher, steeper, more swampy. The heat was the same, only more so ; we walked, drank, lunched, shot (hitting and missing), and bagged nine brace of black-game, sixteen rabbits, a brown owl (— Twister, Esq., thought it was a grey hen), a wood-pigeon, a landrail, and, oh glory of glories! a kingfisher by the stream. This glittering bird was so little injured that it was sent to be preserved, in order that it might be honoured with a perch upon Miss Urchard's coquettish little sailor-hat.

UNDER FALSE COLOURS.

By AMES SAVILE.

YNTHIA! come here ; I want to talk to you.'

Mrs. Blackett laid down her pen and rose from the writing-table. 'What is it ?' she asked, leaning over the back of her husband's chair.

'You acted the *ingénue* uncommonly well at the Beresford's the other night. I dare say more than one man there told you so—eh ?'

'And what then?'

'You never rehearsed at all, did you?'

'Only once regularly. You know Florie's sudden illness only gave me a week altogether to get up my part. What of that?'

'I'm coming to it,' said Captain Blackett. 'Was it difficult?'

'To act the part? Oh dear, no! I dare say I made fifty technical mistakes; but it did not feel the least unnatural.'

'Do you think you could act like that in real life?'

'What do you mean?' asked Cynthia, laughing, as she leant forward and pointed Captain Blackett's moustache with her firm little white fingers. 'Haven't I acted the part of a good wife to you for six whole years?'

'Just this,' he said, leaning back to see the expression on her pretty face: 'I want to take you with me to-morrow to Single-ford, to act as well as you did the other night.'

'When you go to see the chaser? But, Harry, I can't hold a candle to you in judgment on a horse.'

'You've not a bad eye for one,' returned her husband, 'and I want you to use it, whilst you look—you understand?—as if you saw nothing at all.'

'I will look all I can, of course, both ways; but how could I——'

'See here,' and Captain Blackett drew his wife to his side; 'I am not sure that there is not a screw loose with that horse Macedon. If there is not he'll suit us for the Dustyshot October Meeting to a hair; but I've been to see him twice—once, as you know, with Evetts, and once alone. Now, neither of those times could I get a fair look at him.'

'You mean—yes, I see, they've something to hide, and don't show the horse honestly.'

'No; the first time I went he had just come in, and couldn't be stripped, though I had an appointment. I was uncom-monly angry about it. Then, when Evetts and I went, the horse had the " least touch in the world of influenza—nothing to hurt ; " but—you know the sort of thing—could only be seen in the stable. It was a nasty blowy day certainly, but—the stable was dark!'

Cynthia seated herself on the arm of the chair and reflected.

'It is not likely I could see more of the horse than you could?' she observed, questioningly.

'I should think it possible—see or hear; there are two hours between our trains down and up, and I shall probably stroll off to look at something in the paddock. See what you can see, but at all risks don't know anything of a horse. You understand?'

'Yes; if I get a chance I will use it; but you must not be vexed with me if I fail. I am not quick at expedients; there is one chance in every game, isn't there? I will give you your cue if I can, but I would rather trust your wit than my own, any day.'

Singleford was a village nestled among the downs at an hour and a half's distance from London by the Great Western Railway, and frequented during certain months of the year by men of a more or less turfy appearance, bound for one or other of the racing establishments that gave a character, part horsey, part business-like, to the district. Singleford Copse, however, had no pretension to the dignity of a training-stable. It was a small farmhouse lying in a secluded hollow, surrounded by a neglected garden, and flanked by a ragged, unfenced spinney, that suggested badgers, and formed a shelter on the north-east to a paddock that lay a quarter of a mile beyond the house. This was guarded by iron rails, kept with strongly-contrasting carefulness, and tenanted during the summer and autumn months by two or three of those mares whose shortness of price contrasts so strongly with the length of their pedigree at the minor bloodstock sales. Light in bone, soft of heart, or with constitutions that refused to stand the strain of training, their produce, by sires either out of fashion or with some fault of temper that reduced their fee, would occasionally develop a capacity for staying or a turn of speed that raised their names from obscurity; but most of the long-legged yearlings that stalked or streamed across Mr. Terret's paddock went to swell the army of martyrs whose sheets and quarter-cloths, more or less patched, look like the most valuable part of them as they step out of their boxes at some country station, to make a bid for a local plate, and who know so much better the meaning of a punishing finish than of a bolt from the post. Abutting on the rick-yard wall was a low range of buildings, which contained an ephemeral population as various in breeding as in destination. Now the centre stall in No. 2 stable was occupied by an Irishman, whose ragged frame was overlaid by as much concealing flesh as his present owner had been able to persuade a somewhat dainty feeder to put on. There are buyers and buyers, but the greater

number who are influenced by a favourable appearance necessarily over-balance the few who are not unfavourably impressed
by an unfurnished framework, and high-feeding had been freely
bestowed on Macedon (said to be by Alexander out of a
Skirmish mare). Captain Blackett had not asked for a trial, as
it chanced to be as much to his interest as to Mr. Terret's to
keep his possible purchase dark. In the neighbourhood of
Singleford, however insignificant the performer, 'forests have
ears and fields have eyes,' almost literally, for a trial. The
horse, which he had heard of indirectly, took his fancy considerably, but also puzzled him; so, feeling that he had more
than his match against him for a deal, it had occurred to
the Hussar to take his clever little wife down with him for
what must be a final inspection.

'Too neat by half, Cynthia!' he exclaimed, as she came into
the hall, ready for the journey.

'Does it matter?' she asked, looking down at her closely-
fitting tweed dress and jacket, which were surmounted by a
round hat. 'What else could I go to a training-stable in?'

'You look pretty nearly as if you had got a habit on,' he
objected, looking her over. 'Couldn't you have worn a lot of
flounces, or frippery, or something?'

Cynthia laughed. 'Neat dressing does not make one a
judge of a horse,' she said. 'Look at Lady Bee Carr; she
doesn't know a breastplate from a martingale, and think of the
perfect way her tailor turns her out!'

'But then, she'd like it to be thought she did.'

'I am very sorry; it is too late to change now. And then,
if I am to see anything I must be able to get about.'

'Well, don't forget your part,' growled Captain Blackett, as
he opened the street-door.

'The first mistake,' Cynthia said to herself, with grim
philosophy, 'and a proof of the wisdom of the modern stage in
making dress an all-important part of acting.'

A couple of hours later, they were slowly climbing the
last hill before dropping down into the sunny hollow, in
which the farmstead of Singleford Copse lay. It was a long,
steep pitch, and the lad, half stable-boy, half *gamin*, who had
brought a dogcart to the station to meet the visitors, was
walking to ease the horse of his weight, which, moderate as
it was, formed a consideration in the stable economy of the
Copse.

'You are going to have him out, Harry?'

'Most certainly,' was Captain Blackett's answer.

'And you've *no* idea, Harry?'

'Not the ghost of one. Thoroughly puzzled, Cynthia, though it is a feeble sort of confession. Look here! I *think* his legs are sound; I *think* his wind is all right; I *think* his eyesight is good; I *think* his pedigree is genuine; I *think*, which in our friend's case is a consideration, that he is *bonâ fide* his property. What can be wrong?'

There was a long pause.

'He is a winner?' she asked presently, as they rattled down the hill.

'At Letterblancy; five furlongs on the flat: his only entry.'

'What weight up?'

'Seven stone four.'

As they drew up at the gate, Mr. Terret received them with civility. Captain Blackett's third visit, preluded by a telegram, looked like dealing, and Terret had reasons of his own for feeling confidence in the present appearance of the chaser. Twenty minutes were spent in the range of outhouses, dignified by the name of No. 1 Stable, and then Macedon's box was reached and the Irishman stripped. Cynthia had played her part admirably. She had professed fear at a suggested approach to a smart-looking pony that Terret had supposed calculated to take a lady's fancy, had asked more than one vague query about the hunter next door, and pathetically regretted the absence of a swish tail to a well-sheeted varmint-looking mare occupying a stall where a swarm of gnats were manœuvring with confusing tactics in the autumn sunlight that came through the open door; she had testified real seeming disgust at crossing a stable-yard that compared unfavourably with the garden-like appearance affected by private stud-grooms, and now, standing in the rear of Macedon, as her husband passed his hands once more over the sinewy legs of his intended purchase, raised the turquoise-tinted eyes, that had conquered other hearts than Captain Blackett's, to Mr. Terret's hard-featured face, and begged to be assured that there was not mortal danger in such an examination. So far all had gone well, and she felt satisfied with the prologue; but now the play was to be acted. Macedon was coming out of his box, his clothing was swept off, and he strode out of the low doorway, with a swing of his tail and a lift of his heels, that testified ready power.

Cynthia's heart beat high as the horse was led past, and she dropped her eyes quickly lest the flash of keen interest she could not restrain should catch the dealer's sharp glance. Her woman's instinct made her afraid of the man when her husband felt suspicion of the horse, and she was just regretting the part she had been induced to play, and wishing she had come under an honest guise, and without a mask that was so difficult to wear, as the horse passed back again in front of her, showing the whole length of his near flank from forearm to stifle, when she started visibly.

'All right, ma'am,' growled the stableman, who was leading him; 'he don't kick.'

But Cynthia did not hear him, and did not notice Terret's quick glance at her, for her thoughts had gone with a bound to a scene of years before. She saw once more the shady old courtyard at home, where the moss-grey walls of the stables extended in dilapidated length from the side of the old Manor-house to the yard of the Home-farm. She felt once more the cool breeze blowing under the chestnuts, as she stood by her father's side, a freckled sunburnt girl, downcast and dreary, looking at the expression of his face and hanging upon his lips for a verdict. Opposite them, held by a servant, was the little thoroughbred, the last horse she had ever called her own, surmounted by a patched saddle and champing at a rusty bit, a wiry-legged, fretful four-year-old that she had bitted and broken, and that came into her hands as the vixenish mare refused to do into any others.

'Cantered three-cornered, eh?' her father was saying. 'It's all up, little one. I thought she would have lasted our time; but it's a case of sooner or later, and with Ladylove it has come sooner.'

His eye was fixed upon a spot below the short strong quarter. The scene of this great disappointment came back to Cynthia with a flash. And here was Macedon, with his ragged hips and strong wide loins, his huge Irish hocks and flat legs, reminding her of the wiry, short, camel-backed filly that was as ugly and as strong as the Theodore, to which her father was fond of comparing her. A curious freak of recollection!

'What do you think of him now, Captain; and what does the lady think of him?'

Cynthia's intuition was not far wrong. Terret knew men better even than horses, and a practical proof of his knowledge

lay in the account standing in his name at the local bank. He
had guessed from the first moment that the decision hinged
upon her, when he had seen the neat little figure spring down
from the dogcart with hardly a touch of her husband's offered
hand. A man does not bring his wife for the sake of com-
panionship only, he thought, to look over a chaser. Had it
been a lady's hunter, or even a carriage-horse, her veto might
have been of importance, but a chaser was not the affair of a
pretty petted wife, who did not know a cart-horse from a
roadster. The lady, he had decided, was the one to please,
and Terret had expended the full force of what *agréments*
of conversation or manners he possessed upon Cynthia. Her
airs he looked upon as the natural affectations of an 'Aris-
tocrat,' and he had spotted Mrs. Blackett at once through all
her varnish of ignorance.

'A deal too much flesh on him,' smiled the Captain, looking
lovingly at the clean flat legs and deep ribs. 'Suppose you tell
us all about him, Pussy,' he said playfully.

'Oh, Harry, he's *not at all* pretty,' she said, in a tone of
disgust. 'Look at his *quarters*, don't you call them? And
what an ugly thin tail!'

She shot a glance at her husband as she spoke the word
quarters, but he was half facing the dealer and dared not meet
her eye. As it was he missed any point in her words, and
answered generally.

'His quarters are a bit ragged, but they'll do ; and as for
his tail, Pussy, it is a well-bred one enough,' and he laughed.

'I don't like him, Harry ; I should *hate* to see you on him.
He is not *half* pretty enough.'

'Handsome is as handsome does, Mrs. Blackett,' said the
dealer. 'He'd look beautiful passing the post first with the
Captain a-top of him. Now I'll bet you know something of
a horse ; ladies al'us does. See his hocks now, what jumping
power ! and his loins ! Why, as to his tail, it had need to
be thin ; for when he once starts you'll see nothing of him
in front of that but what you can see through it.'

'And he really *did* win a race?' asked Cynthia. 'But
perhaps he'll never win another,' she said childishly, glancing
at her husband, who caught her eye this time. What did she
mean ?

'I should like to show you him winning one,' was his reply.
He was growing more and more in love with the horse. He

approached Macedon. There was plenty of time to get that flesh off between now and the end of October, and there was not a single horse likely to run against him that could touch him, if appearance was to be relied on. Did his wife not like the horse, or was she only trying to seem ignorant of his evident powers? What was she crabbing him for? Only to carry out the game to the end. No doubt she was right. It was not the horse to take the fancy of a woman as ignorant of horseflesh as she was feigning to be; she was right so far. Still, if it were not that, and she disliked him—though he thought he knew her better; a bit of a gallop would show her what she ought to see if she did not, that he was just the horse for the Brigade Cup.

He mounted and walked out of the yard, then, following a line recommended, took Macedon through an open gate on the opposite side of the road, and put him into a canter across the field it led into. Increasing his pace to a gallop he flew a line of hurdles, topped a stiff thorn hedge, and, swinging round half-way down the next field, came flying back to them over both obstacles, only checking his pace within a few yards of home. It was no trial, but he had learnt the horse was handy and temperate, besides showing his wife what a stride he had, and how well those grand thighs lifted the fore-part of him along when once set in motion. The shoulder was good enough to be lifted if it would not have made pace alone. He looked down at her as he pulled up by her side.

'You weren't frightened, Pussy?' he asked, and praised himself for the pretty innocence with which he had put a leading question.

'Dreadfully, Harry,' was the puzzling answer. 'I should never dare to see you on him again! never! How can you like him?'

'But, my dear, I like him particularly,' he said, forgetting her acting in the want of sympathy that irritated him,—Cynthia always liked what he liked.

'Mrs. Blackett will like him when he gets into your stable, Captain,' said the dealer, who had stood silently close behind her during the spin,—'when your groom gets a hand upon him and straps him and shines his coat; he's a bit rough now, but that'll make him look the nobleman he is.'

'I shall *never* like him!' said Cynthia, pettishly, and turned away as Captain Blackett dismounted.

'Well, we'll talk of dealing later,' said Terret, with a quickly
assumed smile. 'Come and see the young ones, Captain; the
lady'll like the foals perhaps, which are sweet, gentle creatures.'

Half-an-hour was spent petting and criticising mares and
foals, which showed all the confidence of good breeding, and
delighted Cynthia with a delight that she dared to show. There
was a promising yearling, and she praised it that Harry might
see she was not out of humour with everything ; but she had
not had so much as a signal from him without a spectator, and
as they walked back to the farm, and he looked at his watch,
she felt the critical moment was approaching, and was at her
wits' end how to prevent his going too far. There had not been
a moment of *tête-à-tête ;* Terret had kept close to him, and now
figures were named, and Captain Blackett looked very much like
yielding 180 guineas for the chaser, and she powerless to prevent
it. Could not the purchase be delayed ? Dare she, ought she,
to make a fool of herself and him by showing in her own
character ? Even that would be better than the misdeal he
seemed likely to make. Why had Harry ever put her into so
impossible a predicament ; and why, madder still, had she ever
consented to step into it ? He had said he could trust her wit,
why then had he not trusted it openly ? But all this time that
she was walking silently by his side, how was he to guess at
her miserable disgust ? 'There is one chance in every game,'
she repeated to herself, with a sigh that was almost audible, 'and
I must watch for it.' There were 200 yards yet between them
and the house and office where the cheque must be signed ;
and Captain Blackett had come to the point in his bargain when
the buyer weighs guineas against sovereigns. Terret now fancied
he must have been wrong all along; and that her judgment, were
he ever so infatuated, could not weigh with her husband, and
felt that the cheque for the sovereigns he meant to drop to, was
as good as in his pocket.

They entered the office, and there the chance came at last :
her husband's cheque-book lay under his hand upon the table.
The ink was low in the stand, and Terret crossed the room to
replenish it from a stone bottle in the window sill. Cynthia had
just time to draw an envelope from her pocket, to scribble four
words in it in pencil, and to pass it over his shoulder. Captain
Blackett read and glanced up at her in surprise, then leaned
lazily back in his chair, as the dealer turned towards him.

'Look here, Mr. Terret,' he said, quietly ; 'I think after all I won't settle with you to-day. A hundred and eighty is your price for the horse, and you won't come down. Now, as I said, I came here only prepared to give a hundred and fifty, and I would rather have another twenty-four hours to think over the extra thirty sovereigns. You *won't* reduce, eh?' he added, to give himself time.

'Not a sov.,' returned Terret, glancing quickly at Cynthia; but her dress had never rustled, and she was standing looking (as she had been before) at an old print of 'The Colonel' on the wall behind her husband's chair; she could not have moved since he sat down. 'The horse is worth every penny of the money, and if I don't get it from you,' he added, with less civility than he had shown hitherto, 'I shall get it elsewhere.'

'Well, if you can get it,' said Captain Blackett, 'that's all right, isn't it? I am not saying a word against the horse, except for the price. Then you shall have my decision by post.'

'A hundred and eighty sovereigns, and you have him,' said Terret, firmly; 'but mind, I don't keep him for you. I have a purchaser coming to-morrow, and if he gives it he haves him.'

'I must take the chance,' said Captain Blackett slowly as he rose. 'I will write to-morrow without fail.' He tried not to speak too positively, but Terret knew he had lost his deal. The by-play had escaped him, but he was morally convinced of the influence against him. 'It's that little jade that did it,' he said to himself, looking angrily at Mrs. Blackett as they drove off; and he is sure of it to this day, though where she beat him he is powerless to discover.

'It wouldn't have done to risk it, would it, Harry?' asked Cynthia, when they were seated in the railway carriage; and her husband had assured her warmly that she deserved having married into the old 23rd.

'Certainly not,' he said; 'the horse might have trained this time, as he did before, in Ireland, but the breakdown might come at any moment, as it did with your poor young mare. But, Cynthia,' he added, 'with all that flesh on him, I believe I should never have found it out myself.' He drew from his cheque-book the broken envelope with the words scribbled on it, '*Near hip let down,*' and looked at it curiously.

Cynthia smiled, half sadly, a tribute to the suffering of the past in the triumph of the present.

'It was too bitter a lesson for me ever to forget,' she said;

'but it was curious the accident should have been again on the near side.   That certainly helped me.'

'A kind stroke of fate for once,' said Captain Blackett. 'I shall keep this scrap of paper in my desk to remind me of the day when you ran so well "under false colours."'

'And was so very near being disqualified on account of them,' added his wife gaily.

AN HONEST MAN ON AN HONEST HORSE.

By 'AN OLD TURFITE.'—CHAPTER I.

THERE is possibly no sport which the British public takes to more naturally than that of horse-racing, the reason being (alas, what a fallacy!) that it has the appearance of being easily understood.   The landlord takes to it because he has nothing else to do, and it has the reputation of being the sport of princes ; the farmer takes to it because he has a knowledge of horses, and breeds one occasionally ; the farrier, for the same reason that made him take to his trade ; the baker, because he has need for one to carry his bread ; the butcher, for he needs one for his cart ; and the publican, because he considers, somehow, that it is a part of his business.   From Land's End to John o' Groats, from the Dogger Bank to the Scilly Islands, men will take an interest in horse-racing, calculate the weights to be carried in the different handicaps, and attempt to vaticinate the results.   The reliance placed upon human nature and on horse nature is terrible to think of ; for there are men who would not trust their next-door neighbour, however well to do or respectable, for a single crown, who would think nothing of 'planking it down,' as they phrase it, on the chance of a horse they never saw, owned by a man they have had no chance of seeing or knowing, and to be ridden by a jockey whose name they pronounce trippingly, as if familiar with him from their youth, but whom they have never been within mouth-hailing distance of.   It is true some are guided by the newspaper sporting prophets, some by their own opinions, but many, it is true, by the information sent them by men who have been guilty of most dishonourable practices—broken-down jockeys, who have been reduced to this by their own disgraceful or sinful actions, and who get business to do through the assurance that they can get hold of secrets which do not belong to the employés but the employers. It is the Turf's misfortune, not its fault, that the sovereigns of the industrious should be chucked in amongst the many idle harpies who congregate where fools abound, and who never did an honest hour of labour except on a treadmill.

Racing must always be the sport of kings, as there is no pastime so exciting, no struggle so interesting to witness, as that between two highly trained thorough-breds, ridden in the most skilful manner by honest and able jockeys. Such a sight can be enjoyed quite as well without a shilling on as with a thousand pounds by a genuine sportsman, one who loves sport for its own sake ; indeed, if there were but the means of finding it out, it might be shown that the majority of the backers of horses never really see the most interesting struggles, being generally engaged in getting their money on. One thing is certain, many of them are so nerve-shaken by the amounts they have risked, that they cannot survey in a cool and impassioned manner the sight of a close finish and a brilliant piece of riding, but get into a fever of excitement, which allows them to see but one horse— the horse they have backed. But it is to tell a story of just such a struggle that I have lifted my pen, not to give a disquisition on the Turf and Turf Morality.

'I tell you, Packington, that if Mowbray rides your horse you will be certain to lose ; so you can just make up your mind early. You're something of a novice at horse-racing, so be advised in time, and take the opinion of a man like myself who has been through the mill.'

'Well, Reynolds, I'm sorry to disappoint you, but my trainer, Naggs, says that Mowbray is the only one who can ride him— that is, with any chance of success. He is a peculiar horse, he says, and if any one is put up who does not understand him he will not try a yard.'

'Nonsense! A child could ride him. But it is not that. If Mowbray rides him he will *not be asked* to try a yard. Did it never strike you, when you were making those big bets about him, that they would try and put themselves on the right side by fair means or foul? The fair is of no use, and so with the foul they have made certain.'

'But Mowbray is a jockey whose very name is above the slightest suspicion. He has ridden for some of the best stables in the country. Naggs would risk his life on his honesty.'

'Don't be a fool, Packington! There's many a man would risk his life, as he calls it, on a man who would not risk half-a-crown. Look here: I know for a fact that Mowbray spent three hours in the company of Brixton, the partner of a man who has laid ten thousand against your horse, and, I may say, the most notorious scoundrel on the British Turf. What does that mean?'

'Be careful what you say, Reynolds, for I heard Lord Buckhurst say that Mowbray was most scrupulously honest and most careful of his company.'

'Lord Buckhurst be hanged!' was the sneering reply. 'If you come with me to-night I'll show you Brixton and Mowbray together, ay, and "confabbing" about the whole business. If you stick to Mowbray after that, all I can say is that you are a bigger fool than I took you for.'

'To-night? And where? and when?'

'Half-past seven o'clock, at the "Blue Dart." Disguise yourself as well as you can, and meet me under the railway arch on this side. Is that agreed upon?'

'Agreed! I will be there.'

CHAPTER II.

IT wanted but two days of the race, and the whole of the sporting writers were commenting on the shuffling movements of the party behind Mr. Ralph Packington's bay horse Fire Escape. He had gone almost to the bottom of the betting list, rebounded to the top, and then settled down at the 'halfway house' of the great Berkshire Handicap. 'If all were right,' wrote one of the leading commissioners, 'we should have no difficulty in naming the winner, but in the face of what we have seen, and the strange rumours afloat, we must decline to recommend the horse. One who is the close friend of the owner of the horse, and is almost daily seen in his company, has made some heavy bets against him, apparently not bogus ones, while the owner himself has backed the horse for an enormous stake in another quarter.' From Newmarket our training reporter wrote to the same newspaper: 'I would not hesitate for a moment in choosing Fire Escape to win outright but for the unaccountable fact that I learn that Sam Mowbray will not be in the saddle, for what reasons are not here known. Fire Escape is a peculiar-tempered horse, and likes a lot of humouring. Mowbray, however, thoroughly understands him, and can get him along when others cannot make him move. Moreover, he is the only jockey who has ever got him to actually win a race. Reflections have been made upon his (Mowbray's) honour, but this can scarcely be credited. However, we shall just have to wait and see.'

So the wise and the wary resolved to wait and see, though Sam Mowbray's reputation was under a cloud. ' You ask me the reason,' my Lord, said the jockey, when questioned as to the remarks of the newspaper writers, ' why such things have been said. Well, all I can say is that I know nothing. If Fire Escape starts, and I ride him, he stands a good chance of winning—*anybody else*, and Jim Shepherd on Nap or Nothing ; and I think it's about a hundred to one on his losing.'

' But has the owner, who has a first call on you, not made any inquiry or explanation ? '

' He has not said a word, my Lord ; but I think somehow that it's all that Mr. Reynolds' doings, and for what reason I don't know—it can scarcely be to get the horse back in the betting. However, we'll see in time, my Lord, only it is a little sore on me in the meantime.'

In due time came the day of the race, and the time for getting ready. ' Who is to ride Fire Escape ? ' was the question asked on all sides. The first two minor events over, and the jockeys commenced to dress and weigh for the great event of the day. One by one, with saddles and leads adjusted, they all turned up at the scale, and had their names, weights, &c., entered by the clerk in his book. Yet Sam Mowbray, who had won the previous race, donned his top-coat, and made his way out of the door, without deigning to notice Mr. Packington, who in a nervous condition was holding a conversation with Naggs, the trainer, and the astute Mr. Reynolds. A northern jockey, by no means fashionable, stood near at hand, and Mowbray quite well knew that it was Reynolds' object, from his remarks and gestures, to get this man into the saddle. It wanted but a few minutes of the time for starting, and the man in charge of the telegraph-board seemed to be waiting only for one wanting number. Mowbray's presence outside seemed to explain what it was, for ' 20 to 1 against Fire Escape ! ' came with a roar from the centre of the ring. He looked to see from whom it came, and immediately recognised it to proceed from the partner of Brixton. Almost before he knew he saw Naggs, the trainer, rush forward and take the bet several times; and then, ere he knew, he dragged him half inside, with the remark, 'There's no time to be lost. Come, get into your jacket—quick! That fool Reynolds has nearly spoiled everything!' The jockey made some show of resistance, but the old trainer's remark, 'For my sake, for your own sake, ride the horse, and things will all come right by-and-by!' In a few minutes more he was in the saddle, his number hoisted, and he made his way out at the gate. As he passed through the little opening on to the course Mr. Packington, with a face greenish-white, like the moonlight, said, in almost a currish voice, 'For Heaven's sake, Mowbray, do your best; my whole fortune depends on your honesty!' A remark to which the jockey replied with a glance which old Naggs said afterwards 'would have withered a gooseberry-bush.'

As the horse, which was smartly wheeled round and sent off on its preliminary canter down to the post, free comment was made on the mysterious movements connected with Fire Escape, which still refused to take its proper place in the betting.

'Do you know this Packington, Duke?' said to his Grace of Cedarville Sir Punter Robinson. 'How's he bred?'

'Oh,' said the former, looking at his card, 'well enough. By Kinmount Willie out of Border Maid.'

'I mean the man, not the horse,' said the baronet, laughing.

'Oh, him! No. Dustman out of Washerman I should think, and pedigree not very certain at that. Father made his money out of a patent shirt-button, after running away from home with the proverbial fourpenny bit.'

'Fourpenny bit, Duke? Don't believe it! I believe he took the whole cash-box. But do you know this Reynolds? I saw you exchange nods rather stiffly.'

'Yes, Punter; I nodded to him mechanically before I recognised him. We were at Oxford together, but his name wasn't Reynolds; what it was I forget now, and cannot get it into my memory.'

'Rather clever, isn't he? Took his degree.'

'His degree? Yes, and his landlady's daughter, and all that he could get down to the last silver spoon; ruined the poor mother, did something wrong on the Turf—I forget what—left the daughter on the dock-side at Liverpool, went to America, and here he is, up to something villainous, I'll swear: you may depend on it. I expect, however, this Packington is his pigeon. But hulloa, they're off! No, they're not; it is only Fire Escape joining his horses from the rear.'

But to see the race we must go to the post and come home with the horses, of which there are half a dozen: Nap or Nothing, ridden by Shepherd; Fire Escape, ridden by Sam Mowbray; Flash, started to make the running for the first-named; Jewel, a four-year-old, thought to have a good outside chance; Frolic, which is not much fancied in the betting, and another.

'You here, Sam?' said Shepherd, not very agreeably surprised. 'I thought they said you was too small a man for to ride a big horse like that. What's come of the great man from Middlebacon?'

'He's backing my mount if he's a wise man, Jim,' was the reply; and then the starter, who had been watching his opportunity, though walking about in a careless, easy manner, as if not at all in a hurry, lowered his flag, and they were off.

Fire Escape was shot into front berth next the rails, but Flash, hard ridden in the middle of the course, soon led by a clear couple of lengths, attended by Frolic, while Nap or Nothing's head lay so close to Mowbray's knee that he literally saw the white of his eyes. For the first quarter of a mile they ran without much change of position, Flash's jockey sending his horse, which was the light-weight of the party, along at a great pace. When the half-mile had been covered, Nap or Nothing was sent forward after him at a great pace, and soon held a lead of half-a-dozen lengths. To Mowbray's consternation he now found that his horse was in one of his queer tempers, and would not try to gain on the other at all. A thrill now ran through him, as he saw the view which would be taken of his riding from the stand. It had been almost broadly asserted that he meant to pull the horse, yet here was the horse refusing literally to go into his bridle; and he knew well that his only chance lay in giving the animal his own way. 'If I bustle him the least,' he said, 'I'm done.' Entering on the last half-mile, the jockeys on the other horses which were beaten dropped back with the remark, 'Go up to him, Sam!' But, of course, that was all nonsense, so long as Fire Escape seemed to think that he was entitled to wait till his own time. At last, when they entered the

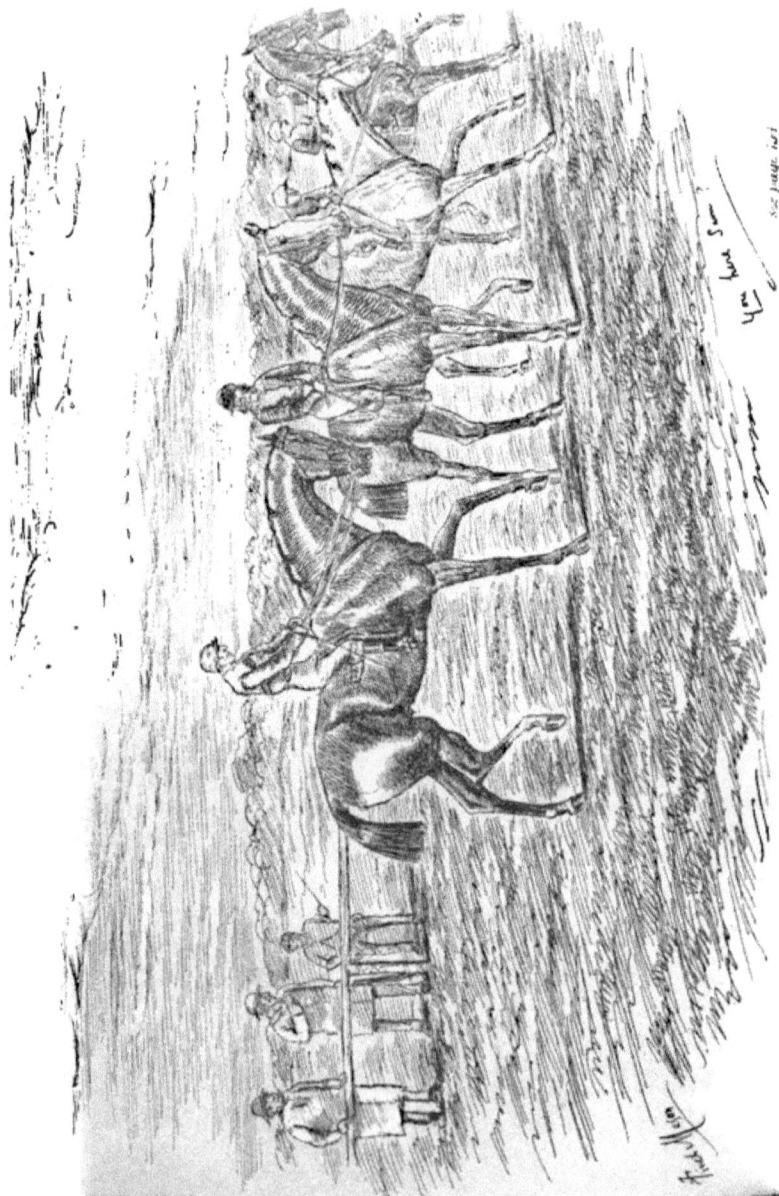

See page 145.

crowd-lined rails, the patient jockey found his horse literally waking into life, as if of its own accord. Stride and stride he closed on Nap or Nothing, while shouts from the stand rent the air. Fifty yards from the judge's chair they drew level, and then commenced one of the most exciting struggles that had ever been seen on a racecourse. Both men seemed to reserve their energies for one finishing rush, and both guessed the judge's eye-line between post and chair to a hair's breadth ; but with a demon effort, in which legs, arms, hands, eyes, and his very soul itself, seemed to become part of his horse, Sam gave him the signal for his last stride, and the shout which followed told that the race was over. Had he won or had he lost ? or was it a dead heat ? He looked to the number-board as he pulled up to walk back, but the man seemed to hesitate in placing the figures within the frame-work. At last up went Fire Escape's number amidst cheers, and his mind was at rest ; still, neither Naggs nor Mr. Packington, nor the latter's friend Reynolds, came forward to lead him to the weighing-room. At last the former made his appearance, much excited, and the jockey soon un-saddled and entered the scales. ' All right !' was the exciting call which followed, whilst the judge, in answer to the query, ' How much ?' said ' The shortest of heads. You just got it on the post—in fact, I could divide you, but no more. I thought you had waited too long.'

' Yes, judge, I did wait, and it was like waiting a week on him ; but he's got his own way of doing things, and if I'd tried mine too soon he'd never have come at all.'

' You did quite right, Sam,' said Mr. Naggs ; ' but I scarcely saw the finish, for Mr. Packington went off in my arms in a fit, and as soon as it was known you had won Reynolds bolted and left me with him in my arms.'

' Reynolds did ? I thought he would ! He had laid the horse to win a fortune, the infernal scoundrel ! I thought I had seen him once before, and it flashed right through me when he was just down below the distance-post there, and I saw the whole game.'

' And who is he ?'

' His name is Jarvis—the James Luke Jarvis warned off the Turf fourteen years ago for pulling a horse called the Gipsy King. But where is he ? and where are the stewards ? for I must get at the bottom of this.'

But Jarvis, *alias* Reynolds, had gone, and the following

letter, addressed to M. Packington, Esq., Turf Hotel, delivered next morning, explains the game :—

Friday.

DEAR SIR,—I return you your racing-jacket, and must ask leave to throw up my engagement, as I could not think of riding for you any more. You have not head enough for racing, and, from what Mr. Naggs tells me, not the heart. The scoundrel Reynolds, whose real name is Jarvis, and who was warned off the Turf fourteen years ago, very nearly ruined you and destroyed my reputation at the same time. I learned all from Brixton, who under the plea of getting a brother of mine—who is not very well behaved—out of trouble, met me by arrangement at two places. The first time I gave him my cheque for an amount necessary to do so. The second time at the ' Blue Dart,' where you watched me receive four five-pound notes, the balance remaining over. Jarvis had laid the horse heavily, besides backing Nap or Nothing ; and if his orders to the northern lad had been obeyed, viz. to send him along the whole way, no stopping would have been necessary. You will see the narrow escape you have had. My advice to you is to sell your horse, and Naggs will give you fifteen hundred for him. I believe I am the only jockey who can ride him, as his temper is a queer one. I will never ride him for *you* again, and if you insist on your rights, I will bring the whole affair before the Stewards.

I am, yours truly,

SAMUEL MOWBRAY.

And Mr. Packington did as advised. Samuel Mowbray rode Fire Escape afterwards in many good races, and found plenty of backers, who are keen at discovering the best of all ' good things'—' an honest man on an honest horse.'

A BAREFACED CASE OF POACHING;

Or, How his Lordship Lost his Bet.

By 'SCRAMO.'

THE Earl of —— is the fortunate owner of a fine estate in Scotland, the beauty of which is only equalled by the great attractions which it offers to the sportsman. The shooting is second to none in the country, and part of one of the best salmon rivers flows through the property. The noble Earl is a very keen salmon-fisher, and never lets a chance slip of killing a fish when the weather and water are in proper condition. His shooting and trout-fishing on a beautiful loch are given up entirely to his

guests; but in the autumn, after the nets are off, a day with the
salmon is not easily to be had, and lucky is the sportsman who
gets on to the river when something turns up to prevent his
lordship fishing it himself. He despises trout-fishing; and who
will blame him, having at his door the nobler sport? Let any
one go out trout-fishing the day after killing six or eight salmon,
averaging 20 lbs. each, when his fly is laid hold of by a trout or
par about three inches long, he will experience a peculiar sensation. His lordship cared not to experience that sensation.

Some years ago I was paying him a visit in the autumn, and
after enjoying some splendid days amongst the partridges I felt
very anxious to try the river; but being in proper fishing order
it was monopolised by his lordship, who was enjoying excellent
sport. However, one morning after breakfast I went into the
smoking-room, and found the head-keeper waiting for orders.

'Good morning, Girvan,' I said; 'how about the river
to-day?'

'It's no use, sir; she's sma' again; and if she was fishable
his lordship would try her himsel'.'

'Then I suppose there is a chance of *my* getting on to it?'
I remarked.

'Oh, yes, sir; but it would just be wastin' time. I ken the
river that weel, that ye might just as weel gang back tae yer
room and fish in yer tub if she's no emptied!'

The door opened and his lordship walked in, puffing at his
morning weed.

'Any chance of a fish to-day, Girvan?'

'No, m'lord; I was just tellin' Mr. R—— that you might
just as weel fish in yer tub.'

I then remarked that I was tired of shooting, and would not
mind trying my luck, especially as I did not see why all the fish
in the river should be sane enough not to rise that day.

'All right,' he replied, 'you can go if you like; and I'll bet
you a shilling (he never bets more!) you don't kill,' well knowing
the worth of Girvan's opinion and his own perfect knowledge of
the river.

'Done with you,' I replied, chuckling inwardly.

Girvan was ordered to send down old Duncan MacSneishan,
the third keeper, to carry my bag, gaff, flask, &c.

In half an hour I started for the river, his lordship standing
at the front door laughing at me, and saying I had better pay
him his shilling before I started.

On our way down the avenue I remarked, 'Not much chance with the rod to-day, Duncan.'

'I could hae telt ye that afore, Mr. R——; and I think ye had better gang back and join the rest o' the gentlemen at the shootin'.'

'I mean to kill fish to-day, come what may,' I said.

'I dinna ken hoo yer gaen tae manage it, sir; the water's doon abin a foot since last neight, and there's no a clood in the sky.'

'I'll manage it for all that,' I said; 'and all you've got to do is to hold your tongue and promise never to let out how it was done.'

Duncan promised, with a suspicious look in his eyes.

Arrived at the river we sat down, and I put on the first fly that came to my hand. I then took the gaff, which was a six-footer, from Duncan, much to his astonishment, and told him to walk up to a small hill about three hundred yards off, and to keep a good look-out, and to whistle if he saw any of the river watchers in sight.

'Goodness gracious!' he exclaimed, 'what are ye goin' to be up to, Mr. R——? You're surely no gaen tae try ony poachin' dodges? If ye do, I'll lose ma situation.'

'Never mind, Duncan, it's nothing to do with you; go and do what I tell you; and here's a "dram" to keep you quiet.'

He swallowed it, smacking his lips (he belonged to the Illustrious Order of Good Templars!), and went off reluctantly, muttering to himself, 'I'm sure he's up tae some devilment.'

Having got rid of him, I proceeded down the river about two hundred yards to the Cruive dykes, and waded across to a small island of gravel covered with bushes. I had noticed on a former occasion that when the salmon were running up through the cruives, especially when the water was in its present state, they very often, instead of getting into the deep water above, came tumbling back quite close to this little island, and within easy reach of a long gaff.

I deposited my rod under a bush, turned up my sleeves, and with gaff in hand prepared for action. I had not long to wait, crouching down like a cat preparing to spring. Up came a beauty, struggling gamely to master the strong current through the cruives, but only managed to get within two feet of the top, and then came rolling over and over within five feet of me. I quickly had the gaff into him, and pulled him on

Clutching frantically at Elsie, I turned thither.

see page 259.

to the bank, which was a very steep and awkward place for
the job I was at, owing to the loose gravel it was composed
of. However, I threw myself bodily on to him, and after a
good struggle killed him with a stone, and put him out of
sight under the bush and took up my position again.

I had only to wait for about two minutes when, with a
tremendous rush and splash, up came a monster as clean and
bright as a new shilling—a fresh-run fish, and looked over 30 lbs.
He went past me, evidently meaning business ; and thinking he
might get over and I would lose my chance of getting him
on his way back, I made a lunge at him, but only managed
to scrape a few scales off his broad back, as he was rather
beyond my reach. But luck was with me : after a desperate
struggle on the very edge of the dyke, his head almost into the
deep water, his strength failed him, and down he came like the
first one, splashing feebly with his tail, right to my feet. I got
the gaff well into him and scrambled up the bank as high as I
could manage to get, and went through the same performance
as with the other, only he being a much heavier and stronger
fish I had a rougher time of it with him. In endeavouring to
get his head steady for killing my foot slipped, and I rolled
down the bank, clutching him in my arms, right to the edge
of the rushing water, but managed with the greatest difficulty
to prevent myself being washed down into the pool below, still
clutching my fish like grim death. Luckily I had got my
fingers well fixed into his gills, otherwise I should have lost him.
However, I landed him on the top of the bank again, and put an
end to his struggles with a couple of blows on the head, and
deposited him in triumph beside the first one.

Within ten minutes I added another to the bag, and if I
had gone on I could nearly have filled a cart ; but thinking I
had a very good show for a bad day, and having more would
excite suspicion, I picked up my rod and waded across to the
mainland, well satisfied with my half-hour's sport.

I called Duncan and said he might come with me now, and
told him what I had done. His face was a picture when he
heard it.

‘ Ma conscience, Mr. R——!’ he exclaimed ; ‘ if ye’d been
catched ye’d hae been fined twenty pund, and I would hae been
turned oot o’ the pairish to-morry.’

‘ Never mind,’ I said, ‘ we’ll run the risk of that.’

Just to pass the time I tried a cast over most of the pools, but, as I expected, I never got a rise, but was quite satisfied with the expectation of the rise I was to get out of his lordship!

After finishing the contents of my flask and smoking a couple of pipes, lying on the bank drawing out poor old Duncan, who was still in a mortal fright about my late performance, I thought it time to be making our way homewards. We got back to the cruives, and I waded over and carried each fish back to the mainland and laid them in a row on the bank, Duncan remarking, 'Weel, this is aboot the *barefacededest* case o' poachin' that has ever come under ma notice, and I've been a keeper for forty-five year!'

While looking at the three fine fish I did feel rather ashamed of myself, especially as no one is more down on poaching than I am. I don't know what put it into my head—simply the love of excitement, I suppose. However, I determined to carry it through; so, having loaded Duncan with the two heaviest fish and carrying the smallest myself, we started for home.

Arrived at the Castle, we took them to the fish-larder and had them weighed. 32 lbs., 22 lbs., and 19 lbs.! 'By Jove!' I said, 'I don't like facing his lordship; he will be in a perfect fury at not having gone down himself.' But there was no alternative but to brave it out, so I went upstairs and found him writing. I lit a cigarette and tried to look as composed as possible.

'Well,' he remarked, 'how about my shilling?'

'How about *mine?*' I said.

'What! you don't mean to say you've killed?' he exclaimed, looking up in astonishment.

'Oh, yes,' I said; 'and had capital sport, too! Got three!'

'Don't believe it!' he remarked, and went on writing.

After he had finished he walked out of the room, and I followed a little way behind him. He went down to the larder, and on seeing the three beauties laid out on the slab, with the water turned on to them, he simply swore at large! Turning round on hearing me behind him laughing, he said,—

'How and where the devil did you kill them?'

'All with the same fly, Jock Scott,' I said. 'Killed the big one in the Parson's Pool, and the two others in Guppy's Stream.'

'D—— you!' he exclaimed, as he fumbled about in his pocket for the shilling.

The next morning poor Girvan caught it pretty hot from his lordship for advising him not to go out.

Five years after I paid back the shilling and told the truth!

CAMPING CASUALTIES.

By WILF POCKLINGTON.

HEN the summer sun is blazing down on the golden sea of corn, and the soft zephyrs meandering through the trees are few and far between; when the river is like an elongated mirror, and the fish lie basking and gasping in the sun; when all nature seems to have suddenly drifted into the land of the lotus-eaters; in other words, when the Oxford Undergrad is fairly well into the 'Long,' I do not know any more enjoyable trip than a camping excursion down the Thames from Oxford to London.

Given a party of four, or (if there are two boats) six men, prepared to take rough and smooth as they come, and bound by a common bond to avoid hotels as they would a pestilence—one of Salter's roomy but light gigs, with the camping impedimenta that he provides—and you have the materials for the most enjoyable fortnight ever spent. I have been the journey six or seven times, and so speak from experience.

The stream runs at about one and a half miles the hour; the scenery is exquisite; you can fish, or swim, or hunt hedges for duck and guinea-fowl eggs; in fact, if you want sport or mischief you will not have far to look for it, whilst if your *forte* lies in the *dolce far niente* you cannot be better situated. I met an old Oxford chum of mine the other day, and his chaffing queries brought the following forgotten incidents back to my mind.

In the August of 1876, Ted Burbidge, Will Wyatt (familiarly called 'Grunter'), and myself, chartered a boat and tent from Salter, and being old campers, found our own stove, lamp, cooking utensils, &c., and on the Tuesday afternoon swept slowly down toward Iffley Lock. 'Youth (*i.e.* the Grunter) at the prow, and Pleasure (*i.e.* Burbidge) at the helm.' I, with my usual luck, had lost the toss, and was straightening my back with the first spell at the oars.

Of course the lock-man at Iffley had to receive his due quantum of chaff, but, through constant scarification, his mental hide is like the skin of a rhinoceros, and requires wit with an extra sharp point to pierce it.

Along we sped on to Kennington Island, deeply enshrined

in all our hearts by the memory of cool cider-cups under the trees, fish-suppers that were an idyllic dream to the uncultured palates of crude nineteen, and last, but not least, by the foaming tankards of mulled beer that greeted us when, in the winter months, we dared the perils of flooded fields, and gaily careened over submerged gate and hedge, straight as the crow flies, to the inn on the Island, which, in these times, we were wont to enter by the first-floor window, leaving our boat tied to the window-sash. Those were happy days, and every now and again a chance meeting brings them all back, with the fresh-ness and piquancy of the sea breeze to an invalid.

A short halt here, and then on through Sandford Lock, past Newnham and its Swiss summer-houses, where we have had tea and 'Commemoration' picnics out of number. We were now fairly under way, and amid such scenes and good fellowship Time sped with winged feet.

On the Friday night we had landed on a neck of pasture land that ran down to the water's edge between two large patches of trees, and after a meal of grilled Thames trout, and a meditative pipe and chat, we had turned into the tent to sleep.

These tents are little structures solely intended for sleeping purposes, being about ten feet long, six feet broad, and four and a half feet in height. The lamp hangs from the centre pole.

About 2 a.m., as we were sleeping the sleep of the just, 'Grunter' suddenly awoke me, saying, 'Old man, there's some-body fooling about with the tent-ropes.'

'Let them fool,' replied I, quite too utterly lazy to move.

As I spoke, a harder tug than before made him and I think the tent was falling.

'I guess I'll make that idiot wish he'd never been born,' said I, crawling out, intent on vengeance dire and deep.

It was quite dark, and I crawled out round to the opposite side from which the shaking appeared to proceed, intending to astonish the intruder. Jumping quickly to my feet, I skipped round the tent.

Ye gods, what a sight was there!

About thirty of the largest bullocks I ever saw in my life, and in the centre of the herd was the leader, stamping with rage, and just performing the one, two, three business with his head that told me a rush was imminent, that would clear our tent to 'almighty smash' like a cyclone.

Rushing straight at the brute with a shout that would

have raised the dead, had there been any in the vicinity, I caught my foot on a tent-peg, stumbled over the culinary department, and turned a somersault right into their very midst. Out rushed my two chums, to find me in a paroxysm of laughter, and the herd some twenty yards off gazing in amazement. I had intended to astonish them, and an unbiassed referee would have owned I succeeded.

After some complimentary passages concerning the *wisdom* displayed in not scanning the field better, we did a starlight flit across the river, and once more courted the drowsy god.

Next day, it being my turn to act as cook, housemaid, and general major-domo, the other two left me for a stroll into the neighbouring village; when, suddenly taking a great fancy for some trout for dinner, I took my rod and fly-book and strolled to the lasher, some little distance above our halting-place, and was soon diligently whipping the stream.

Luck favoured me, and in a short time I had six beauties in my creel, and, satisfied therewith, returned to our camp; when, thinking the fish would be all the firmer if kept in the stream, I fastened the creel lid and hung it over the stern of the boat; then, lighting a pipe, I threw myself down under the shady trees to await my companions' return.

It was a lovely day, the sun was hot as it well could be, the river was almost without a ripple,—the slight breeze that rustled the leaves overhead not being strong enough to stir the surface of the water out of its day-dream. Away up the stream, mellowed by the distance, was the ceaseless roar of the lasher, sounding like the music of an immense hive of bees; and over the river was the not inharmonious hum of a reaper. The sounds blending together were soothing in the extreme, and under the influence I fell fast asleep.

When I awoke it was well into the evening, and, expecting the boys back to dinner, I shook myself together and put the kitchen in order.

I had just accomplished this when they arrived; of course, inquiring about dinner at once.

'I could do with some fish,' said Grunter; 'wish I had gone for some instead of trailing over those scorching fields.'

'Well, I have got six beauties, fully eighteen ounces average,' said I; 'so your wish can be gratified.'

I went down to the boat, and pulled up the creel, opening it with pride to show them my take, when—

'Great Heavens! what's this?' burst from me.

There, in the creel, were six minnows, about two inches long ; and my six trout,—well! I don't know where.

How those boys chaffed me!

' Never knew fish to shrink so in my life,' said Burbidge.

' Are you going to give us anything besides the fish?' said Grunter.

' Been asleep all day, and don't want to own up,' said Burbidge ; 'that's about it.'

Well, it passed over, and we had dinner somehow; but to this day it still remains a mystery as to *who* came and changed those fish.　That they *were* changed is undeniable, and it is considered by me as one of the most successful practical jokes I have known. There were scores of men, I knew, about the river just at that time ; and any one of them would have been quite equal to the occasion.

So we sped along, day by day, always something new to see or to do, until we reached Salter's Yard ; when we returned our boat and inventory card, settled for losses and breakages, and came right along to the Hotel, Charing Cross, where we had ordered our portmanteaus to be sent ; but found, to our chagrin, they had not been sent or heard of.　By the aid, however, of telegraphy, we subsequently discovered they had been left at an hotel of a similar name, but in a different district.

These are some few of the many accidents that may occur on a river-trip ; and those who intend camping out must have plenty of time, and fully make up their minds to allow nothing to annoy or ruffle them: in fact, to follow to the letter the evergreen precept of Lucullus,—

' If the cucumber be bitter, throw it away.'

If this advice be taken, no one will ever regret ' Camping Casualties.'

DEER-STALKING EXTRAORDINARY;

Or, How the Lord Mayor rented Glenyuckie.

By ' ROCKWOOD.'

T was after one of the big dinners at the Mansion House—how many years ago it will not be politic to tell—that Lord Mayor Jinks, who, as he used to boast, was come of a good old Roman patrician, one whose sons helped to build the great Roman wall round

London, but whom less honourably descended members of the Corporation said was an undiluted Cockney, resolved to take a Highland shooting and spend the autumn in Scotland. The cold whisky-punch, which agreed well with the turtle-soup, had no doubt something to do with it ; but the actual cause of this resolution was the rapt attention which was paid by the company to the wonderful capture of a salmon by Alderman Fitz-blether, an old rival, who hailed from the land of cakes, haggis, and snuff. It was no more true than the assertion of the teller that his grandfather had been out in the '45, for the parochial authorities of his own village to this day have as yet proved unable to establish fully his own parentage ; but as he ' birred ' away with the reel, and swung his arms about as if handling a rod, his hearers for a moment fancied ' the monster battling in the mighty deep,' as one of them phrased it, and ' his ludship ' could scarcely get a hearing for his famous cat-hunting story afterwards. Now, as he rather prided himself on the way in which he could tell a good thing, this rather annoyed him, and he then and there resolved to go to the Highlands. He was not much of a shot, it was true, but his son Charlie, who had been at Eton, and was at the time a ' Sub ' in a well-known cavalry regiment, had something of a reputation for the style in which he ' grassed his rocks ' (an expression full of difficulty to the old man, who was heard to mutter as he opened his letters that he would rather grass half-a-dozen horses than a dozen pigeons any day) ; and no doubt they would be able somehow to kill their own grouse, and possibly a salmon or two, as well as Fitzblether. To Charlie he posted a letter that morning, and, rather to his surprise, received a telegram next day from that worthy boy, as follows :—

Jinks, Aldershot.   *To Lord Mayor Jinks,*
                                          Mansion House.

Letter received. Taken Glenynckie Forest for two thousand. Thirty stags guaranteed, four hundred brace grouse, good lodge, salmon fishing. Had to be quick or lose it. Letter will explain.

If the truth has to be told, Charlie, who was busily engaged loading his own cartridges for a pigeon match when the post arrived, shouted out somewhat irreverently, ' Why, you'll not believe that his ludship the Lud Mayor is going to take a shooting ! What a time we'll have of it !'

Knowing the old man's wavering disposition, he then and there telegraphed to take the forest mentioned to the Scotch factor, to whom the advertisement in the number of the *Field*, which lay beside him, said people were to apply for particulars as to rent, and wired back to close at the amount mentioned. It was possibly well that he did so, for the Lord Mayor, when free from the influence of cold punch, had just been thinking of taking a house at Brighton instead, and of spending the season quietly on the Promenade. Charlie's letter settled the matter, though the amount was ten times greater than what he had calculated on. 'It is costly,' the old man said philosophically; 'but I have made my own fortune, and may as well have my own fling, even if it should be a Highland fling.' Having thus wisely resolved to pay the piper, he drew a cheque for the desired amount, and posted it to the factor, writing to his son at the same time to say that he hoped he would see after the looking out of the necessary sporting gear —the rifles, rods, and that, and what dogs he thought would be required : a commission which the boy was not less slow to execute than the first one, throwing in as part of the order to the gun-maker, to be entered in the bill 'kind of promiscuously,' a couple of first-class guns for pigeons, and a large-bore sporting rifle for India. 'It's just one year that his ludship is Lord Mayor,' said Mr. Jinks, junior; 'and when that year's up he may not be inclined to throw the money about so freely, so I may as well look a little bit ahead.'

While Charlie made the necessary sporting arrangements, his admiring mother and sisters sent off hamper after hamper to Glenyuckie, containing all the good things of this life ; and on the first week in August, when the Jinks family set out from London for the north, there was no better-stocked lodge in the Highlands. As Bailie Nicol Jarvie phrased it, it contained 'a' the comforts o' the Sautmarket,' in addition, indeed, to the luxuriousness of the London Mansion House. But good company was scarce, and the worthy Lord Mayor got very soon tired of talking to the gillies, or 'jillies,' as he called them ; and whole strings of crofters visited him daily to ask for compensation for the ravages on their crops by that which he had been looking for in vain for a week—those wonderful stags, of which he had heard so much about. To all his inquiries about their whereabouts (he had imagined, indeed, that the Forest of Glenyuckie was a kind of Scottish Zoo), he could only receive such like replies as,

' They'll be doun the back o' the Ben na Bogle the day, maist likely, or maybe feeding wast ower the Gilnacoble '—places which lay somewhere up amongst the endless and impenetrable mist.

The eve of the twelfth of August brought the irrepressible Charlie, the only son and heir, with all the brother-officers on leave he could get with him, each and all anxious, after much of the snap-shooting at pigeons, to have a day at the grouse. After that, dulness was no longer complained of, for that very night saw a torch-light dance in front of the lodge with pipe music, and heard ' hoochs ' in the reel enough to drive grouse and deer out of the glen.

The ever-glorious morning dawned most favourably for the sport, and ere nine o'clock the Lord Mayor, attired not in his official robes, but in a gorgeous kilt specially made for him by a Regent Street firm, opened the ceremony, as he termed it, by firing the contents of his new twelve-bore without effect into the bosom of the first covey. Disappointed at not killing any-thing, he determined to blaze away at everything that rose, and soon had to be credited with a brace of birds, his first brace, and which, like a genuine Londoner who has killed his first trout or pike, he determined should be preserved in a glass case. All the while Charlie, with his companions, had been putting together a splendid bag, knocking down the first birds that rose with their ' rights ' ere they were fairly clear of the heather, and following on with the ' lefts ' for a second with unerring accuracy. At luncheon-time, when they halted under a bower of birch-trees—the birch bowers of the old Scottish love-trysts—by the banks of a mountain streamlet, they had for four guns sixty brace and a dozen hares, but, much to the Lord Mayor's disap-pointment, *no stag*. In vain did Charlie and the head keeper try to persuade him that they could not expect to kill stags and grouse on the same day; that the former were miles away up in the hills, and that they would have to be stalked in the most unwearying manner for days with the rifle. It was a stag the old man wanted—a stag to tell a story about, which, if the truth were told, would completely take the wind out of Fitzblether's sails ; and a stag he was determined he should have, or there would be no more annual visits to the Highlands.

' The twelfth ' over, and the fever for grouse blood somewhat abated, some of the party resolved upon ' a stalk;' but the stalk, like the late Duke of Athole's sporting treat to his friend whom he had invited to his forest, resolved itself into a weary

walk. 'Yet they were up there, there was nae doot o' that,' said
Donald, the keeper; 'but the gentleman must have perseverance,
as all guid stalkers must have, and must na expect to come on
them the first day, ay, or even the first week.' September was
well in, and as yet no antlers had been seen in the hall or venison
at the table; and the Lord Mayor resolved not to take Glenyuckie for another season—a matter of great disappointment to
his son, who had fallen madly in love with the place. Some
strategy, he thought, must be executed in order to make his
father change his mind, and that without delay.

'I tell you what it is, boys,' he said to his brother-sportsmen,
as he sat in the evening, after a long tramp after grouse, sur-
veying the lovely Highland scene before him, 'we must have
one of those thirty stags at once, no matter how; and not only
that, the governor must shoot one of them.'

There was a pretty general laugh at the latter part of the
assertion, to which the speaker responded: 'Aye, aye, laugh
away; but we must manage it somehow. I know the old man
better than anybody; and what he wants to do is to kill something or other that he can go and tell a long yarn about. I
thought the grouse would have been enough, but he seems fixed
on killing a stag. Once let him kill a stag, or get him to believe
he has killed one, and he'll take a lease of the place for nineteen
years.' 'All very well, Charlie; but how is it to be done, my
boy? A stag *he* never can expect to get within shot of, and
even if he did the odds would be a thousand to one against him.'

'Ah, I did not mean he should kill a stag; I meant to try
and make him believe he had killed one; and if you'll all back
me I'll take Donald and Dugald and two of the gillies into our
confidence, and we're bound to succeed. Donald, who has been
out on the hills after them for two days, says we are almost certain to have one, if not two, to-morrow night, if we're careful;
and if we have them we shall manage to get the governor to
stalk and kill one next day. You just leave that to me.'

Sure enough the next day, after being out from an early hour,
they killed two stags, one of them a 'Royal,' which, for reasons
that were not to be asked, was not taken home. In the evening
the head keeper and Charlie were very much together, and apparently planning some great scheme. And next morning the
former appeared hurriedly at the breakfast-room window of the
lodge with the welcome information that a stag—a grand muckle
beast—was 'feeding jist twa mile up the hill-side; and oh! but

"Up the Course of a Stream."

it was a bonnie chance!' Seizing his glass, his lordship rushed
to the window, and there, sure enough, was a grand stag—a stag
of ten points at least, for Donald could count them standing on
the hill afar off. The ladies, one and all, could make out
the proportions of the noble animal, and so could Charlie's
brother-officers, who could not understand it, and were of opinion
that he must have got hold of a tame deer and let it out on to
the hill-side. Not one of them, however, said a word while
cannie old Donald was repeating that he 'had na seen such a
grand chance of killing a stag for monie a lang lang day.' Attired in his kilt, with silver-mounted powder-horn and belt over
his shoulder, the Lord Mayor was soon ready for to 'take the
hill,' as the old keeper termed it, but not before having a few
words with the clever and cunning Charlie.

'Make it as rough and uncomfortable as ye can for him now,
Donald,' was the latter's parting remark ; 'in fact, give him all
the discomforts ye can think about in deer-stalking ; and, for
my sake, give us time to get that infernal brute well over the
hill and out of sight ere you rush him up to the dead stag.'

'Aye, aye, I'll dae that, Sir, trust to me,' was the reply, as he
made to follow his chief; then added aloud, 'My name's no
Donald McNab if we dinna kill that bonnie beast this day.'

Obeying the directions given him, carefully he made the
esteemed Chief of the London Corporation get down on all-fours
almost from the outset. 'Lord, Sir, keep yer muckle heid
down,' he said, somewhat disrespectfully, 'or we'll never get
anither look at him.'

Up the course of a mountain burn the keeper led him,
making him creep on his hands and knees, though the latter
were all cut and bleeding from the round pebbles. Up to the
neck at another time he forced him to plunge and make his
way through a deep pool, only to find himself crawling with his
chin close to the ground over treacherous and slimy flow moss.
Such a Lord Mayor's procession had never been seen before,
such an one will probably never be seen again.

At length, when he thought they must be getting very close
to him, Donald bade him sit down in a deep pool under a burn,
and no to stir for his 'verra life,' and went off ahead crawling
to reconnoitre. In a quarter of an hour's time or so he came
back with the information that the stag was still there, but in
order not to 'gie him oor wind, we will have to gang back the
way we came.' So off they set down stream again ; and after

another crawling match on hands and knees across the moss heather and rocky boulders, reached another watercourse. Up this, tired and bleeding, the poor Lord Mayor crept behind his guide, who was obeying his son's orders to the letter, and giving the old man all the discomforts he could think of in connexion with stalking.

At last they reached a burn, where the water was rushing furiously, and as they could not go any further Donald determined to have a look. Peering over the edge as if afraid that the few grey hairs on his head might be seen, he took a careful survey of the hill-side ; then bending down, he took off his lordship's cap, and made him get up and have a canny look.

' Eh, but isna he a noble beast ? ' was his remark. ' Oh, but be careful, for ye'll no get sic a chance again for mony a day.'

' He is indeed a noble animal,' was the reply ; ' could we kill him from here ? '

' Ye'll jist have to try. So get up on my shoulders close to the burn, aim well just behind the foreleg, and be quick.'

Planted on the old man's shoulders, so close to the precipice that the water streamed round his neck, the stalker did as desired, pressed the trigger, and the next minute fell, rifle and all, into the pool beyond ; from which, in no hurry, Donald fished him out, remembering Charlie's last injunction to give them 'plenty of time to get that muckle beast out of the road.'

  • • • • • •

How the Lord Mayor killed that stag, and how he took a ten years' lease of Glenyuckie, he loves best to explain at Lord Mayors' dinners, to the great discomfiture of Mr. Fitzblether. Fails he not to tell of his crawling up the burn on his hands and knees, of his swimming through the pools, and of his first sight of 'the noble animal, the monarch of the glen, in all his native majesty standing there sniffing the breeze,' of his unerring aim, of the whistling bullet's message of death (as a matter of fact there was no bullet in the rifle), and of rushing up and finding the noble animal dead with the bullet through its heart.

His son Charlie tells sometimes a scarcely less interesting story, and which relates how he hid a dead stag on the hill-side, borrowed 'a noble animal' (a donkey) from the nearest village, and tied a set of antlers to its head, and set it out to feed on the hill-side, and how by that means he got the Lord Mayor to rent the Forest of Glenyuckie.

Fores's Highly-Coloured Sporting Publications.

FORES'S CONTRASTS.

Illustrative of the Road, the Rail, &c. After H. ALKEN. Price 10*s.* each.

1. THE DRIVER (Coachman) of 1832—THE DRIVER (Engineer) of 1852.
2. THE GUARD (Coach) of 1832—THE GUARD (Locomotive) of 1852.
3. THE DRIVER OF THE MAIL of 1832—THE DRIVER OF THE MAIL of 1852.
4. ST. GEORGE'S (our Jeames)—ST. GILES'S (our Jim).

A STEEPLE CHASE IN THE OLDEN TIME.

After H. ALKEN, Sen. Six Plates, price £3 3*s.*

EXPLOITS OF DICK KNIGHT OF THE PYTCHLEY HUNT.

After C. LORAINE SMITH, Esq. Eight Plates Coloured, price £ . Very Scarce.

FOX HOUNDS.

After T. WOODWARD and W. BARRAUD. Price £1 10*s.* the Pair.

1. COMPANIONS IN THE CHASE.   2. GONE TO EARTH.

AN EXTRAORDINARY STEEPLE CHASE

FOR 1000 SOVEREIGNS,

Between Mr. Geo. Osbaldeston on his 'Clasher,' and Dick Christian on Capt. Ross's 'Clinker.' From Great Dalby Windmill to within a mile of Tilton-on-the-Hill. The five miles were done in 16 minutes.

After E. GILL. Price £2 2*s.*

RETURNING FROM ASCOT RACES.

(A SCENE ON THE ROAD.)

After C. C. HENDERSON. Price £2 2*s.*

EPSOM.

After J. POLLARD. Six Plates, price £3 3*s.*

1. SADDLING IN THE WARREN.   4. THE GRAND STAND.
2. THE BETTING POST.   5. THE RACE OVER.
3. PREPARING TO START.   6. SETTLING DAY AT TATTERSALL'S (OLD YARD).

FORES'S SPORTING SCRAPS.

After H. ALKEN, Sen.   Price 10*s.* per Sheet of four.

1. STEEPLE CHASING.   2. HUNTING.   3. HUNTING.   4. HUNTING.
   5. RACING.   6. COURSING.   7. BOATING.

Sheets 2, 3, 4, form a consecutive series of twelve Hunting Incidents.

FORES'S HUNTING SCENES.

After H. ALKEN. Price 12*s.* each.

PLATE 1.—THE FIRST INTRODUCTION TO HOUNDS.
PLATE 2.—RENEWAL OF ACQUAINTANCE WITH HOUNDS.

FORES'S ANATOMICAL PLATES of the HORSE.

THE AGE EXHIBITED BY THE SHAPE OF THE TEETH.   Price 6*s.*
THE AGE EXHIBITED BY THE TABLES OF THE TEETH.
THE STRUCTURE OF THE FOOT CLEARLY DEFINED.   } Price 5*s.* each.
THE MUSCLES AND TENDONS ACCURATELY DELINEATED. }

LONDON: PUBLISHED BY MESSRS. FORES, 41 PICCADILLY, W

SHIPPERS SUPPLIED UPON LIBERAL TERMS.

b

THE BILLESDON COPLOW RUN.
After R. FRANKLAND.   Six Plates.   Price £2 2s.   Scarce.

THE SMOKING HUNT AT BRAUNSTONE.
After C. LORAINE SMITH, Esq. Six Plates. Price £4 4s. Scarce.

IN LUCK AND OUT OF LUCK.
After T. EARL and W. BROMLEY.   Price 15s. the Pair.
1. IN LUCK.—A Bull Terrier with Pipe and Grog.
2. OUT OF LUCK.—A Scotch Terrier with Empty Platter, &c

ROUGH AND READY.
A Scotch Terrier's Head looking through a broken Hoarding. After G. STEVENS.
Price 5s.

WIDE AWAKE.
A Rough Terrier's Head Watching. After J. S. NEWTON. Price 5s.

MISCHIEVOUS MODELS.
A Puppy and Kitten in an Artist's Studio. After R. PHYSICK. Price 7s. 6d.

FORES'S ILLUSTRATED SPORTING WORKS.

THE SPORTING SCRAP-BOOK.
Forty Plates Coloured, price £4 4s.
HUNTING, RACING, STEEPLE CHASING, COURSING, SHOOTING, YACHTING,
BOATING, COACHING.

SCENES ON THE ROAD.
By C. B. NEWHOUSE. Eighteen Plates Coloured, price £3 3s.
A Pictorial Gallery of Coaching Incidents, spiritedly pourtrayed.

THE HORSE'S MOUTH
(SHEWING THE AGE BY THE TEETH).
By EDWARD MAYHEW, M.R.C.V.S. Demy 8vo. Price 10s. 6d., with Coloured
Illustrations and Woodcuts. 4th Edition.

ROAD SCRAPINGS.
By C. C. HENDERSON. Twelve Plates Coloured, price £2 2s.
Travelling Scenes in England, France, Spain, Flanders, Italy, and Switzerland.
Each Sketch carries a History of the Road with it, truthfully
and artistically detailed.

THE COMBINATION HUNTING AND CARD RACK.
Designed to hang or stand.
A receptacle for the Meets of Three Packs of Hounds; also Documents, &c. Price 15s.

LONDON: PUBLISHED BY MESSRS. FORES, 41 PICCADILLY, W.
SHIPPERS SUPPLIED UPON LIBERAL TERMS.

c

FORES'S STEEL-PLATE ENGRAVINGS.

THE FAREWELL CARESS.
Painted by C. BURTON BARBER. Engraved by F. STACPOOLE.
Artist's Proofs, £8 8s. Prints, £2 2s.

NO FEAR OF THE HOUNDS.
Painted by C. BURTON BARBER. Engraved by W. H. SIMMONS.
Artist's Proofs, £8 8s. Prints, £2 2s.

A PROMISING LITTER.
Painted by C. BURTON BARBER. Engraved by W. T. DAVEY.
Artist's Proofs, £8 8s. Prints, £2 2s.

CHRISTIAN GRACES—FAITH, HOPE, CHARITY.
Painted by G. E. HICKS. Engraved by F. HOLL.
Artist's Proofs, £6 6s. Prints, £2 2s.

IL PENSEROSO.
Painted by G. E. HICKS. Engraved by F. HOLL. Artist's Proofs, £3 3s. Prints, £1 1s.

L'ALLEGRO.
Painted by G. E. HICKS. Engraved by F. HOLL.
Artist's Proofs, £3 3s. Prints, £1 1s.

THE HUNTSMAN AND HOUNDS.
Drawn by Sir EDWIN LANDSEER, R.A. Engraved by H. T. RYALL.
Artist's Proofs, £2 2s. Proofs, Tinted, £1 1s. Prints, 10s. 6d.

HIS ROYAL HIGHNESS THE DUKE OF CAMBRIDGE, K.G., G.C.B., &c.
Painted by JOHN LUCAS. Engraved by T. OLDHAM BARLOW, R.A.
Artist's Proofs, £6 6s. Prints, £2 2s.

Maj.-Gen. The EARL OF CARDIGAN, K.C.B., &c.
(Leading the Brigade of Light Cavalry at Balaklava.)
Painted by A. F. DE PRADES. Engraved by H. COUSINS.
Artist's Proofs, £6 6s. Prints, £2 2s.

A LARGE COLLECTION OF ARTISTS' PROOFS and SCARCE FIRST STATES, after SIR E. LANDSEER, R.A., and other Celebrated Modern Artists.

ALSO,

A GALLERY OF OIL-PAINTINGS AND WATER-COLOUR DRAWINGS, amongst which are choice examples of SIR E. LANDSEER, R.A.; JAMES WARD, R.A.; W. C. T. DOBSON, R.A.; C. W. COPE, R.A.; G. STUBBS, R.A.; C. BURTON BARBER; T. S. ROBINS; J. J. HILL; J. F. HERRING, Sen.; H. ALKEN, Sen.; C. COOPER HENDERSON; WOOTTON SARTORIUS, &c.

LONDON: PUBLISHED BY MESSRS. FORES, 41 PICCADILLY, W.
SHIPPERS SUPPLIED UPON LIBERAL TERMS.

d

TWO SHILLINGS

FORES's SPORTING NOTES & Sketches.

No 4 January 1885

Contents:

EIGHT TINTED FULL PAGE ILLUSTRATIONS,
By FINCH MASON
& R. M. ALEXANDER.

PUBLISHED QUARTERLY BY
MESSRS FORES' 41 PICCADILLY, LONDON.

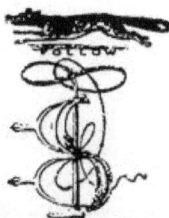

4

FORES'S
SPORTING NOTES & SKETCHES.

A QUARTERLY MAGAZINE.

No. 4.   JANUARY, 1885.   PRICE 2s.

CONTENTS.

LONDON:
PUBLISHED BY MESSRS. FORES, 41 PICCADILLY

SIMPKIN, MARSHALL, & CO.

MESSRS. FORES'S

SPORTING & FINE ART PUBLICATIONS.

THE NIGHT TEAM, by C. Cooper Henderson, forms
Plate 6 of the celebrated Series of Fores's Coaching Recollections, and shows the
night 'Screws' being 'put to,' the duck-toed Coachman looking to the harness,
whilst the Guard affixes the lamps. This is replete with 'character,' and one of
the best of the Series.

Coloured Engraving, 26½ by 17½ inches, £1 1s.

THE FIRST DAY OF THE SEASON, by Cecil Boult,
introduces us to a charming young lady on a well-bred chestnut, preceded by
her father on a clipped bay, who is opening a gate into a lane in which are the
Huntsman, Whips, and Hounds.

Coloured, 19½ by 8½ inches, £2 2s.

THE END OF A LONG RUN, by Basil Nightingale,
Companion to above, presents us with the ultimate of the Noble Sport, 'The
Death of the Fox,' who has just been rescued from the Pack with Brush, Pads,
and Mask intact, the former doubtless intended for the Lady on the well-bred
Chestnut, which forms the centre of the picture. The Huntsman's Bay and
Hounds possess quality and character.

Coloured, 19½ by 8½ inches, £2 2s.

THE SPORTSMAN'S DREAM, by R. M. Alexander,
represents a tired and sleeping Sportsman reclining in his easy-chair before a
comfortable fire, dreaming of the following Sports, which are cleverly depicted in
the wreaths arising from his half-smoked pipe, viz., Hunting, Yachting, Coaching,
Pigeon Shooting, Billiards, Golf, Deer Stalking, Grouse Shooting, Steeple
Chasing, Salmon Fishing, Boxing, Racing, Polo, and Cards.

Coloured, 14 by 11 inches, £1 1s.

SALMON FISHING, by W. Brackett, in four subjects,
entitled 'The Rise,' 'The Leap,' 'The Struggle,' 'Landed,' are clearly the work
of a Salmon Fisher, and being replete with artistic finish, will surely commend
themselves to lovers of the sport.

Coloured, 11 by 8 inches, £1 1s. each, or £3 13s. 6d. the Set of Four

SHOOTING, by Basil Bradley, in four subjects, viz.
Partridge, Grouse, Wild Duck, and Woodcock, will prove acceptable to all
'gunners.' Dogs, game, and sportsmen are thoroughly well delineated by one
who is evidently master of the 'business.'

Coloured Engravings, 23¾ by 14¾ inches, £1 1s. each, or £3 3s. the Set of Four.

'DOLCE CON ESPRESSIONE,'
By J. WATSON NICOL,

Is in this Artist's happiest vein of humour. Two Court Jesters in
motley garb, with cap and bells, are beguiling the tedium of their ordinary avocations with a vocal and instrumental duet, and the admirable
soul-wrapt expression of their faces is inimitably given as they are discoursing a passage 'dolce con espressione.'

COLOURED, 17 by 12 inches, £3 3s. ; UNCOLOURED, 15s.

PUBLISHED BY MESSRS. FORES, 41 PICCADILLY, LONDON, W.

FORES'S SPORTING NOTES AND SKETCHES.

Opinions of the Press.

Fores's Sporting Notes and Sketches. October 1884.—'This is the third number of a new quarterly magazine which has already gone far to justify the reasonable confidence of its promoters. No pains have been spared with the object of securing the sympathy and support of all genuine lovers of sport. The names of artists and contributors are a sufficient guarantee of high-class quality, and the character of the selected subjects hits that happy mean between ponderosity and flippancy which is a sure passport to popular favour. To be bright and sparkling without frivolity, to be entertaining without vulgarity, to be instructive without boredom, demands the possession of qualities whose literary outcome is so apparently spontaneous that the difficulty of the successfully accomplished task is rarely recognised. The difficulty is increased in the case of a publication devoted to the interests of sport, and when we say that *Fores's Sporting Notes and Sketches* has fully surmounted it, we have given the magazine the highest recommendation in our power. Mr. Finch Mason's charming tinted illustrations deserve all the good things that have been written of them by more competent pens than ours ; and Mr. R. M. Alexander, to whom many of this month's sketches are due, has approved himself a worthy coadjutor with the pencil. The illustration accompanying the article entitled "Black-game Shooting on Exmoor,' in which the blundering Twister is detected by Mr. Keeper in the act of firing at a grey hen, who fortunately saved her feathers, is full of humour and life-like movement. This month's number, which includes among its contributors Ames Savile, Wilf Pocklington, "Triviator," "Seramo," and "Rockwood," is bright and readable from cover to cover. The magazine is only two shillings, and when the quality of letterpress and illustrations are taken into account, we have no hesitation in saying that it is very cheap at the price.'—*County Gentleman.*

Fores's Sporting Notes and Sketches.—' The October number of this magazine fully bears out the title the promoters claimed for it in their first number—that of being a high-class sporting quarterly. We scarcely know which to praise the most, the articles or the sketches, for they are all really clever and spirited. A reminiscence of the Devon and Somerset Staghounds will be read with pleasure by all who love the only real sport with the wild red deer now left to us in England ; and who that has ever hunted with these hounds will fail to recognise the truthful and characteristic sketch by Finch Mason of the late lamented Mr. Fenwick Bissett? The rare old stag-hunter is depicted to the very life. "A Day with ' Jock Trotter' with the Royal Meath" is a brilliantly written article anent these hounds and their followers, with all the enthusiasm which may be expected from " Triviator, or the Man at the Cross-roads," whose writings on Irish hunting matters are so well known and appreciated. We hardly agree with the writer that Captain Trotter has the best pack of hounds in the world. Good they are, no doubt, good as can be, but saying they are the best is more than we dare endorse. Two portraits will be recognised in Finch Mason's clever sketch. " Black-game Shooting on Exmoor" is written by a true son of the soil ; the illustration by R. M. Alexander is a very clever one indeed, and the Devonshire keeper's dialect is perfect. " Under False Colours " is a smartly written article, in which a lady's opinion of a horse is proved to be worth something more than common. " A Barefaced Case of Poaching " and " Deer-stalking Extraordinary " are both excellent reading, and "An Honest Man on an Honest Horse " is a well-told racing sketch. The present number of *Fores's Notes and Sketches* will bear favourable comparison with any sporting magazine that has ever been published. Indeed, we may say that the quality of the articles, and particularly the style of the illustrations, have never been excelled.'—*Land and Water.*

FORES'S SPORTING NOTES AND SKETCHES.

Extracts from Opinions of the Press.

'IS brightly written by experts in the several divisions of outdoor sport. Spirited, life-like pencillings by that chief of graphic sportsmen, Finch Mason. As good as anything that John Leech ever turned out.'

Daily Telegraph.

'CAPITAL reading for a railway journey. The really best sketch is the one supplied by R. M. Alexander to "Thames Trout-Fishing."'—*Field.*

'WE heartily commend the book. This bright and entertaining magazine is excellent enough to achieve a great success. The illustrations by Finch Mason and R. M. Alexander are most admirable. A most readable and truthful compilation of sporting events on "Fell and Field."'

United Service Gazette.

'IN hitting off the likenesses of well-known racing men, Mr. Finch Mason has been singularly successful.'—*Illustrated Sporting and Dramatic News.*

'THERE is not a dull line between the two covers, and the illustrations by Mr. Finch Mason are quite beyond the sporting pictures which are usually to be found in pages meant for sportsmen. Indeed we may say that few artists in black and white can compete with Mr. Mason in the delineation of the horse, and the spirit with which he contrives to invest his animals while in movement reminds us of the drawings of John Leech, whose humour he also seems to have caught. Good as was the first number, the second is still better. The third fully sustains the reputation achieved by its predecessor.'

Bell's Life.

'THE articles are all well written, and there is not a dull page in the magazine.'—*The Sportsman.*

'A VERY high-class magazine. The illustrations by Finch Mason are on a scale not often attempted in this class of work.'—*Sporting Times.*

'BIDS fair to form a valuable and welcome addition to high-class sporting literature. Mr. Mason's characteristic drawings are a leading feature. Messrs. Fores, the well-known publishers of Piccadilly, are to be congratulated on the excellence of the third number.'—*Sporting Life.*

'FULLY sustains the high standard its conductors set up for themselves on the opening number.'—*Sporting Chronicle.*

'WE venture to predict it will be extremely popular. R. M. Alexander, who can draw so well, and whose touch is so delicate and yet so full of vigour, is sure to make his mark. The American magazines are so far ahead of us in the matter of illustrations that we gladly welcome a sketch as spirited and as graceful as that of Mr. Alexander.'—*Society.*

8

FORES'S
SPORTING NOTES AND SKETCHES.

NOT NIMRODS BY NATURE.

By CUTHBERT BEDE, *Author of 'Verdant Green.'*

N the letter read by Malvolio, in Olivia's garden, was the saying, so often quoted and misquoted, ' Some are born great, some achieve greatness, and some have greatness thrust upon them.' Similarly, some are born riders, some achieve riding, and some, if they have not horses thrust upon them, are, by force of circumstances, thrust upon horses sorely against their will. Some men are cradled in the pigskin; to others, the saddle is a mockery, a delusion, and a snare. Some are Nimrods, or ' mighty hunters,' from their birth; others most plainly prove, by their ways and manners in the hunting-field, that they are not Nimrods by nature.

The author of *Don Juan* said, ' A fox-hunt to a foreigner is strange.' And Byron could speak from experience. Perhaps he may have read the *Thoughts upon Hunting*, by Beckford—not ' Vathek, England's wealthiest son,' but the accomplished and learned Peter Beckford, of whom it was said that ' he could bag a fox in Greek, find a hare in Latin, inspect his kennels in Indian, and direct the economy of his stables in excellent French.' In his book upon Hunting, Peter Beckford gives an anecdote concerning a Gallic guest of Lord Castlehaven, who, being given a mount on one of the best horses in his Lordship's stud, was taken some miles to be ' shown a fox-chase.' He was duly shown the sport; and, after having been well shaken, dirtied, tired, and run away with, he was asked on his return, ' *Comment il avoit trouvé la chasse ?* ' He shrugged his shoulders, and replied, with much feeling, '*Morbleu, Milord! votre chasse est une chasse diabolique!*' It was clear that Lord Castlehaven's French guest was not a Nimrod by nature.

His sentiments have been shared by many. 'Who hunts, doth oft in danger ride,' says Isaac Walton's *Piscator*, in his 'Angler's Song,' preferring the contemplative man's recreation to that amusement which has been cynically described as 'Riding furiously after a nasty smell.' Pascal could not see what it was, unless it was to drown thought, that should make men throw away so much time and pains upon a silly animal which they might buy cheaper in the market. Honest Sancho Panza observed to the Duke, 'Mercy on me! What pleasure can you find, any of ye all, in killing a poor beast that never meant any harm?' And the courtly Chesterfield, on the day succeeding to that on which he had been supposed to have 'enjoyed' a long run, asked the question, 'Do men ever hunt twice?' Clearly these people were not Nimrods by nature. They belonged to a class of persons who, from deliberate choice and their own free will, and not from the obligations of stern necessity, decline to hunt, and are not moved to any special enthusiasm by the deeds or records of the hunting-field. To them, the sport of hunting seems to be so far removed from the nature of a pastime as to be brought within the category of those things wherein pain and duty are stronger ingredients than option and delight.

Yet, they cannot class it with those pleasures that the Englishman is said to take sadly, for they see it to be a sport that is carried through by its followers with a keen zest of enjoyment, which, if not genuine, is cleverly simulated. And if those who are not Nimrods by nature wish to do justice to those followers of the chase, they are compelled to confess that they really seem to them, in the aggregate, to be a light-hearted race, whose wild freedom of spirits is shared by their horses; so that the hunting-field is certain to exhibit mercurial vivacity in its equine members, if not in their riders. Indeed, from the evident delight of the steeds, it might almost appear to a non-hunting observer that the horsemen were members of a Humane and Anti-Cruelty-to-Animals Society, who, at the risk of their own necks, and with the certainty of incurring great personal discomfort, were exercising the animals, and taking them across country for a day's holiday. Perhaps something of the horsey nature of the fabulous Centaurs may have entered the breasts of the Guy Livingstones

and other modern Chirons, and have caused the riders to participate in the bounding spirits of those

> ' Coursers, than the mountain roe more fleet,'

as, in the words of the laureate of *The Chase,*—

> ' With emulation fired,
> They strain to lead the field, top the barr'd gate,
> O'er the deep ditch exulting bound, and brush
> The thorny-twining hedge.'

Perhaps, too, some high motives may be mingled with the pastime ; for the persons whom Charles Kingsley was so fond of
calling 'God-fearing men' are they who can thrash a bargee,
hold their own at the stumps, fight a poacher, and ride across
country in the foremost flight.

All this may be fine sport to those who really like it ; but to
those who do not, and who are not Nimrods by nature, it must
appear something like an amiable madness. Some may take
pleasure in viewing the sport, regarded as a mere spectacle ; and
may even go the length of sharing the pastime, provided that
they can do so as did John Leech's snob, who pronounced of his
day's hunting, ' It was first-rate ! There were none of your nasty
'edges and ditches, but a good turnpike-road all the way !' or, as
did Mr. *Spectator*, who, when he went out with Sir Roger de
Coverley's harriers, and the critical moment had arrived for his
display of equestrianism, when the hare had stolen away, naïvely
observes, ' This, with my Aversion to leaping Hedges, made me
withdraw to a rising Ground, from whence I could have the
Pleasure of the whole Chase, without the Fatigue of keeping in
with the Hounds.' In such a safe situation, from whence a bird's-
eye prospect of the field might be obtained, they who were not
Nimrods by nature might so far permit themselves to be carried
away by the excitement of the sport as to share the feelings of
Mr. *Spectator*, who, when he viewed the pack in full cry, said, ' I
must confess the Brightness of the Weather, the Chearfulness of
everything around me, the Chiding of the Hounds, which was
returned upon us in a double Eccho from two neighbouring
Hills, with the Hollowing of the Sportsmen, and the Sounding
of the Horn, lifted my Spirits into a most lively Pleasure, which
I freely indulged, because I was sure it was Innocent.' And the
worthy man left the spot, prepared to ' prescribe the moderate

use of this Exercise to all my Country Friends, as the best Kind of Physick for mending a bad Constitution, and preserving a good one.' Though, if the prescription were to be taken after the fashion set by its prescriber, the dose would be infinitesimal indeed.

When Mr. *Spectator* spoke of Hunting in moderation as ' the best Kind of Physick,' perhaps he had in his mind the couplet of Dryden to the same effect :—

> ' Better to hunt in fields for health unbought,
> Than fee the Doctor for a nauseous draught.'

And, in another of his papers—that on ' Planting and Plantations ' —he incidentally mentions that the fact of so many country gentlemen having so entirely devoted themselves to field sports had given occasion ' to one of our most eminent English writers to represent every one of them as lying under a kind of Curse pronounced to them in the words of Goliah, " I will give thee to the Fowls of the air, and to the Beasts of the field."' Nevertheless, Mr. *Spectator* was of opinion that ' Exercises of this kind, when indulged with Moderation, may have a good Influence both on the Mind and the Body.'

But, to those who are not Nimrods by nature, the enforced following of the sport involves much which they cannot regard as otherwise than highly disagreeable. It is not pleasant to them, for example, to be aroused from deep sleep at an untimely hour on a dark winter's morning, and to have to dress by candle-light, and also by it to shave—supposing that you are not ' bearded like the pard.' This is sufficiently unpleasant, even when you are forced to do so to catch an early train ; but, to voluntarily do it to enable you to rail your horse and join a distant meet of hounds, and in their company to run unknown risks for the remainder of the day, and to take a real pleasure in so doing, is, to certain minds, an astounding fact. Yet, if a man rides to hounds, and is not content to be classed with the mere laners, he must make up his mind to brave all the chances of the field, and, philosophically, to set down the mishaps as part and parcel of the sport. But it cannot be pleasant to be propelled into a Leicestershire bullfinch, or to be jumped into a quickset hedge like that in which the wondrous wise man of Thessaly scratched out both his eyes ; for no jumping into another hedge would avail to scratch them in again. Nor can

it be agreeable to be sent a purler over a hidden wire ; or to be
soused in the Whissendine when the thermometer is hastening
to freezing-point ; or to be banged against a stone wall ; or to
be cannoned by a headstrong horse and knocked over ; or to
lose the victory of Waterloo Gorse by being thrown out early in
the run. Nor can it be pleasant to sit shivering on your saddle
on a terribly raw day, with nothing better to warm you than the
anathemas that are directed against the fox for obstinately
refusing to leave the thick covert, where the hounds are getting
all the hunting to themselves. Nor can it be altogether
agreeable to go pounding on through heavy clay, bespattered
with filth and mire ; or to be tearing your flesh and your
garments, 'thoro' brake, thoro' briar,' like Puck in *A Midsummer
Night's Dream ;'* or have to negotiate an awkward fence, on
the drop side of which is a nasty drain ; or, when going well,
and skilfully steering for a practicable gap, to be cut out by
some other craner or funker, and jostled out of your place ; or
to have a horse full of going who makes you override the
hounds, and, thereupon, to be clothed with cursing as with a
garment by the irate huntsman ; or to have your favourite
two-hundred-and-fifty-guinea chestnut staked or maimed ; or to
ride in the teeth of one of those gales that often characterise an
'open' season—a season rather too open for those with limited
steeds ; or to find yourself, after a hard day's run, on a jaded or
overreached horse, in a strange country, at the edge of a dark
and tempestuous night, in the midst of an apparently endless
and decidedly swampy common, and many miles from home,
whether the good accommodation for man and beast be found
at the mansion or hunting-box of a friend, or at some such well-
known quarters as the Leicester ' Bell,' the Grantham ' George,'
the Harborough ' Angel,' the Cheltenham ' Plough,' or the
Wansford ' Haycock.'

None of these mishaps can truly be said to be pastime,
although they occur, from time to time, as unavoidable portions
of the sport ; but to those who are not Nimrods by nature—and
cannot emulate the equestrian deeds of that mighty hunter, the
son of Cush, who, according to Eastern authors, was the first
King in the world, and the first Monarch who wore a crown,—
to such, it seems almost unintelligible that persons who are
not paid to do this sort of thing, and to whom it does not come
within the sphere of their necessary duties—as is the case with

the huntsman and his whips—should voluntarily go forth three or four times—or even five times—a-week during the winter season, and run their chance of so many disagreeables and accidents, from the initiatory days of cub-hunting, to those closing ones when 'them stinkin' wiolets' perfume the air. To many it seems to be nothing less than a matter removed from the sphere of common sense, that, in every part of the country, so many thousands should be found, who, to all appearance, take the keenest delight in riding forth to encounter the dangers and chances of the hunting-field. To such, who are not Nimrods by nature, hunting appears to be somewhat in the nature of an infectious complaint.

If, however, it be a disease, it is one that is very deeply rooted in the Englishman, and is generated in this country as spontaneously as a *goître* would be elsewhere. It is developed, too, at a very early period ; and if the schoolboy who passes his Christmas holidays at a country-house should not be infected by it, it will be wondrous strange. Mounted on an active, scrambling pony, or on a clever cob, the boy who was lately assisting at the 'break-up' of his school, is now found to be equally, if not more, hilarious if he is lucky enough to be one of the fortunate few who are engaged at the break-up of the fox. The master to whom he now transfers his willing allegiance is the M.F.H. ; and his classical readings are limited, by choice, to certain hunting scenes in Homer, Virgil, Xenophon, and other writers, whose works might be classed among the 'Bibliotheca Cynegetica.' He has caught, or inherited, the infectious complaint ; and he returns to school a confirmed, though embryotic hunting Man, possessed of a disease for which, when it has once thoroughly entered into the system, there seems to be no cure. For the cure, such as it is, seems to be on the homœopathic principle of likes curing likes. The severe treatment that is received from thumps and bumps, so far from arresting the progress of the complaint, appears to be analogous to the sanative measures adopted by the late Mr. Harrop, the Brighton 'Rubber ;' or to the Turkish Bath system ; and their effect is to render the body more supple, and the patient more desirous for a repetition of the entire proceeding. It is creative of sinew and pluck, and greatly tends to preserve that *mens sana in corpore sano* which, before and since the days of Juvenal, has been the apt expression for the perfection of health. And so

Galen strongly recommended hunting for its sanative purposes, and, when Somerville describes his company of riders to hounds, he speaks of them as outwardly evidencing not only happiness but health—'In each smiling countenance appears fresh-blooming health and universal joy.'

In short, even those who are not Nimrods by nature, cannot but acknowledge that the good effect produced upon the bodily frame by hunting pursuits is self-evident, despite those ugly knocks and severer accidents which necessarily must attend any sport, whether in the field or on the flood, on foot or on horseback. The liability to such accidents calls forth, indeed, at least one-half of the best qualities of riders to hounds, and prepares them for the unflinching encounter with casualty and danger. That king of fox-hunters, Mr. Assheton Smith, used to say that the most useful accomplishment to a hunting-man was to know how to fall easily; an art that is, probably, as difficult to be acquired by an equestrian in the field as in the circus. The Duke of Wellington, when in the Peninsula, kept a pack of hounds and hunted regularly, knowing that hunting cultivates a correct eye for country; a quality especially useful to a military man; therefore he selected as his *aides-de-camp* those who were good riders to hounds.

The spirit that animated those six hundred horsemen at Balaclava, as 'boldly they rode, and well, into the jaws of death,' is the self-same invincible feeling of British pluck that carries nearly every fox-hunter to the end of a hard run over a difficult line of country. Much that is demanded of the fighter in the field of battle is also required from the peaceful rider in the hunting-field. The field of war and the field of sport have their physical points in common; so that, in the language of Cervantes' Duke, 'Hunting is the most proper exercise for Knights and Princes; for, in the Chase may be represented the whole art of War—stratagems, policy, and ambuscades, with all other devices usually practised to overcome an enemy with safety. Here we are exposed to the extremities of heat and cold; ease and laziness can have no room in this diversion; by this we are inured to toil and hardship, our limbs are strengthened, our joints made supple, and our whole body hale and active. In short, it is an exercise that may be beneficial to many, and can be prejudicial to none.'

They who are not Nimrods by nature may do well to take to heart this judgment of Cervantes' Duke.

A FATEFUL FOURSOME.

By 'ROCKWOOD.'

REALLY do not know,' said Davie, our green-keeper at Powbank, one of the most noted golfing courses north of the Tweed; 'what you'll do, gentlemen, for a foursome, unless——'

'Unless what, David?' said the Major, whose regiment was stationed at the adjoining garrison town.

'Unless the minister comes down in the twelve-o'clock train.'

'Do you expect him?'

'Well, I'll no say that I do, sir,' said the cautious Scotchman in reply; 'but there's a leddy ower the way there,' pointing to the nicely situated residence of a well-known village spinster, 'who, I think, has been expecting him: at least, I've seen Miss MacCawpy twice at the railway station this mornin' to meet the Glasgow trains and go hame disappointed like. But there's the train whistling just noo, and, odds my life! there's Miss MacCawpy coming again!'

As the lady had to pass very close to us, conversation had to be stopped for a moment, the Major and myself taking our 'putters' (to the non-golfing reader I may explain that the word is pronounced like butter), and holing out some nice imaginary strokes. Davie, who was busy with a piece of sand-paper polishing a new club-head, politely touched his bonnet as she passed and bade her a cheery 'Gude mornin', mem;' whispering to us after the coast was clear that it was 'a fair case,' and that, 'bar bunkers, the minister would hole oot an easy winner.' Alas! there was worse than bunkers in store, and that ere the day was over. The guard whistled, and the train, which had been drawn up for some time, moved forward, again revealing to our satisfaction a tall, gaunt figure in black, standing by the side of the lady of whom we had just been speaking. This was the Reverend Donald Dalhousie, of the Free and United Covenanters, a pillar of the church built of 'genuine' Aberdeen granite, and whose training at the Marischal College there was no doubt the cause of his being a keen golfer. Games, like dancing, in the North, are not viewed with much favour; but curling and golfing have long been recognised as orthodox pastimes, and the parsons are, indeed, their best supporters; close confinement to the study making them appreciate a day on the ice or the grass greensward all the greater. But our hero of the pulpit and the 'putting' green was not only a keen golfer; he was, indeed, one of the very best that came to Powbank: for, though novices might laugh at him in his long black 'swinger' as the caddies termed it, and his venerable chimney-pot, for he would not condescend to wear jacket or cap, he could generally prove to them with driver, cleek, or 'putter,' that dress and appearances had very little to do with the game.

Out of his long hang-dog face there was little to be gathered, Moses, indeed, might have gone on striking it with his rod for a century without raising a tear in his eye; while as to smiling, levity and laughter were condemned by his special sect. He had sometimes been seen by the caddies to give the first half-turn of a smile on making a most successful 'putt;' but the countenance seemed at once to relapse into its natural serious condition afterwards. Yet, withal, he was good company over the green; was fond of a pipeful of tobacco and a glass of whisky-and-water, and was as well versed in politics as in Scripture.

On nearing us the lady bade him good-bye, no doubt divining that we were waiting for him, though she was not a great friend of golf, from reasons which have to be explained subsequently. The customary salutations and hand-shakings over, David said that we had just been hanging on for a bit foursome, seeing that the green was in the top of order, and that we would have it all to ourselves; 'and as you've turned up kind o' unexpectedly' (the Major chuckled at this bit of Scotch canniness), 'we could not do better, I think, than arrange that the Major and me will face Mr. Rockwood here and yourself: or, if you like, *you* can have the Major and I'll have Mr. Rockwood; there's no half a stroke over the whole links between them.' It was possibly not Davie's province to propose anything, but old golfers are privileged characters; while it was well known that some of the old East-country feeling that exists between rival greens still made the Aberdonian and the St. Andrew's man 'dour opponents.'

'So be it, David; so be it, sir,' was the dignified response. 'I would rather have a foursome than a single on a nice day like this, when the breeze is so caller and walking so pleasant, though I feel rather fatigued with the heavy duties of the Sacrament week.'

'Deed, sir,' said Davie; 'to speak plainly, I aye feel a wee bit stronger after them.' But the too broad Scotch allusion to the service only drew forth a wooden stare from the divine, which caused the professional to shut up.

Changing his boots for a pair of heavy hob-nailed shoes, but adhering to his tall hat and long black coat, the pastor of the Free and United Covenanters looked out his clubs, and handing them to a caddie we were ready to start—the Major and Davie against myself and the Parson. The two balls were 'teed' on a little nob of sand taken from the hole, and taking hold of our drivers we swiped off, the man of arms topping his, and sending it spinning into a clumpse of green whins, whilst I fared little better, landing my ball in a bunker off the line, and to the right. Davie and the Parson each chose their 'irons,' and it was a matter of opinion as to which handled his club most cleverly—the former, with the top twig of the bush held firmly down with his foot out of the way, lifting the ball with a nice 'click,' and sending it well down the green; while the latter not less dextrously lifted his out of the sand over the face, and well on to clean green turf. Having to play the odds, I chose the 'cleek,' the hole being a short one, and laid my ball close to the hole, which was marked by the customary white disc. The Major, with his 'putter,' played the like, but was strong, and Davie had to play again, which he did, but without success.

'We have this for the hole,' said the Parson, as he smoothed the grass and ran his club along the face of the slight declivity, as if to give his ball a hint as to the road it should take. A gentle tap, and it followed almost as guided, and running to the edge dropped in, to the remark of 'Well putted, sir!' by the Major.

Now, the golfing reader will pardon my explaining to the many that have never seen this game played, that it consists in driving a ball of hammered gutta-percha, less than one half the size of a lawn-tennis ball, over distances of rough and uneven ground, from one little round hole, or rather from within a small circle close to it, to another, in the fewest possible number of strokes. 'Not much in that, indeed!' says the stranger; but until he has played a round or two of the game over one or other of the most famous chains of links in the North, he will not be able to appreciate the many beauties of the pastime. He will not be able, indeed, to know the delightful feeling caused by the clean swipe in driving off when the ball is caught full face by the club, and flies away through the air as if shot from a gun, over dangerous sand bunkers, rough brent grass, or un-yielding whin-bush ; nor will he be able to see the dexterity with which lost rounds are literally plucked out of the fire by the neat, clever play with the 'iron cleek,' for every stroke, be it a hundred yards or be it an inch, counts at golf. Hands must not be used except when a ball is said to be unplayable, and even then under a penalty so heavy as to make it all but impossible for one to win who incurred it.

But the balls have just been freshly teed by the caddies, and the players are ready to 'swipe off' again, the Parson, my partner, having in his hand a driver with a strong family resem-blance—'a verra wonderful club,' as Davie will tell you, for it has had heads on it by every club-maker in Scotland, and shanks for a fact, he knows, by half as many more ; *and a gude club yet!'* he exclaims, without the slightest suspicion of humour. With his trowsers buckled as if to show his silk white socks, his feet planted wide, and his hat set well back on his head, while he shakes his club over the ball and looks well for-ward for a second, as if to measure the distance he means to compass, he is, indeed, anything but a subject for a sporting artist. But his swing is terrific, and as his hat flies off, just as did poor Tommy Morris' Balmoral bonnet, away goes the ball, beautiful for line, and lands clear over the brown edge of a sand bunker, to reappear, having rolled through a hollow into view on the top of a hillock beyond. Davie is not to be beaten, and 'reteeing' chooses a line a little more to the left, and plays a long, beautiful shot also, and a ball which you can know from his manner when he picks up his own clubs, for he is his own caddie, he knows it will leave itself on clear ground..

So on we march again, passing through amongst whin-bushes covered with yellow blossom, or wading amongst the rashes in the hollows of the numerous hazards. It is in early summer, and the soft wind which is coming in over the green sea, which ripples on to the sandy beach, is waving the brent-grass which grows on the little sea-heaped hillocks, larks carol high overhead, linnets pipe to each other amongst the broom-bushes which fringe the burn, which, wimpling, forms the boundary of the links ; and thinking only of the game and our

next shots, and hoping that we may find the ball lying favourable, we tramp, unmindful of all bodily ailments or business
cares. 'No man ever killed himself with ower muckle golf, sir,'
says Davie; 'in fact, the only death it ever caused was a
doctor's, and he committed suicide for want o' patients. But
you must have the sea for golfing,' says the old worthy; 'at
least, I never can play in a match where I cannot hear the
sough o' the waves. Now take the long spoon, Major, and be
careful o't deil's ditch,' he says. And the Major, so advised, takes
hold of the club named, and plays the odds in a manner which
makes me a little afraid of the consequences, for my ball is not
lying so well as I thought. With the cleek, however, I play a
neat, clean, and forward stroke. The Parson and Davie take us
both on to the green with the cleek, and we 'putt' it out, the
Parson just failing to halve by a hair's breadth. Even again—
having gained one hole each—we set out across the links for the
third, and then came home down the side of the sea-beach,
playing a most evenly contested game throughout, having an
alternate hole and an alternate half.

At last came the finishing one for home, when the Major
and myself both swiped off long, clean balls; his, wind-caught,
turning off the line, however, amongst rough ground to the right.
Davie, on following it up, found that it had entered a rabbit-
hole, almost under the roof of the tunnel—a *clearly unplayable
ball*, as he said. The suspicious Parson, however, thought he
would have a look, and expressed his opinion that it was quite
playable, inasmuch as he could see it clearly, and it was strik-
able. In vain did Davie demur; so, after four alternate strokes
from the Major and himself, he kicked the ball up, thus giving
us the hole and the round.

Starting off again, the professional all the time muttering
threats of being even with him, we, never tiring in the least—
the great charm of the game is you can be walking all day and
not know it till the evening—soon finished the second round;
this time the professional and the Major securing the final hole
after keen play, and so making all square. Nothing would do
us, therefore, but that we must start for the rubber. Off we
went again for the third round, as fresh and as keen as when we
started at noon, though the Parson would have liked evidently
to have dispensed with the final. Fortunate, indeed, it would
have been for him if we had done so, but fate willed it otherwise.
The first hole we halved, the second we secured easily, the third

The James Coffee House.

also fell to us, and then our opponents had a run, scoring three holes right off the reel, thanks to my own bad putting and the professional's fine short play. We halved the next two holes, had one about, and in the end stood again, most wonderful to state, on the driving-ground for the game-hole level, each side determined to win. Davie teed the ball for the Major, and laid him off his line for direction, which was right over a bleaching-green, which seemed to have sprung into existence since we started on the last round but an hour ago.

' Noo jist hold on to the left of Miss McCawpy's claes, or we'll never hear the end o't. It's washing-day with her, and all the talkin' in the world would'na persuade her that she should'na dry her newly-washed claes on the whins on the golfing course.'

' The clothes will not do much harm, I think, David,' said the clergyman, feeling bound, no doubt, to take the lady's part ; ' if you were as particular about keeping the cows off you would do well.'

Ere Davie replied, the Major had swiped off well to the left of the clothes, while I, as luck would have it, sent my ball right amongst them. Choosing his driver, the Parson followed in its direction, but could not find, and it was not till after some searching that Davie's keen eyes detected it snugly nestled in the centre of a large white sheet which was bleaching on the top of some young whins.

' There she is, sir ! there she is ! and a playable ball, too. What about the claes noo, sir ? '

Sure enough there it was, right in the centre, and in order to get a fair clean shot at it with the cleek it seemed necessary to do what nobody in Powbank would dare do, in Davie's opinion, viz., get upon the clean cloth, for in washing and bleaching lay Miss McCawpy's pride. After a careful examination the Parson sat down and took off his shoes, and then, with trowsers tucked up and hat on the back of his head, stepped on to the sheet, only to jump back, amidst the laughter of all, as the whins penetrated his tender soles. Whether the Major had pulled the garden-gate bell or not, or Davie had told one of the caddies to do so, till this day has not yet been made known, but just when the cleek was brought up for the stroke Miss McCawpy appeared at the gate, in time to give a scream at the appalling sight. A look of scorn and a slamming of the door in the reverend gentleman's face, as shoeless he stepped forward to explain, let us know the frame of mind she was in, and silently

we played out the hole. The cleek stroke of the Parson was a
clever one, and it would need to have been so, seeing how costly
it proved ; the result being that, with a most deadly ' putt ' from
myself, we secured the victory over the day's play. Alas, alas,
for my partner ! Putting off his golfing shoes and redonning his
boots, he made his way to that door where oft he had been so
welcome—where, indeed, he was invited to take that touzie tea
he could so well do justice to when his game was over. Ex-
planations and expostulations must have been in vain ; possibly
the sheet, which had been taken inside when our backs were
turned, had been cut or marked by the cleek ; but, whether or
not, the Reverend Donald Dalhousie of the Free and United
Covenanters was not accompanied to the station that night by
his affianced one. Nor did he ever play over the Powbank links
again, and the last time that old Davie ever heard about him
was when he sent for his clubs within a week afterwards, and
the shoes which he had been at so much trouble to take off for
sake of fickle woman on that day of the Fateful Foursome.

A MANCHESTER MEETING.

By 'TRIVIATOR.'

HERE was a time—and not so very remote either—
when England felt proud of her Colonial empire ;
when no statesman ever thought or avowed that an
extra island in some remote ocean was an Im-
perial incubus, to be allowed to ' slide ' on the first occasion that
might present itself. And in those days British blood and British
treasure were ever ready and forthcoming to defend such posses-
sions—no matter how remote, no matter how commercially un-
profitable at the moment. Then England was *the Mother Country*
to the Colonists, and not the stepmother which she might now
be deemed by many ; and as the mother afforded protection to
her young brood, the latter looked up with affection and
reverence to the British throne, and the Polity of which it was
their pride and glory to form a part, be it ever so insignificant,
and a little link in that glorious Colonial chain which engirdled the
round world. This affection and reverence is evidenced in a
thousand historical records, and topography sets its seal on the
fact, as it points to the thousands of cities, towns, and villages
on the map, which were called in proud remembrance by the

names of dissimilar cities, towns, and villages from which the colonists or their forbears had taken their departure! Every traveller in the Dominion of Canada, in the United States, in Australia, New Zealand, or the Caribbean Archipelago, can confirm this statement in hundreds of instances within his own observation or purview; for at the time we speak of, *the Manchester School* had not become the governing impulse of our empire, and the Procrustean principles of the Ledger were not applied to our dependencies. Our sketch of a phase of tropical life and manners ' full thirty years ago' illustrates these pre-liminary observations, for the scene is to be laid at *Manchester*, an inland *Parish* of the island of Jamaica (once known as the 'Queen of the Antilles'), and more especially at *Mandeville*, another name, whose connexion with *Manchester* will be recog-nised by the 'intelligent reader' directly. Now *Manchester*, we may state, is the county; *Mandeville* the county town where the assizes are held, and to which the 'Custos Rotulorum' con-venes magisterial and other meetings. 'Our affair,' as the Gauls put it, is with quite a different sort of meeting (though we may feel quite certain that his Honour *the Custos* will be there, and that he will be supported by not a few of his brothers of the bench), so we would try to recall some recollections of those Manchester race-meetings held at Mandeville every year (funds permitting), for they were very peculiar and unlike anything of the sort ever witnessed by European sportsmen, though perhaps fairer trials of the speed and stamina of horses than some of those decorously conducted 'gate-money' *arrangements* that take place continually under the eye and observation of that august and arbitrary body, the Jockey Club of England.

The popular notion about Jamaica is that of a small island set in the Caribbean Sea, where the sugar-cane grows spontaneously like the potato in Ireland, over acres and acres of flat plains, and the negro population — when it will condescend to work—is eternally engaged in the manu-facture of sugar and rum, to sweeten English tea and pudding, and comfort the sailors of the 'British Navee.' This is a very limited and poor conception of one of the most beautiful combinations of mountain and valley, savannahs and sierras, that God ever created and bestowed on man. Long before sugar and coffee became staples of the island, vast herds of wild cattle and horses ranged over the vegas and hills; and the buccaneers made large sums in exporting the hides of the former. Sugar cultivation is, as a rule, limited to the level zones

of fertile land near the littoral, which is studded with bays
and harbours, while the interior of the island rises into either
abrupt mountain ridges—such as 'the Blue Mountains,' that
attain a height of well-nigh 7000 feet above the sea level—or
spreads itself into large plateaux, where the climate is deliciously
cool, and the scenery is, to compare small things with great, like
that of hundreds of English parks rolled into one, so to speak,
and seen at their best in the leafy month of June, while the air
is literally loaded with the fragrance of the pimento groves that
are indigenous to the island, and require no cultivation or original
planting, springing up with seeming spontaneity from the grate-
ful soil. Ill-natured and 'mean whites' say that perhaps this
is a dispensation of primeval nature to correct the *bouquet de
nègre*, which is sometimes overpowering.

'Good morning, massa buckra, come tell me what you tink,
Me hearee Baptist parson say that we poor niggers stink,'

says the nigger minstrelsy : but I hardly think boon nature could
have been so provident in its protection to delicate nostrils, as
we know from history that the *negro* was an imported article,
not like the exterminated Carib, *filius terræ!*

Such a bit of park-like plateau is Manchester in Jamaica.
The air is nearly always deliciously cool and refreshing, verdure is
perennial, and in the valleys, which are watered by many a beck
and brook, there are numbers of cattle and horse-farms—
ranches, to use the western term—where huge oxen are reared
for the use of the sugar-plantations by the coast. And *chevaux de
race*, *chevaux de luxe*, and *chevaux de service*, are bred and trained,
and do no discredit to their thorough-bred 'uncles, cousins, and
aunts' in England. I said 'thorough-bred,' for though there
may be an admixture of the old Spanish and Barb blood, that
has been absorbed and assimilated long ago by the *pur sang* imported from England regularly ; for it has been found by long experience that cart blood is absolutely useless and powerless in the
tropics, melting away under the sun's rays like wax before a hot
fire. These cattle and horse ranches are called *Pens* in Jamaica
language, perhaps borrowed or imitated from the old Spanish
term of *corral*. Their acreage is large, and, curiously enough, all
the stock, whether horses or cows, are branded with the 'Pen'
letters. Hence, when you see a horse with the letters 'F H' on
his quarter, you know that he belongs to such a 'Pen' in Manchester, and you are master at once of some portion of his
pedigree, knowing that such and such thorough-bred sires have
been standing there for some time. In the days to which I

would refer there was a good deal of the Orville, Emilius, and Blacklock blood in merry Manchester.

All soils and climates have their specialties, and it is in these elevated plateau lands that the finest cattle and the best horses are reared, and the most celebrated of the latter come from the various Pens of St. Ann's, St. Elizabeth's, and Manchester, for even in the last-named, the least horsey of the three,

> ' Perchance some seed is sown
> The Heracleidan blood might own.'

The date of our opening scene shall be the 16th of January, and in the fifties, not to be too nice or particular about the Anno Domini—a sore subject with some of us veterans. The hour shall be 5 a.m., and the place Mandeville, a straggling little collection of houses with very white walls, and very green ' jalousies ' to guard the windows, some flower-plots in front of some of the houses protected by a hedge of the Hibiscus, whose red flower does duty at a pinch for blacking boots and shoes. These low, shingle-roofed buildings, not only forming mansions but *stores* of the most miscellaneous character, in which you can purchase a case of Perrier Jouet, a cask of Madeira, perhaps, any amount of rum and negro stores, *qui en* sabe, and George Eliot's last romance. They are mostly kept by Jews, who occasionally combine banking, financing, and hotel business with their more usual mercantile avocations. There is little division of labour, as we understand it ; and the storekeeper will undertake to charter you a ship or get you a pair of fast trotters at short notice. Almost within the extent of the town is a large oval space, nearly a mile round ; it is unenclosed, and a sort of common depastured by hogs and goats, and an odd forlorn milch cow or two. The track round this space is the race-course of Manchester, with a hill at its terminus steeper than Ludgate or Holborn ere they were cut down, and a turn for the grand stand sharper than some of those of our Regent Circi. The *public road* forms a portion of the racing track, and just now a few score of negroes, *strong* in every sense, are clearing away with their machettes the guava bush of the oval, and levelling with their hoes the inequalities of the track, which is literally and truly a turfless road, part lane, part highroad, with gradients that would tax a good horse drawing a heavy load. About sixty horses are walking along this track already, each string being accompanied by a black groom, who calls himself, if you ask him,

a '*strainer*,' *i.e.* trainer, and who gives himself airs of far more
mystery and consequence than all the Dawsons and all the
Scotts combined ever assumed. He wears '*boots*,' but his lads
as a rule wear *none*, sticking the stirrup-irons between their toes.

There is a population of 1500 or 2000 on the race-course,
gathered near the judges' stand, a permanent box, for the Grand
and stewards stands are movable erections, put up each year.
Ginger-beer, spruce, and pepper-punch, are being vended freely;
and pretty coffee-coloured damsels, with good Jewish features
and gleaming white teeth, such as May Fair maidens or Belgravia
beauties might envy; while lots of black and Sambo girls, with
their heads adorned with gay Madras kerchiefs, and very scant
draperies, are showing ebony and bronze figures, so svelte and
lissom that a Gibson or Story would take them instantly for
models. The air rings with 'I'll bet a mac' (the 1½d. silver coin,
for the negro will not touch copper); no odds are asked, as the
favourite is the horse ridden by the lad best known and liked.
The galloping begins at about 5.30. 'The strainer' sends them
along *à discrétion*, but while a few gallop three miles, nearly all,
two-year olds included, do their two, and the last half at score:
finishing in fact, and hence the betting. 'And will these black
monkeys, averaging six stone all round, stick on?' Be sure they
will, as well and better than 'whites,' for they have been on
horses since they could toddle; the rough part of riding they
know well, the niceties are all unknown. So the strings start off
at intervals, each horse with a snaffle bridle, each lad with a
good 'supplejack.' What can have happened? Nine horses
have started for a three-mile gallop, the first round of the course
slow; but one horse has left his mates 200 yards behind, and is
evidently going along best pace! Glasses are brought to bear,
and then we see that the old rotten reins have snapped, and
that the boy is working along his horse's neck to reach the
ring of the bit on one side. 'My King! my King! He's dead!'
No! not for a ducat; for the horse was so much astonished at
the chuck he got that he slackened speed, and gradually stopped.
It was a monkey's trick, and nothing less agile than a monkey
could have done it. Do not talk to 'the strainer' after his
gallops. He is 'the man at the wheel,' not to be lightly inter-
rogated; he is making calculations and mental notes, and,
perhaps, wondering and pondering whether the Obeah man
whom he has propitiated with fowls, yams, rum, and coin, has
worked his spells in favour of his 'tud' (stud): but you will see

that these horses, young and old, though fed on guinea-grass, hay, and maize, look bright and well after their scraping and rubbing, with legs and feet models of soundness, and pipes as clear as Pan's. By 8 o'clock a.m. horses and crowd have vanished, to avoid the sun's rays. But this preliminary *road* racing has already gone on for a week.

The 20th of January is the commencement of the *biduum* of the Manchester Meeting. Mandeville overflows. The horsey 'parishes' of St. Anne and St. Elizabeth have sent some forty representatives to the fray. The *white* regiment of New-castle has sent one. 'The second west,' which claims a sports-man or two among its officers, five. The 'ordinaries' have been splendidly attended. True, two or three duels grew out of hot words, but they were settled in the morning without effusion of blood ; and Lansquenet, known as ' Lammey ' flourished every night in the motley assembly of high officials, soldiers, planters, attorneys,' and storekeepers. The party generally turned out to see the morning gallops, leaving their nigger-boys to pick up the silver coins which had fallen on to the floor ; for men staked silver when their notes were exhausted, and lots of it fell uncol-lected on to the floor, while the owners were intent on ' Company —Self.' All race meetings have points in common : picnicing, jollification, winning, losing, toasting good luck, and drowning or dipping bad in the flowing bowl. The bowl flowed very freely at Manchester, for one good custom was that every steward and official was entitled to share in a ' winning bowl ' offered (voluntary, but you must) as a libation, by the winner of each race, directly after ' All right ! ' was pronounced *ex cathedrá*. It consisted of champagne, cherry-brandy, ice, and nutmeg, mixed up in Sangaree form. Its lowest cost was *a dub* (a Spanish doubloon, 3*l.* 4*s.*), a noble gold coin, and sometimes as-cended to four or five times that amount—a smart income-tax on a 50*l.* stake. N.B.—It might be hinted that the decisions of the stewards, declared final, might not be satisfactory under such vinous influences. As a rule they were ; for the stewards ' had made their heads early.' All races were *in heats*, so the fun lasted with the day.

The maiden race we need not notice. In the Great Breeder Stakes, a good take-up, wherein representatives of Pammon (by ' *the* ' *Priam*), Javelin, Zingaree, and Black Doctor, contended in a two-mile race, run from end to end, the *finishing* process (if we may venture such a *bull*) commencing at the *start*.

The Queen's Plate of 100*l.*, with a free entry and weight for age, was the *pièce de résistance* of the first day—*heats of three miles!* We need not go through the running. A three-year old by Javelin won the first heat. The second was won by a four-year-old mare, called Canezou, by Pammon, from a Moonraker mare. The third by a smart, stuffy black horse, called Antæus, also four years old. The fourth was a duel between Canezou and Antæus, the latter running longest and stoutest, but only defeating the mare by a neck, after a most exciting finish for half a mile—*twelve miles in all.* Antæus carried 8st. and was ridden by a Sambo jock called Charles, who was a full-grown man : the ugliest rider I ever saw, but one of the strongest. He had sweated hard to ride, and of course required food between the heats as well as drink : but to keep his weight right he would go and dance 'the Shay-shay,' a Caribbean Cancan, in the booths during the half hour allotted between them.

In the Corinthian Plate, the rider of a very good-looking welter horse was beaten in the last heat from sheer weakness. He had been 'wasting' for days, but found the night before that all his walking in the cool climate of Manchester was in vain, and he had to take off 14 lbs. in twelve hours. He did it, but failed at the finish, coming in a close second only.

A mule race is not generally very exciting, but the mules of Jamaica from thorough-bred mares, if weedy, could gallop a bit, and perhaps the biggest haul of doubloons at the meeting was made by a gallant young Englishman, who has since distinguished himself in the camp as on the course. He had a mule that used to gallop every morning to the post and back several miles, so her condition was bound to be good, and if she would only run straight and 'try' she could hardly lose. The entry was large, for every planter fancied his own moke, whose breeding and feeding he knew, and it was not likely that a stranger could have a better, so ridiculous odds in 'dubs' were *laid*, and *taken* by the Bold Britisher, who had learnt a thing or two at Newmarket under the mentorship of the famous 'Lord George.' Catch weights and go as you can for the two miles was the mule programme, so 'Fighting Fred' saddled his mule, put a good jock up, as he was too big himself, and at the first turn had a white or grey hack of his own lying in wait to lead the mule team. On they went, but, of course, *more muleorum*, half-a-dozen of the leaders bolted at the turn : not so *Frederika*, lying behind; she spied her stable-mate in the act of starting off on his round, and she followed him as faithfully and fleetly as greyhound pursues hare. Of course she won.

Quijote et Sancho

The departure from Mandeville after the meeting is a curious sight. There are no coaches and but one short line of railway in Jamaica, and planters and travellers go about with strings of led saddle and carriage horses and mules—often seven or eight to each man : it was like the breaking up of a big horse-fair.

THE KING OF THE JUNGLE.

By 'JUGDULLUCK.'

THE King of the Jungle walked out one night,
The sky was clear, and the moon was bright.
    He went for a meal
    To pillage and steal—
For he felt very hungry, as tigers will feel
When they've slept all the day and been dreaming of veal.

He suddenly heard, before he'd gone far,
A small baby heifer call out for its 'Ma.'
    And what does he see
    At the foot of a tree
But that same baby heifer tied up by the knee.
He gazed for a moment, then said, 'It's for me
That that dear little heifer's been tied to the tree !

'Her blood I will drink, and her bones I will crunch ;
I'll make of her breakfast, and dinner, and lunch ;
    And then I will sleep
    'Mongst those nullahs so steep,
Where the trees are thick and the shade is deep,
And the rays of the sun are unable to creep.'

I won't hurt your feelings by telling you how
He killed and demolished that poor little cow.
    He did gobble and stuff
    Till he'd had quite enough ;
And he didn't care whether 'twas tender or tough :
His behaviour was really exceedingly rough.

Then he washed down this very big dinner with drinking ;
And spent all the morning in sleeping and thinking.
    And there he lay,
    Where never a ray
Of the terrible sun dare venture to stray,
Saying, 'No one will come to disturb me to-day.'

But little he knew, as he rolled on his back,
That three tiger-hunters were now on his track.
    For that heifer, you see,
    Had been tied to the tree
To entice him to kill it, and show where he lay
    On that very hot day,
    Where never a ray
Of the terrible sun dare venture to stray.

Now the beaters are ready: the time it has come,
To drive out the tiger with rattle and drum.
> And the old tiger there,
> As he lay in his lair,
Had heard a great noise, but he didn't much care,
Till the sound of the beating began to draw near.
And he said to himself as he cocked up an ear,
> 'Why, I heard a shout !
> What are they about ?
I can't stop here, so I'd better get out.'

Something moves in the bushes, as soft as a cat ;
And the hunter observes, from the tree where he sat,
> The tiger come creeping,
> And crouching and peeping,
And walking quite slowly, because he's so fat.
> From his tail to his head
> He's a fine tawny red ;
> And so white underneath,
> And such beautiful teeth,
And stripes on his body as black as your hat !
It's an elegant skin to make into a mat.

But little he thinks that his end is so near,
When the crack of a rifle sounds out loud and clear.
> What a bound ! What a roar !
> And he feels very sore ;
Such a pain at his heart, he can't go any more,
For the rifle was held by an unerring hand—
And THE KING OF THE JUNGLE lies dead on the sand.

ANOTHER TUNE ON THE SAME
OLD FIDDLE.

By FREDERICK GALE.

MANY of the outward world who stroll on to a cricket-ground on a summer afternoon and, with a knowing smile, criticise and give their opinions and find fault, and run down some player in favour of some Tom, or Dick, or Harry, who is excluded from the eleven, would find themselves somewhat at sea if they were sent on to a village green with six stumps and four bails and a tape, and be told to pitch a wicket without a measuring-frame. ' Dear me !' some of them would say, 'I forget at this moment the length and distances of the creases ; can any one tell me ?' These are the gentlemen who read the reports of matches and who have never learnt the A B C of the game, and talk slang.

I am not talking to gentlemen of this class, but am going to talk with the real cricketers of England about a great change which has taken place in the game, and to submit the question to them whether one or two new fashions have not been carried to a dangerous extent, as regards the simplicity of the game And more than that, whether the example set on public grounds is not doing much harm with the rising generation ? And this question is not much out of place in this winter season, as the Cattle-show week is the time fixed by the Secretaries of all the County Cricket Clubs to meet in London and arrange the programme for the season.

I am not going to blow the trumpet in honour of the men of the past, as their trumpet *wants* no blowing ; and those who don't believe in them need not, and are welcome to their own opinions ; but I am going to play a new tune on what I called my 'Old Fiddle'—on which I played in July last—Lillywhite's *Scores and Biographies*, and to reproduce in black and white a sample of the doings of cricketers thirty years ago, and also of cricketers of to-day, and I shall leave the reader to compare the two together ; and if he has a foregone conclusion and likes to stick to it, let him. He will have before him two official records, which will speak for themselves.

The principles of the game of cricket are, or ought to be, precisely the same as those laid down in the Rev. Mr. Cotton's admirable poem, written in 1775, which are quite as reliable now, as regards cricket, as the doctrines of Izaac Walton about the haunts and habits of fish, the places to find them, and the times and seasons to fish for them are—as regards fishing—to this day.

Many alterations have taken place, of course, but the quickness of hand and eye, nerve and courage, were the mainsprings of the game a century ago, just as they are now.

I am going presently to put before those who really care about cricket, as a science, two lists of 'extras,' one taken from Lillywhite's book of 1854, and the other from the weekly publication, *Cricket*, for this year ; and I shall give the reference to the pages of each, that those may run who read.

It used to be the custom after making a match, in considering how the eleven was to be formed, to secure really good men for long-leg, cover-point, point, and a first-rate long-field and wicket-keeper, and, *above all*, a stone-wall longstop ; and then the most important matches in the field were provided for, as soon as these posts were filled ; and the chances were, that amongst men who were up to their duties at the places named, two at least would be useful change-bowlers. And this was in days when boundary cricket was very rare, and matches were

played on open commons and the ball would run for a week.
I said, *above all*, longstop : this was so ; for before the grounds
were prepared as they are now, although the wicket and
pitch were taken great care of, longstop took his chance of
the ground, and it was very difficult work to quick bowling ;
and a man who made a great name as longstop was sure of the
best engagements.   Some of the most noted were William
Clarke, the old slow-bowler, and Joseph Guy, both of Notts ;
'Jemmy Dean,' the Sussex bowler ; Jack Heath, of the old
Montpelier ;   and William Mortlock, Surrey ;   William Pilch
(nephew of old Fuller), Kent ; Mr. Charles Ridding, of Winchester and Oxford, who was longstop many a time at Lord's
to. Mr. A. Mynn and Mr. Harvey Fellows, and Sir Frederick
Bathurst, in Gentlemen and Players and All England matches ;
the late Rev. J. Randolph, an old Westminster and Oxford.

Where is longstop now ? and Echo answers, Where ?

'Ichabod ! Ichabod ! for his glory is departed.'

A great number of the modern school have followed a
fashion set by the Australians in 1878, when they paid us their
first visit, and play, or rather, try to play, cricket, without a
longstop.   It may be done with advantage sometimes to quick
bowling, but under very special circumstances.

'The Demon' has astonished the world with his tearing
bowling, but the dare-devil wicket-keeping of Blackham without
a longstop astonished them more.   Of course, it was a new
wrinkle, and very advantageous, under certain circumstances,
when it *can* be done ; but, unless success is next door to a
certainty, is the game worth the candle? George Pinder of
Yorkshire followed suit against Allan Hill's and Freeman's
bowling, with as much coolness and effect as Blackham, as have
Pilling, Sherwin, Mr. A. Lyttelton, and other eminent men.

But in 'well-captained' elevens I have observed, when they
do without a longstop to quick bowling, the captain has taken
the precaution to have a man near the boundary behind the
wicket, who can cover the ball so as to give away only one bye ;
and who, moreover, can cover a large tract on the on or off-side.
Briggs of Lancashire is unsurpassed in doing this.

And this, perhaps, is the time to introduce two Schedules,
which will be set out presently, and to explain the principle on
which they are framed.

The first schedule contains the extras given by the All
England and also the United All England Elevens, who in 1854
travelled in different parts of England playing matches against

twenty-twos, eighteens, &c., according to the handicap ; some of them with professionals given to their opponents. I have not specified to which the elevens particular extras belong, as both elevens consisted of well-known professionals.

The second schedule refers to grand matches played at Lord's last season.

There is also a third schedule, which relates to four matches in which schools played.

In the first schedule I have published the ' Police Sheets,' in which the sins of omission and commission of the England sides only occur. In the other schedules I have published the evil doings of *both* sides when in the field ; and the reader will take this as a fact from me, that the opponents to the England sides (in Schedule No. 1), out of thirty-seven matches, completed in thirty-six of them *two* whole innings, and that they won one match, single innings, and on another occasion had nine wickets to fall : so I reckon the sins, &c., of England as occurring during the two innings of thirty-six matches only ; or in other words, during the completion of seventy-two innings, instead of seventy-four, as I deduct the odd innings in the single-inning victory and the half-finished innings in another match.

On the other hand, in calculating the sins of omission, &c., against each side at the matches at Lord's, which numbered nineteen, I multiply nineteen by four, representing the possible number of innings which they would have had in the aggregate, *if* each side *had* had two whole innings each to field against. Four nineteens make seventy-six. Finding that 110 wickets did *not* fall out of the 760 which would have fallen *if* both sides *had* had two full innings each, I deduct those 110 wickets from the 760, which leaves 650, the difference of 110 wickets being equal to eleven full innings of ten wickets each. So I propose to divide the extras in Schedule No. 1, in all 333, by 72, and the extras in Schedule No. 2, 591 in all, by 65.

Any one doing this will find that it gives an average, as near as may be, of 4½ runs per innings to the cricketers of the old style, and 9 runs per innings to those of the new; to say nothing of the gain to the old school of catches made by longstops, leg-byes saved, and numberless tips within his grasp, which go to the boundary now, and are scored to the batsman.

And, *per contra*, you must add to the greater number of extras scored against the players at Lords, the proportionate loss accruing by catches not being held for want of a man at long-stop and tips, which pass the wicket-keeper and go into space.

SCHEDULE No. I.

Page in Lillywhite.	Number of Opponents.	Name of Match.	B.	L. B.	W.	N. B.	Total.
567	15	Sheffield	2	2	0	0	4
571	22	Rugby School ...	2	5	0	0	7
577	22	Upton Park	6	3	0	2	11
580	15	Cambridge University ...	3	5	1	0	9
590	22	Liverpool (with 3 players) ...	2	2	1	0	5
594	22	St. Helen's, Lancash. (with 4 players)	4	4	1	0	9
598	22	*Gloucestershire Club	8	8	0	0	16
602	14	*Undergraduates of Oxford	3	9	1	1	14
603	18	South Wilts (with 2 players) ...	8	4	1	0	13
613	22	Sleaford, Lincoln (with 2 players)	5	3	1	0	9
617	15	Undergraduates of Oxford and Camb.	4	1	1	0	6
619	22	Ld. Stamford's Eleven (1 innings only)	1	1	1	0	3
621	22	Uppingham (with 2 players) ...	0	6	0	1	7
626	18	Maidstone (9 wickets to fall) ...	2	1	3	2	8
630	20	Manchester, Broughton (with 3 players)	1	2	3	1	7
632	22	Yorkshire Gentlemen (with 2 players)	4	4	1	3	12
633	22	Northampton (with 2 players) ...	8	3	3	0	14
635	22	Rotherham (with 3 players) ...	4	3	1	0	8
639	22	Bingham, Notts	2	2	2	1	7
642	22	Spalding (with 3 players) ...	1	4	4	0	9
643	18	Dorchester (with 1 player) ...	2	2	0	0	4
645	18	South Hants (with 2 players) ...	1	2	0	0	3
646	22	Stourbridge (with 4 players) ...	0	1	3	4	8
651	22	New Middlesex and Eton ground	1	2	2	0	5
664	15	*Young Players of Kent	9	5	4	0	18
666	22	Phœnix Park	4	9	0	0	13
667	22	Dudley, Worcestersh. (with 4 players)	5	0	2	0	7
670	22	Rochdale (with 4 players)	2	4	0	0	6
671	22	Birmingham (with 3 players) ...	1	2	1	1	5
673	22	Hungerford Park	4	6	0	0	10
675	22	Preston (with 4 players)	2	10	2	1	15
677	22	Lincoln (with 3 players)	3	4	3	0	10
678	22	Edinburgh (with 4 players)	3	1	1	0	5
679	22	Scotland (with 3 players) ...	0	2	4	0	6
680	22	Reading (with 2 players) ...	6	0	1	4	11
683	22	Chepstow (with 2 players)	11	2	3	2	18
685	22	Stockton	3	8	0	0	11
			127	132	51	23	333

* Probably the Gloucester, Oxford, and Young Players of Kent. Matches were played on rough grounds. The Gloucester match was played in a field near an hotel in Bristol; the Oxford match was played in the Christchurch ground ; and the Maidstone at the ' Bat and Ball' ground, which, though now beautifully laid and kept, was not so thirty years ago. In the Maidstone match over 600 balls were bowled by the eleven, nine bowlers going on in second innings. The Kent was a very strong team, scoring 111 and 226. The United England won by two wickets, scoring 70 and 279 for eight wickets. Hinckley, Willsher, and Holland, amongst others, bowled for Kent.

SCHEDULE No. 2.

Page in cricket. 1884.	Name of Match.	Fifteens.	B.	L.B.	W.	N.B	Total.
117	M.C.C. v. Yorkshire	M.C.C. ...	16	5	0	0	21
		Sussex	23	7	0	0	30
125	M.C.C. v. Kent	M.C.C. ...	9	6	0	1	16
		Kent (for 14 wickets) ...	9	9	1	0	19
138	M.C.C. v. Lancashire	M.C.C. ...	12	11	0	0	23
		Lancashire (1 innings) ...	2	3	1	0	6
140	M.C.C. v. Yorkshire...	M.C.C ...	6	1	0	1	8
		Yorkshire (12 wickets) ...	3	3	2	0	8
156	M.C.C. v. Australians	M.C.C. ...	3	0	0	0	3
		Australians (1 innings) ...	18	6	0	0	24
161	M.C.C. v. Notts	M.C.C. (14 wickets) ...	15	1	0	0	16
		Notts ...	5	5	0	0	10
176	Gentlemen of England v. Australians ...	Gentlemen ...	11	3	0	0	14
		Australians (16 wickets)	22	7	0	0	29
178	North v. South... (Not divided.)	North ...	—	—	—	—	24
		South ...	—	—	—	—	7
198	M.C.C. v. Derbyshire	M.C.C. ...	0	0	0	0	0
		Derbyshire	3	4	0	0	7
222	Middlesex v. Gloucestershire ...	Middlesex	5	2	0	0	7
		Gloucestershire ...	10	19	0	0	29
235	Middlesex v. Kent	Middlesex	9	8	0	3	20
		Kent ...	27	7	0	0	34
241	M.C.C. v. Cambridge	M.C.C. ...	4	2	0	0	6
		Cambridge (1 innings) ...	4	5	0	0	9
246	M.C.C. v. Oxford	M.C.C. (14 wicket)	16	0	0	0	16
		Oxford ...	6	11	0	0	17
258	Oxford v. Cambridge ...	Oxford ...	17	5	1	0	23
		Cambridge (13 wickets)	8	1	2	1	12
271	Gentlemen v. Players...	Gentlemen ...	16	8	0	0	24
		Players (14 wickets) ...	22	4	3	0	29
286	Middlesex v. Surrey	Middlesex (13 wickets)...	13	4	0	0	17
		Surrey ...	12	7	1	0	20
302	Middlesex v. Australians	Middlesex (1 innings) ...	4	3	0	0	7
		Australians	32	12	0	0	44
303	England v. Australians	England ...	6	3	0	0	9
		Australians (1 innings) ...	15	5	0	0	20
315	M.C.C. v. Notts	M.C.C. (1 innings)	2	4	0	0	6
		Notts	5	3	0	0	8
			390	184	11	6	591

Now let us look at the facts. On turning over the sheets of Lillywhite, I find that those who composed either England eleven, from time to time, were amongst the best cricketers of the day ;* and the All England Eleven who went northwards were on their ninth tour since their inauguration by W. Clarke in 1846. They had against them frequently as 'given men,' good professionals, who resided in the districts which they visited.

This was before the days when the travelling elevens had worn out their welcome by advertising great names and substituting second-raters for them.

Of course, some of their opponents, *i.e.*, members of the elevens, were not first-rate, but their matches lasted two and often three days, and they had to put all their power out to secure their victories.

Then again, all the grounds they played on were not, by any means, such as now, and were not beaten and rolled down so as to give a bowler a foothold as firm as a road, and round-arm bowlers on soft and slippery grounds were apt to bowl wide, especially as the overhead movement was unknown, and round-arm bowlers had to deliver the ball with the arm held horizontally—if they took advantage of the extreme limits of the law— below the shoulder. The extreme license now allowed has disestablished wides almost.

It is true that old Clarke bowled a great deal, and although his bowling was called 'Old Clarke's slows,' he would put in a ball quick enough now and then, which would run to the end of the ground if not stopped ; and besides old Clarke there were many terrifically fast bowlers, whose bowling had to be stopped on rough ground. The England men went to 'show the game,' and at Lord Stamford's, when they were beaten in one innings (as Lord Stamford had a real 'hot' twenty-two, including some of the best Marylebone men, Public School, and University men), the England Eleven bowled between five and six hundred balls for three extras. In many of these matches their opponents got good scores.

---

* The principal cricketers in the two elevens were :—T. Adams, G. Anderson, F. Bell, J. Bickley, T. Box, W. Buttress, G. Chatterton, Julius Cæsar, W. Clarke, W. Caffyn, J. Grundy, Joseph Guy, T. Hunt, A. Haygarth, Esq., W. Hillyer, R. Iddison, John Lillywhite, T. Lockyer, F. P. Miller, Esq., A. Mynn, Esq., W. Mortlock, W. Martingell, G. Morton, T. Nixon, G. Picknell, S. Parr, G. Parr, H. Sampson, H. H. Stephenson, T. Sherman, C. T. Tinley, J. Wisden, H. Wright, E. Willsher.

There were only 127 byes in the England's seventy-two innings of their opponents, and mind you, as I said before, on much rougher ground. And consider the number of catches which longstop must have made, and the hundreds of runs which he must have saved, off tips, or draws within his reach, all of which now count to the batsman, but are practically given away for the want of a man behind the wicket-keeper.

Those in the country who found the money would not have thought much of them if they had not had good longstopping and smart all-round fielding.

Then, again, there were only 132 leg-byes given by the England men against 184 at Marylebone, and 127 byes against 390 there. I think any cricketer must observe how easy it is for a quick runner to steal a bye when the wicket-keeper lets the ball go only a few yards from him when there is no longstop, and how leg-byes are given because there is no longstop to dash in.

The wides were more numerous, and so were their no-balls; but *this* is *not* the age for no-balls; and I say this with a sly chuckle; but, at the same time, honestly and thankfully confess that I am very glad that our 'no-ball' difficulty—now almost of the past—was in the hands of well-bred gentlemen at Lord's, men of position as fellow-members of M. C. C., and fellow Public School, or University men, who, although differing *toto cælo* in opinion, by courtesy and good-breeding can settle a difficulty without quarrelling and abuse; which is so common now amongst under-bred nobodies, who have been pitchforked into Committees of Clubs, and who are utterly ignorant of cricket and the breeding of a gentleman.

Every one must see what I am driving at, which is—speaking for a very large section of old cricketers, of whom I know as many of all classes as most men—we should like to see the longstop back again to quick bowling; or at any rate, as half a loaf is better than no bread, a man near the boundary, behind the wicket on one side or the other, to cover the ball and prevent more than one bye, and to save the tips which pass the wicket-keeper.

It saddens us to see a ball just turned aside off a quick bowler and running into space to an unguarded boundary, whilst the batsman, instead of being obliged to run, has a word or two with the wicket-keeper or 'point' till some man in the crowd throws it up. No one except those who have steadily

studied the game can tell how fatal it is to a match allowing
batsmen with impunity to score boundary hits. The actual
running, and the chance of being run out, all tell on a man's
nerve and wind.

We believe that the England's game thirty years ago was
more like the old English cricket in the field than that shown
in the 'Police Sheet' from Marylebone this year. The game of
thirty years back was clean cricket, and I belong to a school
who think that a long list of extras means slovenly cricket.
Giving away extras is gambling with the game.

Has it paid with the Australians? (True, Blackham was not
always with them.) 117 byes and leg-byes, at Lord's, in four
matches!

Is it worth copying? Were we not better off than we are
now when Mortlock went through a whole season (I believe)
with one bye, and Alfred Mynn, and Harvey Fellows, and Sir
Frederick Bathurst 'thundered' at the players' wickets with
Charles Ridding behind the wicket as longstop?

Do we not all see, because occasionally a very brilliant
wicket-keeper, on a very hard, true wicket, *can* succeed, some
jackdaw in peacock's feathers, who calls himself a captain, sets a
second-rate wicket-keeper to work with an utterly unguarded
boundary behind him, and ruins a match? It is no good for the
so-called wicket-keeper to put himself in the attitude of a man
'giving a back,' and to look very knowing, and let a lot pass,
even off the medium bowling. He is simply a lubber in everybody's way.

If longstop is taken off at all to very quick bowling, let the
captain tell wicket-keeper to stand five yards behind the wicket,
and, if worth his salt, he would make four catches out of five,
instead of two, perhaps, as he does *at* the wicket.

The fact is, that there are very, *very* few really first-class
wicket-keepers at any time in England. Wicket-keeping is a gift.

A good thing cannot be too often repeated, and I believe
this has been put in print before by myself.

In 1883, at Gravesend, Kent beat Lancashire on the post by
somewhere *about* twenty runs.

The ground is rather small, and there was a boundary (a very
easy three-er), a kind of somewhat near 'long on' to the batsman. Tom Adams, the old Kent veteran, pointed it out to me,
and remarked that it wanted well covering. The same idea
evidently struck Lord Harris, as he had a consultation with Mr.

Tylecote, and longstop was sent away to the boundary, and Mr. Tylecote went five yards behind the wicket to the bowling of Mr. Christopherson and Collins—who both bowled at a tremendous pace—and he only let one ball go by him in the second innings; and he was so wonderfully quick and sure that I firmly believe, if the batsman had gone out of his ground, he could have thrown the wicket down almost as quick as he could have stumped the man, if behind the stumps.

'I like to see a good man north, south, east, and west, to guard the boundaries,' old Fuller Pilch used to say; 'those fourers run up very quick, like a butcher's or a lawyer's bill, and I can't abide them.'

I am not the only one who believes that playing without a longstop, and no one to cover a boundary, which reckons four for every ball running to it, takes fifty per cent off the value of wicket-keeper and short-slip, who both ought to be able to dash at anything with impunity.

For what it is worth, let me, as 'an old buffer,' beg young captains to go back to the old fashion of priding themselves on almost a clean sheet of extras, and to guard their boundaries well; and to remember the golden rule, ' Change the bowling at both ends, if necessary, after twenty runs or so are got, without a wicket, no matter if the change is not so good as the man you take off: it gets the batsman's eye out, and lets him know that he is carefully watched.

I say it without fear of contradiction, that it is a sickening sight to see runs given away through causes which are avoidable, and to see a bowler kept on whilst thirty, forty, or even fifty runs are got without a change.

I don't pretend to compare past with present general cricket here, but I quite agree with the late Mr. Grimston's oft-repeated remark: ' I can't bear to see those byes going away for four: it *ain't* cricket !'

Once only in my life have I applied personally to an amateur captain on behalf of a bowler. I knew the bowler well, and had taken him about to matches with great success, as he was a *really* good all-round man. He was ' shoved down the throats ' of the county for which he played by extreme outside pressure. The Incapables who managed (?) the county did their best to shelve him, but he was played and *made his mark*, and was landed, and they did not dare exclude him.

The utter neglect of his bowling powers was a scandal to the real supporters of the club, and at the last moment before the most important match of the season I wrote a very nice letter to the captain, and begged him to give the bowler a chance.

As luck would have it, we had the best of the match in the first hour, and for another mortal hour the bowlers who commenced were kept on till dinner-time, and the bowling was smashed all over the ground, and runs accumulated by dozens.

After 178 runs were got, the bowler for whom I pleaded *was* tried, had three overs, got *two* wickets. If he had been put on after the first hour we should have had a fair chance. That match was pitched into the fire.

'You were too late, old fellow,' I remarked, 'trying that bowler.' '*Humbug!*' was the answer. Yes, it *was* 'humbug' in the captain's obstinacy, if you please.

No captain knows what his eleven *can* do unless he has them with him at practice and in bye-matches, and puts a shilling on the wicket for them to bowl to.

Turning now to the School Matches at Lords, let us plunge *in medias res*, and produce

SCHEDULE No. 3.

Page in Cricket, 1884.	Name of Match.	Elevens.	B.	L.B.	W.	N.B.	Tot.
283	Eton *v.* Harrow, about 2 innings and a half played (wet)	Eton ...	2	4	0	0	6
		Harrow ...	4	1	0	0	5
319	M. C. C. *v.* Clifton Coll.	M. C. C. ...	11	2	0	0	13
		Clifton ...	1	4	0	0	5
330	M. C. C. *v.* Rugby	M. C. C. ...	18	3	0	0	31
		Rugby ...	11	12	0	0	23
335	Marlborough *v.* Rugby	Marlborough	9	5	1	0	15
		Rugby ...	6	4	2	1	12

Three cheers for Clifton! One bye only, although they lost their match single innings. This comes of training.

Richard Humphrey, who is their coach, and who was one of my Mitcham colts, told me last season that he taught the boys on the old village green the rule of 'first learning to be "a good longstop," and the fielding will follow.' That is the sound principle of learning—do the hard work first.

So pardon me at this Christmas-tide, ' my Christian friends,' if I submit to some of you cricketers at Lords that it may do you good to go to Clifton College and learn long-stopping from Richard Humphrey in the spring; and submit to you also, if you have not a *really* good wicket-keeper who can stand up to the wicket, and you want to increase your out-field, whether it would not be wise to put a good man five yards behind the wicket *instead* of *at it.*

And so a happy Christmas to all, and more power to long-stop's elbow next season, and let bygones be byes no more.

A QUEER DAY ON LOCH LEVEN.

By R. M. ALEXANDER.

OUR old family doctor is one of the best of his sort who ever felt a pulse or ogled a tongue ; and he has put me under many an obligation to him, having pulled me through more than one serious illness.

He is a keen fisherman, and can cast a trout-fly and kill his fish in a workmanlike manner, as he can burn a throat or vaccinate a baby. He is a great authority on orchid growing, and no man in the country is better known in connexion with them. You can always tell him a mile off, as he invariably wears an orchid in his button-hole, generally about the size and shape of a china teapot, and with a name to it long enough to crack the jaw of an alligator.

One day he called to ask me if I would go with him the following week to try our luck on Loch Leven, as the papers were giving fabulous reports of the number of trout being killed there that season. Although I don't care particularly for loch fishing, I agreed to go to please him. One does not get the exercise nor half the sport standing or sitting in a boat all day long, whipping away at still water, and when one does get hold of a fish it has not the life of one half its weight hooked in a running stream. For all that, the loch angler does get hold of trout that fairly test his skill in the gentle art, especially on Loch Leven. We agreed to meet at the station on the following Tuesday, so I set to work to dress some flies for the occasion, and to get my loch tackle into order. The day arrived, and turned out to be one of the right sort for the water we were going to fish, viz., cloud and sunshine, with a steady east wind.

I drove up to the station at the hour fixed, and found my friend the Doctor awaiting me, as usual adorned with an orchid that made you blink to look at it. He was accompanied by two friends, of whom he had made no mention before. I did not bargain for this ; however, we were introduced to each other, and I looked them both over. One was a sportsman I could see at a glance, with a bronzed complexion, a very old coat, green about the shoulders, showing signs of having weathered many a rough day ; his basket was worn out, and the cover of his rod ditto.

The other I was not so favourably impressed with. His name was Mudford ; everything he owned was brand new : his rod had evidently never been out of its case except for examination in the shop, his basket was new, his hat was new, he had on a pair of new patent leather boots and a black coat, and I expected to see him put on a pair of lavender kids every minute ! It was needless for him to inform me, which he did when we got into the railway carriage, that he had never killed a trout in his life, but that he had killed a few gudgeon and eels when he was a boy—and he certainly looked like it !

' Have you engaged boats ?' I asked the Doctor.

' Oh, no!' he replied ; ' we are sure to get them all right : there is never a run on them at the beginning of the week.'

I hope you are right,' I remarked ; ' but I doubt it ; and if there is a club competition on there to-day we are done for.'

However, we hoped for the best, and made the journey to Kinross pass quickly by trying to outdo each other in the biggest Munchausen-like stories of fishing adventure, told in the way only fishermen can tell them !

On drawing near to our destination, the Doctor, in an insinuating way, asked me if I would mind his friend Mudford going in my boat, as I knew something about fishing and could show him how to work the oracle. Of course I could not say no, but inwardly blessed the Doctor, as there is nothing I hate more than being bottled up in a boat all day with a perfect stranger, and especially one who is not a sportsman.

Arrived at the loch we were not agreeably surprised to find that my surmise had proved correct, and that a strong detachment from a neighbouring fishing-club were going to compete that day, and all the boats were engaged except one !

'Well, who was right?' I asked the Doctor.

'Oh! never mind,' he said; 'we can all get into the same boat, and take it in turns to fish.'

He was one of those who always tried to make the best of everything, and quite right too, but it did not suit me on this occasion.

'No, thank you,' I replied; 'I would sooner take my chance casting off the bank.' But while we were talking a friendly labourer, who had been listening to our conversation, said, if two of us would not mind using 'a rayther lairge kind o' a coble, which was half foo o' water,' he could get the loan of it for us: so I thought that would be better than nothing, and agreed to take it, thinking at the same time it would put Mudford off coming with me—but no such luck!

When the craft was produced it was about the size of a Thames coal-barge, and about as dirty. Our friend said, 'If ye would just tak a seat on her for a wee and get yer flees put reight,' he would go and try to procure a couple of hands to man the barge. In the meantime the Doctor and his companion had started in the only available decent boat, and we saw them in the distance already hard and fast into a big trout, which was certainly tantalising.

In about half an hour back came our new acquaintance, followed by two queer-looking individuals. One was a very ancient specimen of humanity, who had evidently been having his 'mornin,' or at least several 'mornins,' as he could hardly walk, and staggered up to us with his hands well shoved into his pockets, a quid in his mouth, bloodshot, wrinkled eyes, and a nose like a Chinese lantern. I asked him if he could row a boat.

'And what for *no?*' he replied.

Did any one ever hear a Scotchman give a direct answer?

'All right, then,' I said; 'jump in, and we'll see what you can do: there is one consolation, you can't upset *that* boat.'

The other hand was a youth about fifteen, with a Balmoral bonnet pulled well down over his eyes, ears like two Japanese fans, and a mouth like an open carpet-bag; and he also had his hands shoved well down to the bottom of his pockets. He had evidently been captured on a ploughed field, as he had about a ton of clay attached to each hoof.

'Can *you* row?' I asked severely.

'Na!'

'Were you ever in a boat?'

'Na!'

'Did you ever see a trout caught?'

'Na!'

'Does your mother know you're out?'

'Na!'

I believe he would have said 'Na' if you had asked him if he would like to go to heaven when he kicked the bucket!

He was an uncouth youth! The only thing for it was to make the best of a bad bargain, so I got this mongrel crew on board after fixing up my own rod, and also that of my unwelcome companion, who couldn't even do that for himself. I asked him to show me his fly-book, and looked through it. It was evidently filled by the stationer, or toy-shop owner, from whom he had bought it, with 'real killers!' There was not a single fly in it that would raise a trout in a month of Sundays. Anyhow, I put on two of them, and one of my own, to give him a chance, and, screwing on the top of my landing-net, gave the order to shove off.

I was informed before starting that Davy was the name of our ancient boatman, and that when he was sober, which was the exception to the rule, he was as good a man as one could have in a boat, and knew the loch well, and the favourite haunts of the speckled beauties. It was a sight to see the first attempt the two made to row; the uncouth one splashed his oar into the water each time he took a stroke fit to drive every fish out of the water. Old Davy got along pretty well for about fifty yards or so, when he caught his oar in some weeds, and over he went on to his back, knocking over the youth (who was rowing, or at least trying to row, bow) at the same time! Although I was in a bad humour I could not help roaring with laughter to see these two extraordinary looking creatures floundering about at the bottom of the boat, old Davy utterly powerless to get up by himself, and sending forth volley after volley of good honest Scotch oaths, tinted with a sprinkling of Gaelic. I was at last obliged to go to the rescue, and got the old man on to his seat again, and took the bow oar myself to show the uncouth one how to use it, and after a little tuition he managed to get along tolerably well by keeping his gimlet eye fixed steadily on the blade of his oar the whole time; his mouth, as usual, wide open, and his tongue playing round the corners. We got on to the fishing-ground and found the trout rising well all round, so I

thought it was time to get to work and see what was to be done.
I took possession of the bows, and told my would-be sporting
companion to stay in the stern of the boat and to do as I did
in the way of casting and working his flies. While he was
getting ready for action I tried two or three casts over a trout
that was rising near to us ; he came at me twice, but short both
times ; and now, bad luck to it ! Mudford began. He watched me
attentively, and certainly did as I did, as he cast exactly at the
same time that I did ; and the consequence of course was, that our
lines caught behind and got into an almost hopeless entangle-
ment, which, of course, I had to undo. All this time the trout
were feeding greedily all round the boat, and old Davy was
getting more and more impatient, as I had told him he would
have a 'dram' after the first blood if he kept steady ; so, of
course, he was anxious that we should hurry up and kill a fish.

'Eh, mon! for guidness' sake, look shairp,' he exclaimed ; 'the
water's jist like bilin' porridge wi' them troot, and yer no catchin'
ony. I never see'd sich a pair o' daft-like fishers in a' ma born
days !'

'Look here, Davy' I said, 'if you don't keep a civil tongue
in your head I'm hanged if you'll get a drop out of us to-day.'
He kept quiet, but looked as if he thought a lot !

After a great deal of bother I got our lines straight, and told
Mudford he had better fish by himself for a short time, and I
would sit down and smoke a pipe and tell him what to do. He
commenced thrashing the water as if he was using a flail.
Crack ! crack went his flies behind him, but I let him go on till he
seemed to be getting tired ; then I said,' You had better look at
your flies, to see that they are all right ;' so he rolled in his line,
and was very much astonished to find all his flies off except one.

'The trout have been biting hard at you,' I remarked ; 'and
big ones, too !'

'Have they really ?' he credulously replied.

'I think you had better try and put on some fresh flies yourself this time, and get Davy to help you,' I said, knowing they
would take a precious long time over it, and that I should get a
chance of killing something while they were busy ; so I told
them to row round the island a short way, so as to get out of
the water that Mudford had thrashed into foam. While they
were fumbling and bungling over the flies I managed to land
three nice trout, averaging about a pound each, Davy, of course
reminding me of his 'dram' after the death of the first one.

Mudford became fearfully excited over this, and was dying to be at them again. He managed with difficulty to get two more flies fixed on after a fashion, and once more commenced the attack, when, wonderful to relate! he got hold of a trout, and a good one, too. Directly it took his fly he lowered the point of his rod, and let the fish run to its heart's content, which it did with a will.

'What am I to do, now?' he yelled.

'Hold up the point of your rod,' I roared; which he did with a jerk enough to pull up a team of galloping horses, and snap went his line and off went the trout, whisking his tail, with twenty yards of line fixed to his gills. Poor Mudford's face became livid with disappointment. I was really sorry for him, and so gave him the use of a spare reel and line I had with me, and once again I fixed him up, this time with some of my own flies.

Just then I noticed a heavy trout come lazily to the surface of the water within a few yards of the boat. I knew by the boil he made he was one worth having, so threw my line over him and up he came, but only to look at me, as he never touched. I tried him again, and this time he meant business, and came at me with a rush. My line tightened, and I drove the barb into his jaw. Off he went with a splendid burst for about thirty yards, and jumped two or three feet out of the water. He certainly was a beauty as far as shape went. Just at this moment Mudford, who had been casting viciously all this time, managed to put his flies clean over my line, and got one of them tightly fixed on to it. I could not stand that, so let out at him, which made matters worse, as he lost his nerve, if ever he had any: when I told him to slacken his line he rolled in, and *vice versâ.* At last I was obliged to take his rod out of his hand and work both reels myself, and no easy matter I found it, with a heavy and lively fish fighting determinedly for its life. After some minutes' careful manipulation of the two rods my trout began to show signs of distress, so I told old Davy to get the landing-net ready. Mudford was most anxious to try and land him for me, but I politely declined his services, telling him that he might practise when I got hold of a smaller fish. I gradually drew my trout to the side of the boat, and sang out, 'Now is your time, Davy! and for goodness' sake pull yourself together.' But Davy had not steadied down yet: he gave a lurch over the side of the boat, and if I had not caught him with my right

hand by the scruff of the neck he would have been clean over into the water. I yelled to the uncouth one to come and take the net from him, and see if *he* could manage better. After a desperate struggle with old Davy, who refused to give it up, he at last got possession of it, and made a lunge at the trout, who had begun to revive again, and was plunging about in a dangerous manner. The clumsy lout missed it and struck my line, but, fortunately, the tackle held. By this time I had fairly lost my temper, and the air reeked with language not of the choicest. I snatched the landing-net from him, as I saw the only way out of the difficulty was to do everything myself. There I was, with two rods in one hand and a net in the other. By this time half the boats on the loch had crowded round to see what the excitement was about, and their occupants were all laughing at me.

The trout was now completely finished, so I got the net well under him and whipped him into the boat, and great was our delight when we saw him lying motionless at the bottom. The fly actually dropped out of his mouth when I took him out of the net, so I certainly got him by the skin of his teeth! He turned down exactly four pounds, and was the heaviest fish killed that day.

After this the flasks were passed round, and I held up my fish to the envious gaze of those who had been jeering at me.

Notwithstanding many difficulties, I killed over nineteen pounds of beautiful fish during the day, and Mudford, to his great delight, managed to land two to his own hook; and as I made him a present of all those I had caught except the big one, I have no doubt he paraded them all before his friends, and took all the honour and glory of killing them to himself.

The Doctor and his friend had also a good basket of fine trout, and he thanked me for showing Mudford such good sport, and screamed with laughter when I recounted my adventures to him. I have never taken any of his friends out since, and nothing will ever persuade me to have Mudford in my boat again.

THE DUKE'S BONSPIEL.

A Curling Story.

By T. Dykes.

SCARCELY less interesting than the accounts of the numerous battles are the descriptions of the many peaceful 'bonspiels,' as the great curling games are termed, which have been fought in Scotland on the ice field. If Bannockburn has its broadsword and claymore contests, stirringly described by the old minstrel chroniclers, Carselbreck has as thrilling accounts in prose and verse of the many fights with the besom and the curling-stone. In winter, indeed, all over the North, John Frost, though he may pinch the trees, tingle the ears, and make auld wives huddle close together round the fireside, is an almost universal favourite, for it has to be remembered that the strong and healthy inevitably make the stakes ; not curling dinners of beef and greens only, but coals to replenish the fires of the poor, and meal with which to make,—

> 'The halesome porritch,
> Chief of Scotia's food.'

One of the most historical games ever played in the North was that between a rink raised by a former Duke of Hamilton against a rival Clydesdale laird, Lockhart of Lee. The game was then in great favour amongst Scottish noblemen, and on the Borders the old feuds were settled in a bloodless, though at bloodheat manner, on the ice. Lady-loves, not the meek, mild-mannered dames of the present day, but the grim Lady Grizels of the old ballads, who defied Fause Argylls from the castle-walls of the 'Bonnie House of Airlie,' and whose sole anxiety was to have families of sons to fight for Scotch King or Southern cattle, would have nought to do with a man who could not take his own part in a bonspiel, and handle his broom in the style of a modern crossing-sweeper. Broad acres and herds of cattle sometimes depended on the passage of a stone, and defeated men have been known to have gone home with icicles at their eyebrows, the frozen tears of vexation. It was during such times

that Lockhart of Lee was dining with the Duke in the ancient
castle which has now been merged in the modern palace, the
finest building in Scotland, that conversation turned on curling,
for it was in the third week of December, and the red glow of
the setting sun in the west proclaimed the likelihood of a visit
from the frosty King. Dry winds had cleared the lands of all
surface moisture, and farmers were certain that if frost set in it
would last all over the Christmas, and they would have a rare
time of it on the ice. It was natural, therefore, that Sir Norman
Lockhart, a keen curler, and the Duke, should, after the wine-
cup had been passing freely, commence to boast of their curling
achievements.

'Look here, Lee,' said his Grace, naming him in Scotch
fashion after his estate, 'we have a rink here that will play any
one in all Scotland, and for any stake you like.'

'Any one but the Lanark Laddies, Duke: that's my own
rink, and they're invincible.'

'Come now, for a hundred guineas, if the frost sets in hard and
holding, I'll meet you on the Haughs of Avon outside there, three
good men and myself against three Lanark Laddies, as you call
them, and yourself, and we'll curl the best of twenty-one heads,
rink against rink, stone against stone, broom against broom,
and the best men to win.'

'With all my heart, Duke: if there's aught o' luck left in
the Lee Penny I should have no trouble in winning. Come, a
bumper to John Frost ; a hearty welcome and a long stay.
Keen ice and keen curlers.'

'Keen ice and keen curlers,' said the Duke, raising a beaker
of claret to his lips. 'I join in the toast with all my heart. But
how shall the meeting be ? when shall I let you know the ice is
strong enough?'

'The old way, Duke ; the old castle tower will stand the
brunt o' a tar-barrel as well as it did in more stirring times.'

'By my soul and it shall, Lee ! and if it burns the place
down, there will be no great odds. At midnight I'll give
you a beacon to tell you that you must be on the Haughs
there at daylight in the morning, you and your three Lanark
Laddies.'

'So be it, Duke. And now I must go, my horse is waiting,
and though he be as stout an old-fashioned Clydesdale as ever
tramped a hillside, he'll have hard work before him, for the road
is not in the best of order, and we must try by the ford. Good

night, Duke, and remember, if frost sets in, the midnight beacon, for I shall keep a watch for it.'

In a few minutes the hoofs of the baronet's Clydesdale horse rang out in the castle court-yard, and were lost to hearing as in the moonlight he disappeared in the direction of the town of Hamilton.

Next morning John Frost held everything within his close embrace. The ploughman retired from the lea field without so much as turning a single furrow, so rock-firm was the ground. The wild geese and ducks all gabbled together in a corner of the pond, angry at this rude interference with their liberties ; the little teal came down from the Strathaven moor-ponds in flocks to the Clyde, where it rolled past the woods of the Hamilton grounds : the rooks, with the plough stopped, and no worms to pick up, sat disconsolate on the trees, and the wee birds crowded in close to the barn-doors in order that they might have a chance of picking up some stray seeds. It was hard frost, there could be no doubt, from appearances without, and as the Duke said, while he sat at breakfast in the old hall, hard frost from 'appearances within ;' for the pine-log in the old-fashioned brazier blazed and laughed and sputtered out showers of sparks every moment, making the whole apartment warm with the very brightness of its smiles. Two days more of John's reign and the geese and the ducks abandoned the ice-clad ponds and winged their ways to the river. The wild cattle of Cadzow, tamed in spirit, sought food on the edges of the last of the old Caledonian forests, and after another night old Douglas, the forester, was able to walk across the ice which lay on the grounds in the Haughs of Avon, formed by the floods from the Avon, at the point where it joins the Clyde.

'You can well play Sir Norman Lockhart to-morrow, your Grace,' was the old forester's answer, on being asked, when called into his presence ; 'but how about Tam Pate ?'

'Do you mean Tom Pate the fish-hawker ?'

'That I do, for the Laird of Lee Castle, I hear, has put on as skip Jock o' Carstairs, and there is not a curler save Tam Pate, in the whole of Scotland, fit to face him. With Tam we stand a chance of winning, without Tam we stand every chance of losing.'

'And where is Tam ?'

'Tam is the Lord knows where ; some say he's off on a poaching job, for he's a wild character, but his wife says he went off to Greenock after haddocks, herrings, and such-like fish as he can get : but she says, if ice can hold him above water better than the Lord can hold him out of mischief, he'll be at the curling.'

'Say you so, Douglas ? Well, then, light the pine-fagots and the tar-pot on the tower at twelve midnight, sharp. And here, Douglas, I say, send some horsemen about to see if they can find Pate. I mind not whether he be poaching or preaching or selling fish, but let's have him, for Lee seems determined to win this hundred guineas. I meant to play skip myself, but seeing he's got a better than himself, then Tam Pate must captain us. If he can't be found, we'll do our best.'

At midnight the beacon blazed from the top of the old tower, as if to rouse the surrounding farmers and peasantry against some clan foray. Brightly it lighted up the Clyde windings far up amongst the trees, as if to waken, as it would have done in days of yore, with sounds of alarm, the warder on Craignethan, the renowned Tilletudlem of Sir Walter Scott. On Bothwell's ancient walls it shed, too, at times, its fitful glare, and the men of St. Mungo's city, who were sitting late over their rum punch from the Indies, blinked, and said it was the moon. There were no blazing iron-works in the Clyde valley in those days ; no heaving and soughing and smoke-giving coal-pits, but all was in summer, peaceful cornfields and apple orchards, from Lee Castle to the old oaks of Hamilton ; the most happy and peaceful scenery then in all Scotland. Alas for the race, for riches, and its rumbling of coal trucks ! Let no man say what it looks like now. As the pine-knots crackled on the roof the flames shot up into the darkling sky, while men with beakers of good ale watched the horizon afar. At last there burst from all a cheer, as a light shot high against the horizon in the direction of Lee Castle. Quickly Douglas found his way into the hall, where still sat the the Duke, poring over a despatch from the South.

'Well, Douglas, what news ?'

'Sir Norman has answered your challenge, Sir ; there is a beacon blazing on Lee Castle.'

'Ah! then get to bed, and try and find Pate the fish-hawker : we must meet him on the Haughs in the morning.'

And so, as the beacons were dwindling down to feeble rush-lightings, the old forester, a staunch and true henchman to the house of Hamilton, joined his companion curlers, and all sought their way to bed, to enjoy that repose which a true sportsman always needs before entering upon a great struggle.

In the morning the frost was more intense than ever. It had
frozen, the old butler asserted, the wine in all the bottles, let
alone freezing the bottles to the bins. Worse than that, the
cook said that the kettle had been frozen to the hob. No doubt
each and all of them were exaggerating, but there could be no
doubt whatever as to the fact that Jack Frost had been most
intent in his wooing during the night-time. According to an
old song.—

> 'The music of the year was hush'd
> In bonnie glen and shaw, man,
> As winter spread o'er nature dead
> A winding-sheet o' snaw, man.
> O'er burn and loch the warlock frost
> A crystal brig has laid, man ;
> The wild geese screaming with surprise,
> The ice-bound wave hae fled, man.'

Still the invincible Tam Pate was missing, not one of the
horsemen who had been despatched for him on the previous
evening having been able to find him. 'He must have gone to
Newhaven for his haddocks instead of Greenock,' said some.
'It's more than likely,' said others, 'that he's joined some curlers
at a road-side pond, for it's scarcely possible for him to pass
one,' said others, who knew his fondness of the game.

No time was to be lost, however, for the noble Laird of Lee
and his men, headed by the valiant Jock o' Carstairs, carrier,
salmon-leisterer, and general ne'er-do-weel, were trying their
stones on the glassy ice, but the roaring, reverberating sound of the
polished granite blocks seemed to have awakened the chief, for
in the pauses was heard the well-known voice, echoing from the
town streets, crying, 'Herrings, fresh from Loch Fyne. Herrings,
the real Glasgow magistrates.'

'Bring him, herrings, barrow, and all, forester, and lose no
time over it,' said the Duke : 'we want him here. Send for a
pot and we'll boil his fish for luncheon.'

Tam Pate wanted no second invitation to come and curl for
the Duke, more especially when he knew that his market was not
to be spoiled by delay ; and speedily sought out from amongst
the bracken on the edge of the woodlands a pair of heavy
Crawfordjohns, with oak handles, which seemed to have well
stood the warm summer moisture.

'Oh! and it's you that's to face me, Jock o' Carstairs !' he
said, looking to the latter. 'Well, and if I don't do my best my
name's no Tam Pate. Say, now, we're ready.'

As arranged by the forester he was to lead himself, followed by Jamie the gardener; the Duke playing third against the Laird of Lee, and Tam Pate skip against Jock o' Carstairs. The toss between the two latter resulted in the forester leading off with a shot which went clean away, raging beyond the tee, and, as the skip said, 'roaring as if it meant to jump the Clyde.'

The Lee opposing man, a burly farmer from Tintoch side, was more careful, and placed his stone exactly as requested, a yard in front of the tee; by far the best place. It is no use explaining to the curler, though to the non-curling reader it may be explained, that if it lay on or past the tee it would be sure to be played against and forced out.

'Now, forester, draw a cannie shot past that one, and spare some o' your strength for the big trees in Cadzow—a nice gentle draw, with your elbow out for a bit curl at the finish.'

'You are well laid down, Sir! beautifully curled, Sir! you're a rare one when you finish: but, oh, ye're weak! Bring him on, Duke! soop (sweep) him up. Soop, soop, soop! for ye're lives soo-oo-p him! Bring him on every inch. Eh! the shot, Sir! well curled! and well done. Well soopit, Duke! He's half gairdet by their own stane.'

It was now Jock o' Carstairs' turn to direct his men, and so he took a good survey of the situation for himself.

'Look here, Hyndford,' was his call. 'Draw a gentle shot past your own stone; if ye take it ye'll do no harm, if ye miss it ye'll have the shot. A gentle draw, but be up, for you must not be their guard.' But the Hyndford man was not straight, and rather too strong, for Tam Pate, by hard sweeping him, took him out of the counting circle altogether.

The result of the second men's play completely altered matters, however, for the gardener was no match for the Lanark Laddie, a knight of the loom, who opposed him, and earned the remark from Tam, who was a man who cared for nobody, 'that he might be a great man amongst cabbages but he was nothing amongst curling-stones.' The weaver with his last shot having left about three parts of the face of a stone bare, it was the Duke's duty to knock it out.

'Come down on it,' said the skip to the noble player, 'with a rattle as hard as ye can swing.'

There was no doubt about the swing and the roar, for down came the stone with a noise which made the welkin ring; and as Tam, with an ecstatic yell, jumped back, waving his broom aloft, it struck its object full in the face and sent it spinning down the ice, whilst it cannoned down the pond full fifty yards. 'Curled like an angel!' 'Weel played, your Grace!' were amongst the numerous salutations which followed. Sir Norman Lockhart failing to draw a shot, left it open to his Grace for a draw, and Tam most earnestly enjoined him to be careful. 'If ye can only give me a nice canny draw to my feet, ye may have half the herrings for nothing. You're well laid down again. Oh! he's a rare one, gentlemen! not a broom; he's strong enough; wait on him, jist! oh! but he's a rare one! never was better. Ye may have half the herrings, my lord. Oh! fetch him on now; he's lagging! Soop! soop! oh! he's a good one! Ye may have the whole of the herrings. Soop him up! soop him up! Soop! soop! soop! Hurrah! ye may have the *barrow*, my Lord. Tee shot drawn! Hurrah! you for a curler!'

The Laird of Lee left matters undisturbed, Tam Pate putting down guards which could not be passed, and the result was that the Hamilton rink won the first end by one shot.

In the clear frosty air and the brilliant sunshine they played with varying success, till far on in the afternoon; refreshments— not to forget the herrings, which were boiled on the ice in huge cauldrons, or kail-pots—being supplied from the castle, not only to the players, but to the excited townsmen of Hamilton, who were gathered around. It was truly a lively scene of Clydesdale in the olden times, with its oaks hanging with frosted tassels, its long winding valley, with uplands gently sloping from the river, with whitewashed walls of farm-houses surmounting the brows. and the top of Tintock, white, with snow shining in the far distance. But the players saw little to admire in the scenery. Both sides stood 14, 15, at the second last head; and the last head they started to play *par*, equally confident. There had been many splendid shots during the game, which Tam Pate had warmly commended, and some which he fiercely condemned. winding up an expostulation to a stone with the words, 'Oh! soop him up, he's a hog! Oh, your Grace! your Grace! oh! you're a *dis*-Grace!' a remark which made the Duke roar with laughter.

Shot and shift, and shot again, was the order of the play, for the first four stones of either side in the finishing head; and the next stones, those of the Duke and Sir Norman, resulted in the latter leaving a nice shot well guarded, only about a quarter of it being visible. Jock o' Carstairs almost covered it up com-

"Hurrah! you've got him!"

pletely, and the result was that Tam Pate had to waste his first stone making the way clear. The Carstairs man tried to shut the road up again and failed, and it now remained on Tam Pate to win or lose the game. If he could lift the stone of the opposing side his own side lay toward, they were victors, if not they scarcely could think the word!

'Can you do it, Tam?' cried the Duke, who was down on his knees to watch the result: 'if ye can, ye'll ne'er need to hawk a fish nor pay a rent for man or mare as long as ye live!'

'I can but try, your Grace. Stand by with your brooms, in case I catch our own stones.'

So saying he balanced his stone in his right hand, swung it behind him, and delivered it on the ice as evenly and as flatly as if he had raised it but an inch.

'You've got him!' said the Duke; 'you have him fair!' he cried, as down on his knees he watched the path it was travelling. Down past the outside guard it came, so close to the first guard that a sheet of paper held between them would have been rubbed off, the forester and the gardener trembling with anxiety. On past the second, the Duke still crying, 'You have him!' 'Hurrah! you've got him!' was his final exclamation, as he flung his broom in the air and commenced to dance the reel of Tulloch, while Tam Pate was busy down the rink at the Highland fling.

That night the pine-knots again blazed on the old tower of Hamilton, and the Lady of Lee retired without waiting for the return of the Laird, for she knew the result. Need it be said there was rejoicing in house and hall, or that Tam Pate had ever to hawk herrings, or that his mare ever wanted a bite of grass on the Haughs of Strathaven?

TALLY-HO!

THE FIRST DAY OF THE SEASON.

By CAPT. ALEXANDER CLARK KENNEDY, F.R.G.S.

THE sound of the horn and the ring of the gun
Proclaim that the reign of fair Summer is done;
And Autumn the forest in beauty reveals,
And jolly old Winter comes close on his heels!
Then a health to the Fox, and a health to the Hounds,
Good luck to the covert where 'music' resounds!

And here's to our Master, his horses and men !
Tally-ho ! for the first of the season again !

' Tally-ho ! Tally-ho !' Oh ! what memories steal
Through the heart of the hunter ! what joy doth he feel
When the chorus resounds in the woodland below !
To the Meet, if you love the sweet sound Tally-ho !
   Let all foreigners know
   How we love ' Tally-ho !'
   We are Englishmen—so
   ' Tally-ho ! Tally-ho !!'

Your foot in the stirrup, your hand on the rein,
And the seat that you love in the pigskin again,
No lark in the heavens more happy and gay
Than you—on the first of the season to-day !
Let them gallop their best,—they shall gallop in vain
To catch the best steed that your stables contain !
As a youngster you rode—may you ride as a man,
Never fear,—the best fellows are found in the van !

  Chorus—' Tally-ho ! Tally-ho !!' &c.

Oh ! gay is the life that we lead in the North,
Where grouse-cock and black-cock inveigle us forth,
Where the salmon runs up to his death from the sea,
But in winter the pastime of hunting for me !
So, each to his fancy, and each to his love !
There's fun for your money where'er you may rove ;
Then take up the racquet, the rod, or the gun,
And leave me my joys in the cream of a run !

  Chorus—'Tally-ho ! Tally-ho !!' &c.

Let the fences be ' hairy,' the hedges be high,
You're as bright as a bird as you over them fly :
Be the brook in the valley forbidding and wide,
We shall see you, be sure, on the opposite side !
Though, splashing and dashing, pop some of us in,
No worse can befall you than wetting your skin !
Then, away ! in a twinkling, go sportsman and horse,
For you'll dry in the air as the pasture you cross !

  Chorus—'Tally-ho ! Tally-ho !!' &c.

Come, tell me the joys that the cover-sides bring,
Come, strike up the air we are longing to sing,

Come tune up the chorus of sweet 'Tally-ho!'
For the pack have a fox in the spinney below!
And clust'ring around—be it sunshine or rain—
Are the cheery, familiar old faces again;
For the glance of an eye, and the grip of a hand,
Make the yeoman as proud as a lord of the land!

Chorus—'Tally-ho! Tally-ho!!' &c.

The Peer whom we dote on, the Squire from his Hall,
With faces so cheery and welcomes for all,
The Doctor, who's given his patients the slip,
The Sailor ashore for a day from his ship
(And who than the sailor more sporting can be,
As he rolls in his saddle like yacht on the sea?),
The Parson whose parish has gone to the wall,
The Soldier, the Farmer—'Hurrah for them all!

Chorus—'Tally-ho! Tally-ho!!' &c.

Though gardens in summer with flowers are gay,
And roses bloom only for lovers they say,
You can talk to your flame as you ride through the gorse,
And make up the match from the back of your horse!
And many a matron and many a maid,
In the workmanlike garb of Diana arrayed,
To grace the first meet of the season are here,
So you've only to follow your fox or your *dear!*

Chorus—'Tally-ho! Tally-ho!!' &c.

When summer is here there are birds on the wing,
And the woods in their glory with melody ring;
But what would you wish now the covert is bare?
Why, of course, you expect that the 'varmint' is there!
So be it! my sportsman! a moment restrain
Your ardour, I pray you; it shall not be vain;
For soon shall you hear the proud cry 'Tally-ho!'
And then, noble sportsman, hark, for'ard! you go!

Chorus—'Tally-ho! Tally-ho!!' &c.

Bestir you, my young one, nor longer delay,
Hark, hark! to the halloo! he's for'ard, away!
Now, now for a 'spin,'—like an arrow we speed
Away o'er the fallow! away o'er the mead!
And when the first day of the season is done
We'll tell o'er again the delights of the run,

As we sit round the table, contented and gay,
For the sport that we love is *beginning* to-day.

Chorus.

'Tally-ho! Tally-ho!' Oh! what memories steal
Through the heart of the hunter! what joy doth he feel
When the chorus resounds in the woodland below!
Then away to the Meet if you love Tally-ho!
And let foreigners know
How we love 'Tally-ho!'
We are Englishmen—so
'Tally-ho! Tally-ho!!'

THE POINT TO POINT STEEPLECHASE
OF THE T. V. H.

By 'DERVISH.'

HE Timbermore Vale is one of the happiest hunting-grounds in England. With as large a proportion of grass as any of the crack countries in the Shires, it is fortunately not so fashionable in the eyes of the general public, and is consequently frequented only by sportsmen and sportswomen, who give the hounds every chance, partly from their own sense of the fitness of things, partly from the discipline generated by long years of the judicious but firm rule of the best of masters. Few countries could furnish a larger percentage of followers who mean riding straight to hounds—where riding straight is often not an easy matter—and if the road division is at times a bit swelled during a quick thing, this may be put down rather to bad starts or wrong turns than to any repugnance to the negotiation of obstacles. Though fairly well-gated, it is essentially a jumping country; the enclosures are small, and the fences, which are mostly of an on-and-off nature, take a lot of doing, not so much from their size as from the strong hedges and stiff binders that surmount the banks.

It is not unnatural that, towards the close of each season in this sporting country, the 'customers' should be disposed to try conclusions as to who is the best man, and which the best horse out of a hard-riding field, under circumstances where none can complain of a bad start, or any other such disadvantage. Accordingly it has been the custom in the Vale for some years to hold a small meeting of a couple of races over a natural country, one for the gentlemen and the other for farmers. Four miles from point to point to be got over as the rider pleases, provided he do not go a hundred yards along a road or through a gate, is not quite such plain sailing as a flagged course; but it is far more suited to testing the powers of a good hunter; and knowledge of the country, and judgment in picking his place, will stand a 'rider to hounds' in good stead, where a crack jockey might, in spite of all his knowledge of pace, find himself sadly pounded.

It was to take part, then, in one of these annual meetings that I arrived one wet afternoon in the middle of March, not many years back, at the 'Delveby Arms,' the principal and sporting hostelry of the charming town of Sherminster, in the centre of the Vale country. I had made the above my hunting quarters during the early half of the season, and though I had been obliged to return to duty with my regiment at the expiration of my leave in January, my horses were entitled to run in the Point to Point race, as having been regularly hunted with the Vale Hounds during a good portion of the season. The pick of my little stable, Harbinger, had been given some pipe-openers during the last three weeks on the Downs, adjoining the town where my regiment was quartered, and sent down forty-eight hours previous to my own arrival, to the care of Toddy Hunter, my pal and brother-officer, whose guest I was to be at the 'Delveby Arms.'

As I passed the bar I met Toddy himself, wet and muddy, having just come in from hunting.

'Well, old boy,' he said, 'you've lost nothing by not coming down a day earlier. We've had a pottering day, very little scent, and no sport to speak of. This rain is doing a lot of good though. The east winds had begun to dry up the land rather too rapidly, though three weeks ago the Vale was as deep as ever I saw it. Of course you want to see Harbinger. He's all right. Come and look at him.'

Right enough he looked, certainly, as he stood stripped for a minute for my inspection in his roomy, well-ventilated box. His kind, game eye stood out clear and healthy, and there was a reassuring gloss on his bright chestnut coat. He looked, indeed, the model of a fourteen-stone hunter. Fifteen-three, with grand sloping shoulders, deep, well-rounded ribs, a roach back, wide hips, muscular quarters and second thighs, well let down into big, flat,

clean hocks, and a straight dropped hind leg. Rising eight and
sound as a bell of brass I knew him to be, too; temperate,
clever, and bold, he had proved himself in many a good gallop.
What could the heart of man desire more? Well, one little
thing. With all his grand points he was not *quite* fast enough
for my fancy. He should have been, he looked it, but he wasn't.
Anything but a *slow* horse, he was fast enough for hounds in
most countries, especially a close one like the Timbermore Vale,
and he could *keep on* going, but he was not exactly a flyer.
And this, I think, was the reason he came to be in my hands, and
not carrying a first-flight man in Leicestershire. But I had
entered him for this race, as I *knew* he would go straight, and
he was not *likely* to fall.

'He had a steady two-mile gallop round the close below the
town this morning, Sir,' said my lad, whose special charge he
was just now, 'and pulled up as fresh as anything. I thought
best not to give him any more.'

'Quite right, Jem.' Then we had a look round Toddy's little
stud, and he pointed me out especially the horse he was going to
ride on the morrow.

'Old Gaylad ought to have a chance with eleven seven up'
(two classes of competitors, riding 13st. 7lbs. and 11st. 7lbs.
respectively, were to start in the same race); 'you know his speed,
but I'm afraid of his uncertain temper without hounds. He'll be
likely enough to refuse. I hope not.'

We then adjourned to the comfortable sitting-room, shared
by the five or six votaries of Diana staying at the 'Arms,' and
over a cup of tea we examined the 'correct card of the race,'
just sent round from the printer's. The entries for our race were
as follows :—

WELTER-WEIGHTS—13st. 7lbs. each ; black coats.

1. Mr. Cropperton's b. mare 'Chance It.'
2. Mr. Fiddlemore's roan g. 'Banker.'
3. Captain Lilbourne's ch. g. 'Harbinger.'
4. Sir John Mead's gr. g. 'The Friar.'
5. Major Fitzjames' br. g. 'The Novice.'
6. Captain Splinterbar's b. g. 'Down Again.'

LIGHT WEIGHTS—11st. 7lbs. each ; red coats.

7. Mr. Todmorden Hunter's b. g. 'Gaylad.'
8. Major Brown's roan m. 'The Witch.'
9. Mr. Skeffington's bl. m. 'Kilkenny ;'

and five others which I cannot remember now, in all fourteen

starters, over four miles of country to be pointed out on the
ground.

There was a second race, with some half-a-dozen entries for
farmers and members of the Yeomanry residing within the
limits of the hunt.

By-and-by we sat down, a largish party, to a capital dinner,
washed down by the sparkling wine of France in free circulation.
One or two of the red-coat division regretted enforced abstinence
on account of their weight, notably my friend Toddy, who, in
order to ride 11st. 7lb., had supplied himself with a red flannel
coat and racing nether garments; also a six-pound saddle. I was
at my ease, as I knew that in my ordinary hunting clothes and
saddle I should scale within a pound or two of what my horse
had to carry. So I did not spare the good cheer; and by the
time the cloth had been removed, and one or two pocket-books
produced, I felt brimful of confidence and desperately inclined
to have a trifle on Harbinger's chance amongst the Welters. I
should have stated that the stakes, which were trifling, were to
be divided between the first of each division to pass the post.
The honour and glory was, of course, the main point; but if there
was a little wagering to be done, why should I not back my
opinion? And that opinion was, that among the six Welter
entries 'Harbinger' and his owner would be an ugly pair to dispose
of when it came to a stiffish line over the Vale. I had thought
over what I remembered of the other five *before* dinner, and had
deemed mine an excellent chance; *now*, of course, it seemed
better than ever. 'Chance It' was a well-bred speedy mare
enough, but hardly as much at home in this country as she
would have been in a flying one. Cropperton generally sent her
too fast at her fences, and they were constantly coming to grief
in consequence. 'Banker' was a grand, clever, weight-carrying
hunter, and able to gallop, but his owner never seemed to find a
place in the fence to suit him; or, if he did, the good horse, from
having been messed about, was apt to refuse. The 'Friar' was
a real patent-safety conveyance, but troubled with 'the slows.'
'Down Again' was the model of a weight-carrying hunter for
any country, but he made a bit of a noise, and his forelegs were
none of the best; so, being a gross horse, his owner had not been
able to get him fit to race, as the ground, until this last splash of
rain, had been a bit hard. Fitzjames' mount, too, I thought I
held safe. The only one of his lot I had seen him go on with
real confidence this season was a young horse he had bought

from a farmer in the neighbourhood, a very clever one certainly,
but, in my opinion, not fit to be mentioned in the same breath as
'Harbinger,' either for quality or for speed. I presumed *this* was
the 'Novice,' but forgot to ask.

In the whole of the British Cavalry there was no better fellow
or cheerier companion than Willie Fitzjames. He and I were old
friends, and would, I am sure, have either of us gone a good way
to get the other out of a scrape. But for all this there had long
been a great rivalry between us, which dated from the time when
our respective regiments had lain together at Newbridge, and we
two, as reckless cornets, had tried to break each other's necks for
the honour of the said regiments. Our elders, too, enjoying the
fun, had not failed to egg us on to out-Herod each other, whether
in negotiating large obstacles or in recounting our exploits over
the mahogany. It had been 'Where were you to-day, Fitz, when
George showed the way for five whole minutes?' or, 'George,
my boy, you wouldn't have looked at that ravine that Willie had
this afternoon. To be sure it took the wreckers half an hour to
get him out.' And sad-eyed, weary men, who *could* think of
other things than hunting, had left us to talk each other down, if
possible, over bumpers of military port. Fitzjames had during
the last summer won a hatful of money from me at *écarté*; but,
more than ever, our rivalry had been increased by our both
paying marked attentions to the same young lady during the early
part of the present hunting season.

He was making a small book on the Welter race now, and
after accommodating Cropperton and Fiddlemore with what he
was pleased to call the market price of their respective mounts,
he turned to me.

'What about Harbinger? I'll lay you ten sovereigns to one.'

'Ponies,' I said, 'if you like!'

'No, old man; *four ponies*, if it comes to that.'

I ought to have seen he had only been chaffing, but I was
nettled at his having seemed at first to decry my horse, and then
drawing back when challenged. Blinded by pique, and perhaps
jealousy as well, I exclaimed—

'I'll lay you an even "monkey" on Harbinger against the
Novice—first past the post!'

'Done,' said he, and booked the bet.

'Well,' said Toddy to me quietly, 'you *have* put your foot in it
now, George. If the Novice stands up he ought to finish in front
of Harbinger. He has the legs of him, I really think.'

'You don't mean it, surely?' I replied. 'He's very clever, I grant, particularly for a young one——'

'It's not his young one at all. This is an old horse he bought out of Leicestershire on purpose to win this race. He was rather rash at first, but having been bred in Ireland, he soon remembered the days of his youth, and took to doubling his fences right enough. Dear me! I thought you knew about the horse. And I didn't think you were such an owl as to go lumping down your money like that *without* knowing.'

This was not very consoling; but I felt he was right, so I held my tongue.

The party broke up early, in view of the next day's doings, and I was winding up my watch in my bedroom when Toddy looked in.

'I want to speak to you, George, about one or two things now we are alone. First, about this race. You *mustn't* drop five hundred to Fitzjames if it can be helped. I can't make the running for you if it were wanted, as I'm not in your race; and the pace is sure to be good enough for Harbinger, anyhow. But I know the country a good deal better than either of you, or *ought* to, as I've hunted here since I began on a pony. So you can't do better than follow me. It will serve both our turns; for if Gaylad refuses, Harbinger will give him a lead directly after. And I may show you a better line than perhaps Fitzjames will choose. Now another thing. The Wildairs will be there on their coach, and we'll go to them and see the farmer's race from it. I know this is quite as interesting a subject to you, George, as the race. You told me, when you first met, how much you admired Constance, and though you grew so reserved about it, after a while, of course I wasn't blind. Now, between ourselves, Marion has as good as promised to take your humble servant for better for worse, though it is not to be given out just yet. So, being behind the scenes a bit, I can see a thing or too, and I know, as no doubt *you* know better, that your chance with Constance is a good one. Well, you know too what a lot they both think about good riding; so, if you win the Welter Race, it ought to be any odds in your favour for the other event. If you could but bring off the *double* event, win back your money from Fitz, and end your friendly rivalry, for good and all, by carrying off the one great prize in life, what a *coup* it would be!'

'Too much good fortune I fear, old man, to come to one

chap all in a heap. But I must hope for the best. Now go and turn in, I want to get to sleep. Good-night.'

I could not sleep just awhile ; but I wished to be left to my own reflections. It was quite true that I had fallen deeply in love with Constance Wildair, whom I had met for the first time in November. She was by a long way the handsomest and nicest woman I had ever seen ; and I had not the slightest doubt but what she would make me the happiest of men for life, if she would only have me. But, though we had got on capitally during the short time we had been acquainted, I had not ventured on the all-important question. However, as Toddy had suggested, my success in the Steeplechase would be all in my favour, so I determined to propose on the morrow if I won ; if I lost, it would be time enough to consider then what else to do.

The next morning broke grey and cold. The rain was gone and the east wind had set in with renewed vigour. The morning passed not too pleasantly. I think every one was more or less fidgety and nervous. I know I was, for one. And I had reason. It would make a difference of a thousand pounds to me whether I beat Fitzjames or not. I could pay up if I lost, but it would cripple me considerably for a while. It was a relief to put on my ulster and get into the fly, which was to convey Toddy, myself, Splinterbar and Cropperton, to the King's Oak, a favourite meet of the Vale Hounds, about six miles off on the London road. Thither our horses had been sent on, and we were to meet there at three o'clock, so as to ride to the starting-post, as yet unknown to us, where the course would be pointed out.

About half-past three, which was punctual under the circumstances, the starter had us all duly marshalled, and we trotted away to be made acquainted with the journey before us. Then it was we found that the course rather belied its name, and that we had to go about two miles away from home, wheel to the left round a tent, cross the London road, round another tent, and return nearly parallel to the road, finishing in a field about half a mile from the Oak. It was a capital course for the spectators, but not strictly Point to Point.

To be sure, if you kept a certain spire in view on the homeward journey, you could hardly go wrong ; but the day was none too clear, and it was easy to lose sight of the beacon.

It was a relief to be off at last, and all my nervousness vanished as I felt Harbinger sailing beneath me, with his strong,

easy stride, just laying hold of me to show that he relished the job. I could see Fitzjames making play and forcing the running on the extreme left. Toddy, more to the right, was lying about fourth, and I kept from ten to fifteen lengths behind him, so as to avail myself of the places he selected in each fence without fear of jumping on him if he should fall. The pace was a cracker, but the going was very good, and many of the banks hereabouts being lower than is the rule in the Vale, might be done at a fly. I observed the Novice trying that game on and devoutly hoped he might do it once too often and drop his hind legs in the far ditch of a double. Harbinger was not losing much ground either, for when sent a good pace at his banks he could kick back with great rapidity, and you barely felt the thud. There were no mishaps till we came to the brook, after going for rather more than a mile. Here Gaylad, going best pace, whipped sharp round to his left when he came near the brink, shooting his rider over his off shoulder, but, fortunately, on to *terra firma*.

'Go on, old man, I'll catch you up,' said Toddy, scrambling to his feet, bridle still in hand, as Harbinger, whom I had pulled off to the right, glided not the least disconcerted over the water.

Now that I had lost my pilot, I turned my attention to Fitz- james, who was still leading nearly a field ahead of me; but I was pleased to observe, as we neared the tent which indicated the first turn, that he had been going so directly in a line for the same, that it took him more than a hundred yards after passing it, before, with the way he had on, he could turn his horse to the left. Having lain wide I could incline to the left, and just skirted the tent-pegs as I completed my wheel and faced the drop into the road. I pulled Harbinger into a trot, and it was well I did, for it *was* a drop and no mistake, and made me sit back all I knew. Fortunately the landing was on to a turf siding. Just here a lane ran across the road, and down it trotted the Witch, Kilkenny, and Chance It, their riders on the look-out for a low place into the field where the second tent was pitched. Remembering the conditions of the race, I thought best to leave the bank where we were, and Harbinger, with a mighty effort, scrambled up the perpendicular rise, nearly coming on his knees, but righting himself at once. Then the other three turned back and followed me. But I was first round the tent, and I looked for the spire which was to guide me home.

The day had grown thicker, and I could not see it. It would
not do to skirt the road exactly, as I knew there were two or
three quite impracticable places near the edge. So I inclined
somewhat to my right, taking a pull, in hopes of being passed
by some one who knew the country better. I had not crossed
two fields ere I was passed by my three late companions in the
lane, and Fitzjames, the latter now rapidly resuming the lead,
thanks to the Novice's speed. They seemed to be bearing too
much to the right, but I was preparing to follow them, when I
heard my name called from behind and to my left, and looking
over my shoulder I saw Gaylad overhauling me hand over hand,
and his rider stretching out his whip to his left front. I obeyed
the signal and presently Toddy, as he passed me, said,—

'They are all going wrong, we shall gain a quarter of a mile
on them.'

A long, narrow spinney hereabouts separated us from the
leading division; so they were lost to our view for the present.

The next fence was a stopper. The blackthorn hedge on
the top of the bank, to all appearance, perfectly impervious.
You might as well ride at a seven-foot brick wall. There was
nothing for it but to jump a gate which lay but little out of our
course. It was no great height, but the gateway was poached,
and Gaylad, when sent at it, pulled up short and tried to chest
it. Not so Harbinger, who, as soon as the take-off was clear,
poising himself one moment on his powerful hind-limbs,
bounded high and safely over like a deer. Gaylad made a
better offer the next time of asking, but hitting the timber all
round he landed on his head and knees in the mire; Toddy, by
sitting well back and leaving him alone, just saving a roll over.
One more easy fence, then came the brook again, over which I
led, when Toddy passed me again, and we could see two black
and two red coats fully four hundred yards behind and to our
right. Having perceived their mistake they were bending towards us; but, bar accidents, they were too late. All went well
till we reached the last field but one, which was intersected by
narrow open drains. We were close to the crowd of spectators,
and I could not help looking about for the Wildairs' coach. I
saw it, and saw Constance gazing, as I thought, with a pleased
look; when Harbinger, undoubtedly a bit blown (from the pace
at which he had been shoved along at first), and grown careless,
put his foot in a drain and rolled over, just as Gaylad was
cleverly topping the last fence. If my good horse was blown

before, he was still more so by his fall, and as he lay motionless
for half a minute I groaned in despair. I could see the Novice
coming on full of running, and not two fields from us, when
Harbinger, having caught his wind a bit, gave a struggle, then
scrambled up and shook himself, and I was in the saddle in an
instant; but not an instant too soon, for Fitzjames was now in the
same field, and as we scuttled through the gap that my leader
had made, was not thirty yards behind me. Fortunately the
run in was of no great length, and poor Harbinger, who had not
much left in him, just got home, the winner of the Welter Race
by a length.

I don't think I ever enjoyed looking on at a race more than
I did at the one which followed ours. My *tête-à-tête* with
Constance was not disturbed, as Fitzjames, somewhat crest-
fallen, passed on after a few words of greeting. He paid up like
a man within a week, and we are better friends than ever. Altogether, when I tell you that Toddy and Marion are now respectively my brother and sister-in-law, I think I may safely say I
never did a better day's work than when I rode in the POINT TO
POINT STEEPLECHASE OF THE T. V. H.

SPORT UP THE NIGER.

By F. W. BENNETT.

KNOW no part of the world where shooting is more
difficult to be obtained than the West Coast of
Africa. True, at Sierra Leone red-legged partridges,
also a few snipe and duck, can be got without much
trouble, and at Prince's Isle guinea-fowl abound, and an occasional deer, but down the whole coast, from Sierra Leone on the
north to Great Fish Bay on the southern division of the station,
shooting can only be obtained with difficulty, with the almost
certainty of a severe touch of fever. Nevertheless, naval officers
condemned to serve on that infernal station contrive somehow
or other to get a fair amount of sport, although the bags are
but small and the labour immense. Some years ago, when in
command of one of Her Majesty's small vessels employed on the
prevention of the then almost extinct slave-trade, I was directed
to take charge of an expedition up the river Niger, and although
it was too late in the season to hope to get very far up, yet I

congratulated myself upon the chance of getting a little wild
sport of a better description than that to be obtained near the
sea. Accordingly, one afternoon in November, I took the B——
across the bar, one of the worst on the coast, and anchored in
the then mouth of the river for the night, off the factory at
Baracoon Point. This factory consisted of two long, low houses,
built of wood, one for a store, the other for clerks and Kroomen
to live in ; behind was a long shed for storing palm-oil.

From the fact of the season being so far advanced, and the
river falling rapidly, I saw that it would be necessary to lighten
the B—— as much as possible ; and as it would take a day or
more before she would be ready for the ascent I organized a
shooting-party, and the morning after our arrival in the river
Mr. W—— (the trade agent), my surgeon, Dr. E——, and
myself, with the Kroomen for beaters, left the factory soon after
daylight.

The bush was excessively thick, but we soon struck a native
path, and after about two hours' walking came to a large plain
covered with Guinea-grass and small, thick bush. Here we
found quantities of Guinea-fowl, but as it was next to impossible
to get them to rise, we had very considerable difficulty in getting
sport out of them, added to which, unless killed outright (and
they can carry off a heavy charge of shot) their extraordinary
running power made the retrieving of them extremely difficult.
In addition to the fowl we put up two small antelopes, one of
which I killed, and the other, wounded by E——, was pulled
down after a short chase by our only dog, a pure-bred English
bull slut.

After working the grass well, the intense heat proved too
much for us ; so, giving most of our guns to the Kroomen to
carry, we started for home. Shortly before reaching the forest,
Rose, the slut, picked up the scent of some animal, and dashed
off in sharp chase. We followed, and after a run of about a
quarter of a mile, found her barking and leaping at the foot of a
large tree. Looking up, I caught sight of the hind-quarters of a
large tiger-cat. My gun, a 12-bore muzzle-loader, had two
ounces of swan shot in the right barrel and a ball in the
left, and. as I could not get a clear sight of the brute's
head, I let him have the dose of shot in his stern. He
sprang out of the tree like lightning, clear over Rose, and
was off without turning, but a quick snap shot from my
remaining barrel put a ball clean through his head, and

'dropped him in his tracks.' Rose at once fixed on his nose, but, fortunately for her, the animal was past fighting. However, we had hard work to get her to let go. Leaving a couple of Kroomen to skin the beast, we retraced our steps to the factory. Our bag for three guns consisted of 16½ brace of Guinea-fowl, two antelopes, one tiger-cat, and a few small birds of rare plumage, shot for preserving.

In the evening we had a couple of hauls with the seine net, and got a quantity of fish—a great treat, as fish are very scarce on the coast.

Next morning we started up the river, but as our journey was not marked by any extraordinary circumstance I won't inflict it upon my readers, but will at once proceed to Angama, a large town about eighty miles, as the crow flies, from the coast, but nearly double that distance by river. Here we had our second day's experience of Niger sport.

The Niger here is a lovely river. The banks, where not cleared for native farms, are wooded with magnificent trees, among which the lordly cotton towers like a monarch, filled with birds of the most beautiful plumage ; and monkeys of a dozen species, from the wee *Mangrove* to the big 'dog-faced,' gambol on the branches and run up and down the pendent leaves with ten times the agility of the smartest topman.

I was very anxious to add the head of a hippopotamus to my curios, and as they abound in this part of the river I determined to try for one ; but knowing the difficulty of securing the huge body if killed in the river, not only on account of the swiftness of the current, but also of killing so large a beast in its native element, I directed our interpreter to find out from the natives if they knew of any favourite feeding-ground where we might have a chance of getting a pot-shot at ' Mr. Behemoth,' with a reasonable certainty of bagging him ; and as he found a native hunter who said he knew a good place, I organized a party, consisting of my own medical officer, the trade agent and his medico, and two of my marines. We left the ship at mid-night in a large canoe, lent us by the King of Angama, paddled by thirty men, all of whom were said to be noted hunters. A cold wet fog hung like a pall over the river, and as the fitful gusts of the ' terral ' came off, loaded with heavy, sickly miasma, an indescribable feeling of nausea came over me, which took a strong dose of quinine and brandy to remove.

After paddling for about five miles we landed on the right-

hand side of the river, and following a broad, beaten track for
nearly a mile, arrived at a place of dense bush, thickly interspersed with banana and plantain-trees. Here 'behemoth,' we
were told, was accustomed to sup. Choosing a position on each
side of the path, and concealed in the bushes, we spread our
waterproof sheets on the ground, and, lighting our pipes, loaded
our rifles, and having sent our dusky companions to beat up the
quarters of our anticipated prey, resigned ourselves to the attack
of musquitoes and midges innumerable. Slowly passed the
time. Once or twice a troop of chattering monkeys came and
had a look at us, bolting off the instant they found we were not
of their 'kith or kin,' and twice an antelope presented a
splendid chance to us, standing within twenty yards 'sniffing
the tainted air,' but escaping, as we wanted bigger game. Some
two hours passed, and just as the day was beginning to break
one of the natives, who had remained with us, gave me a slight
touch with his toe. I could hear nothing, but the savage's ear
had not deceived him, and in a few moments we could distinguish the tread of a heavy animal approaching. A feverish
feeling of excitement came over me, and whispering to my companions not to fire until I gave the word, I kept my eye fixed
on the path, my finger ready on the trigger, and my rifle (a
service Enfield) well above my hip. A few seconds more, and a
dim huge form heaves in sight, panting and blowing down
the path. He is now not twenty yards from us, and the
moment is come. I cry 'Now!' and three Enfield bullets crash
into his skull: for an instant he stands, then turns and bolts
back. To snatch up my double, and send two more balls after
him, is but the work of an instant, and I hear distinctly the
'thud, thud,' as they strike, and immediately after with a crash
he falls. Three of the natives rush out, and bang! bang! bang!
go their three guns, and a wild yell proclaims that all is over.
We join them, and find our prey to be a full-grown bull, with
very good tusks. Leaving the natives to get his head off, we
seek a clear spot, and, having found one, light a fire and make a
jorum of coffee, as we purpose beating the bush for an antelope
before going on board.

After a light repast, consisting of well 'laced' coffee and
pipes, we commenced to beat back towards the river and after
nearly two hours' fruitless work, hit it about a mile and a half
below the spot where we had left the canoe. The sun was now
getting very powerful, and not feeling inclined to retrace our

steps, we sat down under the shade of an immense cotton-tree, and sent one of the natives up to collect our crew and bring the canoe down to us.

The tree was growing almost on the extreme edge of the river's bank, which was here quite clear of vegetation, and sloping down at an angle of about forty-five degrees to the water, a distance of about thirty feet. We were quietly awaiting the canoe, when, accidentally casting my eyes upwards, I saw an agitation of the foliage immediately above me, and in an instant caught sight of a panther engaged in watching us. My rifle was, of course, beside me, and snatching it up I drove a ball through the beast's head, and he fell plump in the middle of us, so astonishing E—— that he threw himself back, and rolling head over heels down the bank fell into the river. For a moment the rest of us were convulsed with laughter, but the next instant the thought that alligators abound there, and the difficulty of our friend being able to crawl up the steep, muddy bank, struck us all. The current was sweeping him down, and it seemed any odds that our sport would have a tragical end, when, with an effort that seemed superhuman, he threw himself half out of water, and managed to dig his hands sufficiently deep into the mud to hold on, while we cut a liane long enough to reach him, and with a hearty 'one! two! three!' we hauled him up—not hurt, but considerably scared.

Shortly after the canoe arrived, and embarking, we paddled back to Angama without any further adventure.

GURDOM'S GHOST ;

A SHORE SHOOTING ADVENTURE.

By WILF POCKLINGTON.

A FEW years ago there was probably no more attractive ground to the shore shooter than the immense saltings that line the estuary of the Wash, on the Lincolnshire coast. Stretching away for miles, and in many places giving at low water a breadth of two miles of mud, or mud and sand, intersected by creeks, ditches, and drains, tenanted only by the wild fowl, and the few men who went in quest of them, a more desirable place for shore shooting cannot well be imagined.

About the best place along the coast was a village called Frieston Shore. I call it by courtesy a village; but it was then simply a dozen or so farm-houses scattered loosely around two large hotels, which, to a stranger, seemed a most incongruous alliance. These hotels depended upon the trade arising from the vessels of large draught, that, being bound for the port of Boston, some seven miles away, were unable to enter the somewhat shallow river, and consequently discharged their cargoes by means of lighters from the deep-sea moorings known as 'Clay Hole.'

In the famous duck winter of 1870 I received a letter from an old friend of mine named Gurdom, asking me to make definite arrangements for a long-deferred wild-fowling excursion, and a week from the receipt of his letter found us both comfortably settled at 'Plummer's Hotel,' at the 'Shore.'

Gurdom was a perfect stranger to these parts, but I, having been born almost on the very borders of that part of the Wash, had known every creek and ditch from boyhood.

Our host provided us with a capital dinner, and during the evening we loaded a supply of cartridges; afterwards we had a chat in the bar of the hotel with some of the fishermen, and the one professional fowler of the district.

As soon as it was light next morning we were moving, had breakfast, filled our flasks and sandwich tins, and started down the rude roadway that led us a mile or so into the desert of mud.

We were both carrying 12-bore guns, weighing about eight pounds and a half, both barrels full choke.

At the time I write, the useful 10-bore introduced by 'Wildfowler' was still *in embryo*, and, of course, for shore shooting in heavy mud, this is *the* bore to carry.

Arriving at the end of the road we began business in earnest, and, slipping into our mud pattens, we made our way towards the water's edge with that peculiarly graceful, undulating motion common to the shore shooter in pattens.

A bleak north-easter was blowing straight in from the German Ocean, keen enough to cut a pole in two, and it came across those dreary flat saltings with an added keenness. The same weather had prevailed for the previous week or two, and, as usual under the circumstances, the birds were somewhat easier to approach. We held a consultation, and agreed to work up the coast towards Leake, I taking the higher shore, and

Gurdom the lower one, thus giving him an off-chance at any birds I missed. The old retriever and I worked every creek systematically, and some very fair sport was obtained.

Towards noon I shot a large curlew that Gurdom flushed out of a very deep creek, and I declared my intention of sticking him up as a decoy, and waiting in the creek for results. Gurdom declined, saying it was too cold to wait about, whistling the retriever to follow him. He made his way along the coast towards Leake.

I hunted about for some drift-wood, and, cutting two suitable skewers, soon had my curlew fixed, beak in the mud, apparently very busy. I then retired to the creek, which was deep enough for me to stand upright in, and waited.

Not long, however.

Before a quarter of an hour passed there was the once-heard-never-to-be-forgotten 'skreek' of a curlew, and one came flying over the creek to cry 'halves' with my decoy. Bang! and down he came, almost at my feet.

I kept perfectly still for some little time longer, and then the sound of wings reached me. I peeped cautiously between the two hillocks of mud I had made on the edge of the creek, and my heart nearly came into my mouth, for there were four ducks and three mallards inspecting my curlew from a distance of about fifteen feet.

I have never had 'buck ague,' a disease common to our transatlantic sportsmen, but it could not be worse than the feeling I experienced for the space of half a minute. Then it passed, and I was all right.

One old duck was eyeing the curlew in a very suspicious manner, and I could almost imagine she was turning up the tip of her bill and saying contemptuously :—

'Well! I never saw a curlew on crutches before! Don't believe it is a curlew at all!'

To these sentiments a general 'quack' and preening of feathers seemed to reply :—

'Quite right! guess it's a fraud. Let's go.'

However, I cut the picnic short at this juncture, and just as their heads were all wisely wagging together I pulled, and two lay dead; a third, hard hit, went floundering down towards the water; the other four rose. I just caught the leader under the wing as he turned in his flight, and brought him down with that 'thud' that has such a charm to a sportsman's ear.

I climbed out to gather up my spoil, but having no dog, my wounded bird was in a fair way of getting off without further damage.

'Confound it! Where's Gurdom and Nell?' I muttered. I could not see them anywhere, and concluded he had worked up the saltings to the ' Shore.'

It was now about 3.30 p.m., and the inner man was making a piteous outcry, so I gathered up my bag and turned my face homewards, well satisfied with my share of the day's sport.

As I reached the bank I passed the coastguard.

'Just off in time, sir,' said he : 'this north-easter is bringing the tides in full thirty minutes early, this last day or two!' And turning round, I saw that the tide was well over half the saltings, with a depth of about three feet already at the place where my decoy had stood.

Have you seen my friend pass in ?' I queried.

'Well, no, sir, I can't say as I have ; I saw him down opposite the Toft Sand about two hours ago, and I have not seen him since.' After a few more words we parted, and I entered the hotel.

Gurdom had not come in.

Nothing in that fact to give me any uneasiness, perhaps my readers will say, but to any one knowing that coast as I did there was every cause. The two-mile trail over those flats is a good hour, or hour and a quarter's work ; and if, having good sport, he had driven it to the last minute before starting, the fact of the unwonted early tide, and the dangerously swift sweep with which it covers those flats, almost at one unbroken roll, rushing up the deep ditches and creeks like a rapid, and spreading simultaneously on every side, made it a question almost of life or death.

I ran out on to the high bank and swept the saltings with a glass, but no figure was in sight.

It was now nearly dusk, and knowing how bewildering a strange shore is, I had a lantern hoisted up on the flagstaff of the hotel, and away I ran towards the coastguard station, nearly a mile down the coast. I reached there nearly breathless, and in a few words explained matters. The men wanted but a few seconds to throw oars into the boat, light a lantern, and run the boat down into the water. Then three of the coastguards and myself jumped in, and bent to the sternest race I ever rowed.

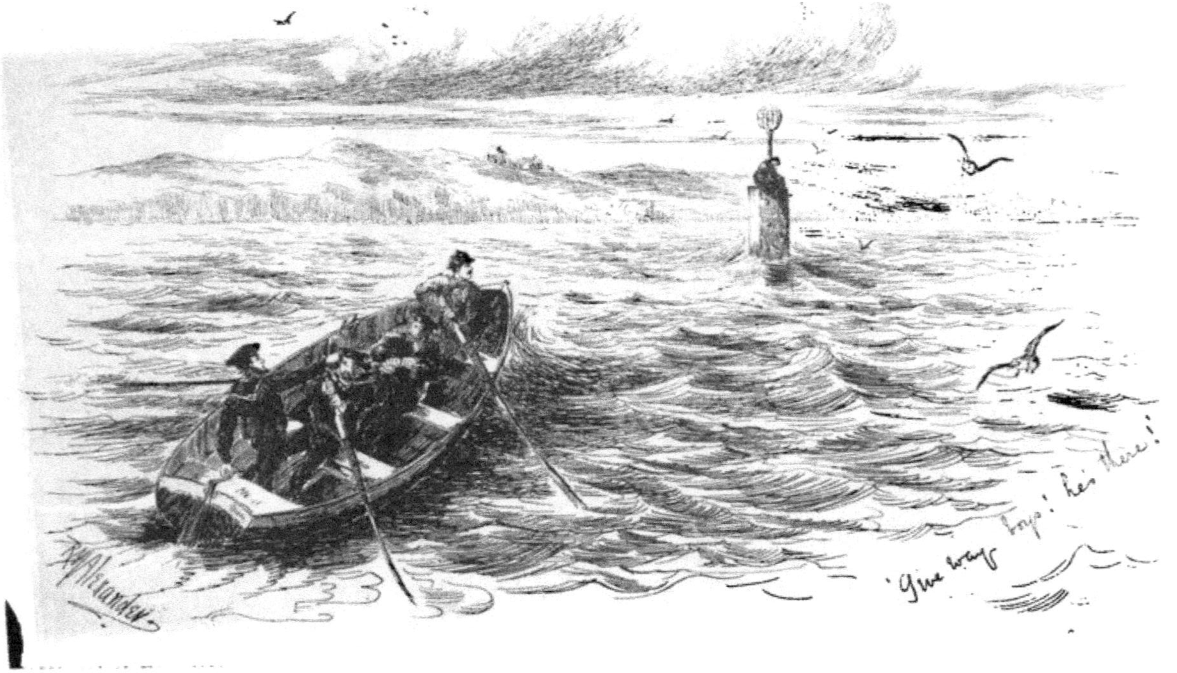

'Give way boys! he's there!'

' Reckon we'd better make for the line of beacons, sir,'
said the leader of our party; 'it's our only chance, if he's in the
water.'

The wind was colder than ever, and as the spray from the
lipping waves flew over us now and again it froze on our clothes
and hair. Away sped the boat, almost flying through the water,
and in a very short time, which seemed hours to me, we reached
the first beacon, which was merely a long stout pole with a
basket on the top, placed at intervals along the coast to show
the position of the sand-banks.

' We had better work up the coast, sir : there is the Shore
Beacon, which will be the most likely spot.'

Away went the boat in the direction of the ' Shore Beacon.'
This differed from the others in having been built for a lantern,
instead of a basket, and was a solid oak post, four feet square
and twelve or fourteen feet high, with a pole and basket at
the top, and rude steps still remaining in its side, by means
of which the men had climbed to light the lantern in the old
days.

Suddenly the man at the tiller called out, ' Give way,
boys! he's there! I can see him on the beacon!' We gave
way with a will, and a few strokes ran us alongside.

There was Gurdom at the top, insensible, crouched all of a
heap.

I climbed quickly up to him, and found him as I feared,
nearly dead. He had climbed up, and, becoming numb, had
placed his arms around the pole, and tied his wrists together
with his handkerchief, to which circumstance he undoubtedly
owed his life. I cut the handkerchief, and we lowered him into
the boat. Then three of us rowed for the bank, and the other,
stripping Gurdom to the skin, dashed salt water over him and
rubbed his arms and body as hard as he could.

Arriving at the bank, the inmates of the hotel were all
waiting to assist, if necessary. So, wrapping him in a blanket,
we carried him into the hotel to find a hot bath and everything
ready. It was evidently not the first case of the kind they
had had.

Slowly and painfully life returned, and some two hours
afterwards we laid him in bed, and he was soon fast asleep; and
when he awoke next morning there was little the matter with
him.

' A trifle stiff, old man! nothing more; but, by Jove! that

was a near go. You thought me insensible when you found me, but I saw and heard you as in a dream, and only became totally unconscious after reaching the hotel. Where's Nell? The faithful old beggar stood it as long as she could, but was at last driven back, half wading, half swimming, by the incoming tide.'

I hastened to assure him that Nell had turned up at the hotel later on, and was just at present very busy downstairs with a great pile of bones.

As may be expected, the coastguard men had no reason to regret the exertions they had made on his behalf, and he is well remembered among them, as I understand every Christmas a little genuine Scotch whiskey finds its way to the station. But this is strictly *entre nous.*

The old beacon is still standing, and instead of 'The Shore Beacon,' is generally known as 'Gurdom's Ghost.' Such is fame!

It stands on the salting between the Toft Sand and the shore, and is the only beacon for miles that can be mounted. If any of my readers visit the neighbourhood, any fisherman will point it out.

The following morning his gun was brought in, and we finished the week with a splendid total. But *tempora mutantur.* Of late years the number of birds here has decreased beyond belief, what with the erection of docks lower down, and the new laws making the fishermen riddle their fish in deep water, the wild fowl appear to have sought a more secluded and better feeding-ground, and the winter before last I tramped over these saltings for six hours, and never emptied a single barrel.

END OF VOL. I.

LONDON:

Printed by STRANGEWAYS & SONS, Tower Street, Upper St. Martin's Lane.

JOHN MORGAN & CO.
5 ALBEMARLE STREET,
PICCADILLY, W.

SPECIALITY:

'The ALBEMARLE SHOOTING COAT'
(REG.)

ADVANTAGES.—Obviates the fatigue and heat of a cartridge belt, and ensures dry cartridges and gun locks in the roughest weather.

THE ALBEMARLE WATERPROOF TWEEDS FOR ABOVE.

MELNOTTE ET FILS,
REIMS,
1880 CHAMPAGNE.

84/-

PER DOZEN

BOTTLES.

45/-

PER DOZEN

HALF-BOTTLES.

HEDGES & BUTLER,
WINE SHIPPERS AND MERCHANTS,
155 REGENT STREET, LONDON.

a

FORES'S STEEL-PLATE ENGRAVINGS.

THE FAREWELL CARESS.
Painted by C. BURTON BARBER. Engraved by F. STACPOOLE.
Artist's Proofs, £8 8s. Prints, £2 2s.

NO FEAR OF THE HOUNDS.
Painted by C. BURTON BARBER. Engraved by W. H. SIMMONS.
Artist's Proofs, £8 8s. Prints, £2 2s.

A PROMISING LITTER.
Painted by C. BURTON BARBER. Engraved by W. T. DAVEY.
Artist's Proofs, £8 8s. Prints, £2 2s.

CHRISTIAN GRACES—FAITH, HOPE, CHARITY.
Painted by G. E. HICKS. Engraved by F. HOLL.
Artist's Proofs, £6 6s. Prints, £2 2s.

IL PENSEROSO.
Painted by G. E. HICKS. Engraved by F. HOLL. Artist's Proofs, £3 3s. Prints, £1 1s.

L'ALLEGRO.
Painted by G. E. HICKS. Engraved by F. HOLL.
Artist's Proofs, £3 3s. Prints, £1 1s.

THE HUNTSMAN AND HOUNDS.
Drawn by Sir EDWIN LANDSEER, R.A. Engraved by H. T. RYALL.
Artist's Proofs, £2 2s. Proofs, Tinted, £1 1s. Prints, 10s. 6d.

HIS ROYAL HIGHNESS THE DUKE OF CAMBRIDGE, K.G., G.C.B., &c.
Painted by JOHN LUCAS. Engraved by T. OLDHAM BARLOW, R.A.
Artist's Proofs, £6 6s. Prints, £2 2s.

Maj.-Gen. The EARL OF CARDIGAN, K.C.B., &c.
(Leading the Brigade of Light Cavalry at Balaklava.)
Painted by A. F. DE PRADES. Engraved by H. COUSINS.
Artist's Proofs, £6 6s. Prints, £2 2s.

A LARGE COLLECTION OF ARTISTS' PROOFS and SCARCE FIRST STATES, after SIR E. LANDSEER, R.A., and other Celebrated Modern Artists.

ALSO,

A GALLERY OF OIL-PAINTINGS AND WATER-COLOUR DRAWINGS, amongst which are choice examples of SIR E. LANDSEER, R.A.; JAMES WARD, R.A.; W. C. T. DOBSON, R.A.; C. W. COPE, R.A.; G. STUBBS, R.A.; C. BURTON BARBER; T. S. ROBINS; J. J. HILL; J. F. HERRING, Sen.; H. ALKEN, Sen.; C. COOPER HENDERSON; WOOTTON SARTORIUS, &c.

LONDON: PUBLISHED BY MESSRS. FORES, 41 PICCADILLY, W.
SHIPPERS SUPPLIED UPON LIBERAL TERMS.

d

PERILS ABOUND ON EVERY SIDE

Railway Passengers Assurance Compan

No. 64, CORNHILL,

INSURES AGAINST

ACCIDENTS OF ALL KINDS,

ON LAND OR WATER,

AND HAS

THE LARGEST INVESTED CAPITAL,

THE LARGEST INCOME,

AND PAYS YEARLY THE

LARGEST AMOUNT OF COMPENSATIO:

Of any Accidental Assurance Company.

Chairman   -   **HARVIE M. FARQUHAR**. Esq.

Apply to the Clerks at the Railway Stations,

the Local Agents, or

WEST END OFFICE,

8, GRAND HOTEL BUILDINGS, CHARING CROS:

OR AT THE

Head Office, 64, CORNHILL, LONDON, E.C. ·

WILLIAM J. VIAN, *Secreta*

www.ingramcontent.com/pod-product-compliance
Lightning Source LLC
Chambersburg PA
CBHW030914270326
41929CB00008B/691